THE NAKED GUIDE TO CIDER

By James Russell and Richard Jones

www.tangentbooks.co.uk
Tel: 0117 972 0645
email Richard@tangentbooks.co.uk
Unit 5.16 Paintworks
Bristol BS4 3EH

The Naked Guide to Cider by James Russell
First published 2010 by Tangent Books (978-1-906477-32-5).
Second edition published 2012 (978-1906477-79-0)
Third edition published 2015 (978-1910089-13-2)

Editor: **Richard Jones**
Design: **Joe Burt & Alex Dimond**

Thanks to: Martin Thatcher for sponsoring *The Naked Guide to Cider*, and for lending us his technical expertise. Many other people across Ciderland gave us their time and helped us with information, stories and pictures, so a big thank you to all of them too. Special thanks to Dayna Stevens and Sean Busby for valuable assistance in researching this book.

Print Management: **John Garrad** (Akcent Media)

Printed using paper from sustainable sources

WELCOME

Welcome to *The Naked Guide to Cider*, where you'll find all the information you need to start making your own cider, along with suggestions for places to go and ciders (and perries) to try. It isn't hard to make good drinkable cider. In fact, there's no reason why everyone shouldn't have a go, and you'll discover in the following pages that people all over the country are doing just that. We've included some of their stories so you can see what cidermaking entails.

We've also gathered advice and stories from people who make excellent, award-winning cider and perry. To do this consistently requires years of work, with regular testing of the product, so be warned: when you gather your first sack of apples and fire up the scratter for the first time, you're probably starting out on a lifelong adventure. Then again, there are worse ways to spend your time. And the cider you make yourself may well be the best you ever have...

James Russell

CONTRIBUTE TO THE NAKED GUIDE TO CIDER

If you have any comments about *The Naked Guide to Cider* or would like to suggest a pub, cidermaker, supplier or website for inclusion in the listings section, get in touch with us via the contact form at **www.tangentbooks.co.uk**

ABOUT THE AUTHORS

James Russell is an acknowledged authority on cider and orchards, who has written on the subject for *Geographical Magazine*, *The Daily Telegraph* and other publications. *Manmade Eden* (Redcliffe Press, 2007), his groundbreaking history of orchards, was dubbed 'a hugely enjoyable read' by *BBC Countryfile* magazine. Fruit expert Joan Morgan called it, 'a thought provoking, engaging and informative book that everyone interested in the countryside will enjoy.' James's other books cover environmental issues, history and art; they include *How to Turn Your Parents Green* (Tangent Books, 2007), *Discovering Harbourside* (Redcliffe Press, 2010) and *Ravilious in Pictures: Sussex and the Downs* (Mainstone Press).

Richard Jones first came to the public's attention as the fresh-faced pop page editor of the *Bristol Evening Post*. From here, he introduced the city to exciting new beat combos such as Massive Attack and Smith & Mighty and was one of the first to document the arrival of the so-called Bristol sound. He now runs Tangent Books in Bristol and specialises in titles about popular culture and also publishes *The Naked Guide to Bristol* and *The Naked Guide to Bath*. He started making cider with his friend and neighbour Sean Busby in 2008 using apples collected from orchards in the West Pennard area of Somerset and pressed by hand on the slopes of Totterdown in South Bristol.

FOREWORD BY JOHN THATCHER

Being born into a Somerset cider-making family there has never been any doubt in my mind that cider deserves every accolade available. It brings warmth to my heart when I talk to people around the country who have gained a genuine interest in cider thanks to the renaissance the industry has experienced over recent years.

Cider has a worthy place as our national drink. We have taken it to our hearts, particularly in the West Country, where the climate lends itself perfectly to the cultivation of bittersweet cider apples. Throughout our social history there are mentions of how cider played its part in people's every day lives – we are told that back in the 14th century babies were baptised in cider since it was cleaner than water, and in the 19th century it was even advertised as a cure for gout. No such claims today, but with cider still one of the most popular alcoholic drinks in the UK, there is a thirst to know more, not just of cider today, but of its rich history.

There would be no cider without apples. One of the fondest memories I have of life in cider country is enjoying happy hours out into the orchards with my grandfather harvesting the apples. Those same orchards are of course still here, and as the generations roll on, I now take my own grandchildren out into the orchards and together we enjoy the Somerset countryside. Together we marvel at the sight of a deer, or hare, staring at us from the end of a row of apple trees.

At the time when my grandfather was pressing cider in the early 1900s, it was commonplace to give cider to the farm hands as part of their weekly wage. That was certainly the case on the Thatcher farm – the cider was produced by my grandfather and then my father for this very purpose. I recall as a child one occasion when my father had the barrels of cider standing in the paddock and a young rep came to visit on business. He asked my father what would happen to all the cider, and was given the reply that the family would drink as much as they could – and he would then have to sell what was over. And the rest, as they say, is history.

In those days, people would use recipes that had been passed down the generations – or they would use their instinct, experiment and come up with something that was to their own taste, or suited the apples that they grew on their own farm. We're very lucky that the recipes that have been passed down to us through our family have really stood the test of time, and while we might have adjusted little things here and there, some of the ciders we produce now are basically the same as those my grandfather enjoyed. Whatever means to create your cider you choose, the basic method remains the same as it has done for hundreds of years. And by experimenting, you find the method and style that is right for you.

Pressing cider is a way of life. So be warned, once you've read *The Naked Guide to Cider* you might get hooked. Not only will the book take you on an informative but light hearted tour of cider making country, it will give you a taste for what making your own cider is all about, and why enthusiasts throughout the country just can't get enough of their Dabinett, Tremlett's Bitter or Yarlington Mill.

John Thatcher
Chairman, Thatchers Cider

EST. 1904
THATCHERS

Contents

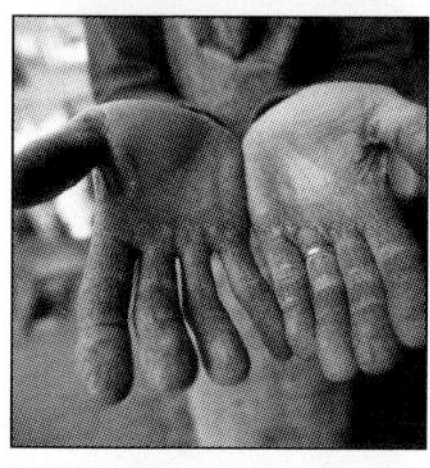

CIDER AND PERRY

AREAS

Introducing Cider & Perry

How the fermented juice of apples and pears have given so many people so much pleasure for so many years...

Cider is our national drink, the most versatile alcoholic beverage of them all. There's a cider for every taste and pocket, from farmhouse scrumpy to fine bottled ciders made by the champagne method. Best of all, cider is easy to make. Given a certain investment of time and effort anybody can make a barrel of decent cider, and it isn't unknown for beginners to steal the prizes at major national competitions.

Somehow we've allowed our drinking culture to become dominated, over the past half-century, by imported lager and wine. In response, cidermakers tend to market their wares either as competition to mass-produced lager or as an alternative to wine, but cider and perry have their own distinctive character. Products of native orchards, these drinks have their own strength and flavour, their own rituals and traditions, their own cultural and historical associations. A cider house is not the same as

"I be 80 and never drinks nothin' but cider."

Cheers! Let's hope we're all still enjoying a pint of cider when we're 80.

The Cidermaker's Art

"First and foremost, the cidermaker gave his closest personal attention at every stage of production. The fruit came from his own orchards, the vintage quality of the varieties used and their blending requirements had been learnt by experience, the necessary care in the harvesting and storage was exercised and the right moment in stage of ripeness was selected for milling and pressing."

BTP Barker of the Long Ashton Research Station on what made a good cider in 1904 – the same is true today.

a pub. Champagne-style cider or perry is not the same as Prosecco. Real cider is not the same as real ale.

WHAT IS CIDER?

There is so much variety in cider and perry, and so much debate about juice content, alcohol strength and duty, that it's easy to forget that good cider can be made very simply.

If you crush and press apples, then store the juice in a clean, air-locked container for several months, the yeasts that live on the skin of the apples will transform the sugars in the juice into alcohol leaving you with a delicious, strong, dry cider. People have been doing this for more than a thousand years, and the basic principles haven't changed much; visit a Somerset farmhouse cidermaker and this is what you'll get.

Anyone can make this kind of cider, and one of the aims of this book is to show you how. But simple as they may be in principle, cider and perry have evolved over the centuries into a fascinating range of regional styles, brands and variants. Herefordshire cidermakers tend to have a different approach to producers in Somerset, while makers in Kent and East Anglia have their own tradition – one they champion fiercely – that uses cookers and eaters rather than specialist cider varieties.

If you explore the Cider aisle of a supermarket you'll find a bewildering range of drinks: some are colourless, others are pink and come in a wine bottle, others still are honey-coloured and a bit hazy, and beside them you might find sparkling pale drinks in beer bottles with crown caps. The curious thing is that, apart from differences in price, packaging, and alcohol content, there's often no way of knowing what these very different ciders are like – how they're made or what's in them. Buy a packet of sweets and it will tell you the ingredients and their nutritional value; buy a bottle of cider and all you will learn is that it Contains Sulphites. One bottle might contain 100% English apple juice, while the one next to it is 90% water and glucose.

In France there are strict rules governing different kinds of cider. 'Cidre Traditionnel', 'Cidre de Fermier' and 'Cidre de Cru' have legally binding definitions, while in Brittany and Normandy ciders are protected by Appellation d'Origin Controllee (AOC), the same kind of legislation that prevents any old sparkling hooch being labelled 'Champagne'.

Definitely not rocket science – anyone can make cider.

Some of the best cider you'll ever taste is made in the traditional way on Somerset farms. This is Parson's Choice...

Introduction

So what are the rules in the UK? Legally, cider and perry are defined as alcoholic beverages between 1.2% and 8.5% ABV (anything over 8.5% is fruit wine, which attracts a higher level of duty), made from the partial or complete fermentation of apples or pears. Cider can contain pear juice, but not more than 25%, and perry may contain apple juice in the same proportion. Cider and perry may contain any quantity of potable water or sugar, which can be added before or after fermentation, plus a range of permitted additives to enhance flavour or colour. You're not allowed to add alcoholic liquor at any time.

It isn't a particularly restrictive definition, is it? On the one hand, this means that cidermakers are free to experiment without a lot of meddling bureaucrats coming along and saying 'That's not cider!' On the other, it makes life tricky for artisan producers who would, in France, enjoy the legal protection of an AOC or Cidre de Cru designation.

White cider may face extinction if the definition of cider is tightened up, so get some while you can. Or not.

As of September 1st, 2010, the UK has a new legal definition of cider. Essentially the juice content before and after fermentation must be at least 35%, while the Specific Gravity of the original juice has to be at least 1033. This definition was agreed on by HM Revenue and Customs and the NACM and is likely to affect only the very worst industrial ciders. It leaves us with no distinction between factory cider and full-juice artisan cider and has the unfortunate effect of confirming the worst opinions of UK cider's critics – that our cider is a feeble, factory-made imitation of the glorious French beverage. Would you willingly drink cider made with only 35% juice?

A traditional cider jug – part of the collection of cider artefacts at Barrington Court in Somerset.

At the time of writing debate is raging about the duty levied on cider and how different kinds of cider could be defined so as to protect artisan producers from tax rises aimed at curbing the production of cheap, strong cider. Another debate is going on in Europe about the labelling of alcoholic drinks, with wine producers resisting calls for ingredients to be displayed on labels. If you buy an imported can of Gaymers Original or Strongbow in Canada it will bear a detailed, and not very inspiring, list of ingredients. Maybe this will one day be the case here, but for now we can't rely on labels or product information. We have to find stuff out for ourselves – find the pubs that sell good cider, visit cidermakers and test their wares. Sometimes life just doesn't seem fair…

REAL CIDER

CAMRA HAS COME UP WITH A DEFINITION OF 'REAL CIDER'. WHAT DO YOU THINK OF IT?

Cider served straight from the barrel in the days before carbonation.

When the Campaign for Real Ale (CAMRA) started taking an interest in cider they immediately ran into a major problem – there was no definition of 'Real Cider'. So, since it's very hard to campaign for something when you don't know what it is, they invented one.

A. INGREDIENTS

1. The liquid content before fermentation must consist entirely of non-pasteurized cider apple or perry pear juice.
2. No apple or pear juice concentrates.
3. Normally only the sugar naturally available in the fruit should be used to cause fermentation, but in years when the level of natural sugar in the fruit is low the addition of extraneous sugar to aid fermentation is acceptable.

B. PROCESS

1. No pasteurization to take place during the production process in relation to the cask product.
2. No added colouring to be used.
3. No added flavouring to be used.
4. There must be no artificial carbonation for draught products.
5. Sweetener may be added to fully fermented Cider/Perry to make it sweet or medium.
6. The addition of water is permitted to bring the alcoholic content down to the level required by the producer. Ideally however the minimum juice content should not be lower than 90% volume.
7. No micro filtration allowed (this takes all the yeast leaving a "dead" product)

This is an odd set of rules for a 'real' drink, since it implies that you could enter a CAMRA competition with a bottled cider or perry that has been sweetened with saccharin, carbonated and pasteurized. But perhaps it's a realistic definition. Many respected cider makers use saccharin, and have done for 100 years. Besides it can be difficult to taste sweetener in cider, and who wants to see cider trials judged by bio-chemists?

HOW MAGNERS LAUNCHED A CIDER REVOLUTION

It was fantastic: the simplest of USPs – put ice in drink – promoted with the simplest of advertisements – shot of Timeless Orchard followed by another of happy young people drinking. Thirty seconds of brilliance that kick-started a cider revolution.

The fortunes of cider have fluctuated violently over the centuries. New apple varieties and advances in milling or bottling may give cidermakers a boost, but so too do war, recession and other factors that effect the import of wine or the availability of grain for beer-making. Cider and perry tend to prosper in hard times.

And then there are the moments of brilliance, the dazzling bursts of inspiration in product development and marketing that spark a nationwide enthusiasm for cider and perry. In the 17th century wine-strength cider became the national drink, with both Royalists and supporters of Cromwell keen to support a homegrown industry. And in the 1880s Herefordshire cidermakers began mass-producing cider of a uniformly good quality that was bottled and distributed nationally on the back of increasingly sophisticated advertising. During and

Love it or loathe it, you have to credit Magners for kick-starting the great cider revival. But where did they get that cider-over-ice idea?

You can make cider from any apple variety.

after World War I, when grain shortages and reduced wine imports gave cider a lift, Bulmers, Whiteways and numerous other makers came up with dynamic brands and ingenious ads. Post-war, Babycham stole the scene, but then began a long, slow period of decline.

By the 1990s cider was deeply unfashionable and orchards were being grubbed up at a fantastic rate. Concerned about this loss, the environmental charity Common Ground launched Apple Day. The genius of Magners lay in noting the massive popularity of this new cultural phenomenon, and in reconnecting cider to its origins in the orchard.

Once upon a time Whiteways promoted the concept that their cider was 'Bottled Orchards'; a century later Magners did the same thing, ensuring the right balance of leafy apple boughs and bright blue skies by filming the 'Irish' countryside in New Zealand. For a long time cider promoters had tried to distance their product from its rustic homeland, assuming that up-and-coming youngsters would associate orchards with scrumpy-glugging yokels. But these aren't West Country orchards. This is (sort of) Ireland, a country at once ancient and venerable but modern and go-getting. Just the sort of place where you'd expect the cognoscenti to transform an age-old drink with a few chunks of frozen H^2O.

Industry people acknowledged that the Magners approach was, to borrow a phrase, pure genius, pushing up profits across the spectrum of cider companies and encouraging the nascent revival in small-scale cider making and – importantly – orcharding.

As outspoken Somerset cider brandy pioneer Julian Temperley put it: "It's down to them that cider is now getting the respect it deserves. They have changed the image of cider and completely transformed the perception of it as the poor man's lager. Cider has become female friendly and it is now considered cool to drink it."

Subsequent ads had more mixed success, with one TV commercial banned in February 2009 by the Advertising Standards Authority. This ad stood the famous 'over ice' schtick on its head, by promoting a draught cider – wait for it – with no ice in it. A brilliant idea – you make a gimmick out of adding ice, then another out of taking it away. Unfortunately someone complained that the

Advertising has always played an important role in the cider business. Ads like this one encouraged women to try new ciders designed to be light and sweet.

wordplay designed to communicate the message – 'the perfect icebreaker' and 'making sure the conversation flows' – suggested that drinking Magners could boost confidence and aid social skills, and the ASA upheld the complaint.

Undeterred, Magners hired hip comedian Mark Watson to advertise its pear cider; these ads make the uncontroversial claim that pears are the only fruit used in the beverage's manufacture. They don't have to tell us what else is in there – or whether Mr Watson would drink the stuff if he wasn't getting paid.

Meanwhile, interest in cider and perry has blossomed. At the National Cider and Perry Collection in Sussex, Rod Marsh has noticed that people drawn to cider by Magners are now exploring other ciders and developing the palate you need to enjoy dry artisan cider. Orchards are being replanted across the West County as demand for apples – and, even more so, for perry pears – increases.

But the most exciting thing for us is that people all over the country are now venturing out to gather apples and getting together to press fruit. Everywhere, from western Wales to Norfolk, and from Cornwall to southern Scotland, novice cidermakers are setting up shop in allotment sheds and garages, cellars and air raid shelters. Cider competitions and shows are attracting more and more people. New cider houses are opening. These are exciting times.

A good perry is hard to beat. To find the best, head for the Three Counties or buy online (see Listings for retailers).

WHAT IS PERRY?

"Besides Cider, there are many other curious Drinks that may be prepared out of our British Fruits: as perry, whereof is a great quantity made yearly in several places of this Kingdom"
(J. Worlidge, Vinetum Britannicum, 1676)

Perry has similarities with cider but is more complex and difficult to make, since it requires not only great skill on the part of the maker, but also expert knowledge of orchards and fruit. People sometimes describe it as the 'wine of England', but if you open a bottle of perry expecting it to taste or feel like white wine you'll be disappointed. Approach with an open mind and you'll be in for a treat. Like cider, perry has its own identity, its own flavours and mouth-feel and its own culture. It is also extremely fickle. The same maker using fruit from the same trees can create a world-class perry one year and fail the next.

Simon Day of Once Upon A Tree is one of the new wave of perry makers.

A SHORT HISTORY OF PERRY

Indigenous to central Europe, the wild pears Pyrus communis and Pyrus nivalis have been cultivated for perry-making since Roman times. The drink's purgative

Perry Pear: Ancient Giant

Of the many differences between cider and perry one of the most striking is this. While a cider apple tree has a maximum life span of a century or thereabouts, a perry tree can still be bearing fruit after three hundred years. And whereas popular cider apple varieties tend to lose their vigour over time and get superseded by new favourites, perry pear varieties show such resistance to diseases like scab and canker that they go on and on.

Perry pioneer Andrew Knight noted at the beginning of the 19th century that the variety Red Longdon was approaching the end of its useful life. Two hundred years later the tree can still be found scattered around the Severn Vale, while many of the varieties beloved of modern craft perry makers were equally popular during the Napoleonic Wars. The Taynton Squash may be rare now, but individual trees still grow around the Gloucestershire village that gave the variety its name; we can only imagine what the famous ciders of the 17th century tasted like, but the perries are still being made today.

Individual trees of 60-feet plus are common, and can be mistaken at a distance for limes or other woodland trees. A solitary giant in a field is probably a Barland, a variety widely planted in the 17th century; single trees survive from larger orchards, saved for the farmer's press when demand slackened and the other trees were cut down.

The Holme Lacy Pear

The mother of all ancient pear trees is at Holme Lacy, the estate where Lord Scudamore cultivated the Redstreak before the Civil War. This monster tree, which is of no known variety, covered three-quarters of an acre in 1790 and produced 5-7 tons of fruit a year. Though the main trunk has disappeared, secondary trunks and branches survive and still crop today.

TEN TOP PERRY PEARS

ALMOST ALL THE COUNTRY'S PERRY TREES COME FROM ONE AREA. HERE'S THE PICK OF THE PEARS

If you want to make good perry, you need to know your pears...

In recent years Dunkertons, Olivers and others have planted hundreds of acres of perry pears. But demand is increasing fast so don't expect to get your hands on vintage fruit without a major effort. This being said, here are some favourites:

Blakeney Red
Planted in huge numbers at the end of the 19th century, in west and south-west Gloucestershire as a perry and cooking pear. During World War I it was canned and also used to dye uniforms khaki. One proud grower said, 'Thic pear won that thur war – it gave the Tommy good drink, good food, and clothes for his back.'

Taynton Squash
Venerable old variety used in the 17th century to make a champagne-style perry that was sold as champagne. Rare today.

Brown Bess
Large tree and a heavy cropper, common in south Gloucestershire.

Coppy
There's only one mature tree bearing this excellent variety, although it has recently been propagated by grafting. Do we know where it is? Maybe, but we're not telling.

Butt
Not the most romantic name, but valuable because the fruit is slow to rot. 'Gather your Butts one year, mill them the next and drink the year after.'

Gregg's Pit
Large, vigorous tree and a good cropper, producing a good, fruity perry. Still grown in the orchard planted around the old marl pit of the same name.

Barland
The solitary giant often seen standing in a Herefordshire field. Barland was recommended in the 18th century as a remedy for kidney disorders.

Yellow Huffcap
One of numerous, similar Huffcaps. A large, spreading tree which crops heavily, if often biennially. Fruit must be shaken down before it is ripe, otherwise it may rot on the tree.

Moorcroft/Malvern Hills/ Stinking Bishop
Perhaps the most popular variety for perry-making, giving a high gravity juice and excellent perry. Known as Malvern Hills east of the Severn, and Stinking Bishop in Newent. Used by Charles Martell to soak the cheese made famous by Wallace and Gromit.

Arlingham Squash
An ancient variety still found alongside the tidal Severn, and producing a good, full-bodied perry. May have been the Green Squash Pear noted by John Evelyn in the 17th century.

qualities made it a popular choice among early Christian ascetics, who enjoyed the challenges of a perry-only diet. We don't know exactly when perry was first made in its present heartland of the Three Counties, but William the Conqueror's barons certainly liked their pear juice and most likely planted perry orchards in the latter part of the 11th century.

Subsequently, perry has had the same sort of roller coaster ride through history as cider: a golden age in the 17th and 18th centuries was followed by a long period of decline, with the new possibilities of factory production encouraging a 20th century resurgence. Bottle-conditioned perry from the Taynton Squash pear was sold as champagne during the Restoration of Charles II; 400 years later the makers of Babycham were protesting that the bestselling drink's name came from 'chamois', not 'champagne'.

Apart from these brief forays into the national scene, perry has mostly been made and enjoyed in the West Midlands, where it played a similar part in the rural economy as cider did elsewhere. Fine vintage perries were enjoyed by the gentry, while working men and women drank copious quantities of the rough stuff. Tom Oliver recalls that his grandfather made perry for the workforce of Moorland Farm, until tractors and other machinery made drinking on the job too dangerous.

The three pears sable on the Worcester coat of arms were awarded by Elizabeth I in 1575.

PERRY AND THE THREE COUNTIES

About 95% of perry pears are grown in the Three Counties of Herefordshire, Gloucestershire and Worcestershire, and the relationship between pear and place goes back centuries. The arms of the City of Worcester includes 'three pears sable', added at the instigation of Elizabeth I after she visited in 1575; it's most likely that she enjoyed her pears in liquid form, fermented to perfection.

According to legend, perry pears only thrive if planted within sight of May Hill, which dominates the landscape north-west of Gloucester, but why is this? Nobody is entirely sure, but there seems to be in the region a happy coincidence of good rainfall, enough sunshine – perry pears need more sun than cider apples – and heavy clay subsoils that apple trees don't much like, but which suit perry pears just fine. Then there's the culture of the region, especially around the Forest of Dean, where smallholdings were common. Given a small plot of land, a cottager might plant a single tall perry pear rather than an orchard of cider apple trees, especially as many common pear varieties make an excellent, mildly bitter-sharp perry without needing to be blended.

Whatever the origins of Three Counties Perry, it remains a distinctive, local craft, preserved and practised by the region's farmers through long periods of obscurity. In the mid-1990s there were around 40 small-scale producers, with the likes of Kevin Minchew and Dunkertons making a particularly important contribution, and that number has steadily increased as interest in perry has blossomed in the last few years. To an extent this growth has mirrored that of cider, but perry remains distinct and is one of few English drinks recognised as a genuine artisan product.

Made in Ocle Pychard, Herefordshire, Oliver's Perry is made using rare local perry pears and natural yeasts.

> *'About Taynton, five miles beyond Gloucester, is a mix'd Sort of Land, partly Clay, a Marle, and Crash, as they call it there; on all which Sorts of Land there is much Fruit growing, both for the Table and for Cider; But it is the Pears it most abounds in, of whch the best Sort is that they name the Squash-Pear, which makes the best Perry in those parts. These trees grow to be very large and exceeding fruitful...'*
> **Evelyn, Pomona, 1670**

As increasing numbers of people try their hand at making perry, the Big Apple Cider and Perry Trials have launched a class for Novice Perry.

Not only do the producers of Gloucestershire, Herefordshire and Worcestershire enjoy the protection of a Protected Geographical Indication (PGI), but Three Counties Perry as a whole has been recognised by Slow Food, the international organisation set up to preserve local culinary traditions and foods around the world. With its distinguished history, ancient, slow-growing trees, awkward fruit and production methods that have resisted transfer to the factory (Babycham is another story), perry is an ideal Slow Food product. To people who aren't Slow Foodies the whole thing can seem a bit, well, odd, but the idea is that there is an Ark of Taste to which groups of producers can ask to add a Presidium. Bristol, incidentally, has the world's first Slow Food Market, where you can buy cider and perry from Orchards and Olivers. It's on the first Sunday of every month. Anyhow, the Presidium for Three Counties Perry is built on these principles, which are a bit more refined than CAMRA's real cider definition:

1. That 'true' perry is a unique product – which when well made from carefully selected varieties of 'genuine' perry pears and without the unnecessary addition of additives – is capable of standing alongside a fine wine and should be valued as such;
2. Safeguarding biodiversity. It is critical that the current decline in the stock of perry pear trees is reversed and individual varieties are protected;
3. That perry has its roots in England's West Midlands and should be protected and encouraged as one of the traditional arts and crafts of this region;
4. Individual perries should reflect the specific terroir of the region;
5. Perry making is a highly skilled operation involving considerable time and endeavour on behalf of the producer;
6. For the consumer, it is critical that the products promoted and marketed are of the highest quality, safety and reliability – reflecting the best of the values upheld during the late 17th century.

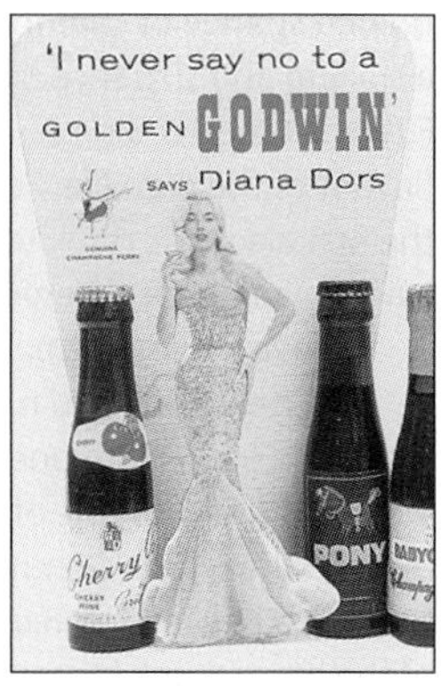

Babycham had its rivals, like Bulmers' Golden Godwin, but not even Diana Dors could persuade the nation to switch brands.

I'D LOVE A BABYCHAM

Perry hasn't always been quite so rarified, however... For people living in post-war austerity, 1953 was a year of good news. The rationing of sugar and petrol ended, a Queen was crowned and women across the country found a new reason to go to the pub. Packaged in a diminutive bottle smothered in sky-blue foil, with a picture of Bambi's mildly wicked cousin on the label, this new drink had the

The English Ladies Perry Making Association:

In the 1980s and 90s, when cider and perry were languishing in obscurity, Jean Nowell was doing her bit to keep the culture going. When she and her husband moved to Lyne Down Farm in Much Marcle they brought the old stone cider house back into production, using a belt-driven 1904 scratter they found in a shed. After her husband's death, Jean continued pressing a ton of fruit a day in season until she was well into her seventies, retiring in 2002; she is also a founder member of The Big Apple Association.

She once described herself as the founder and only member of the English Ladies Perry Making Association.

"My father made cider and we children were allowed free access to the barrel, as long as we didn't leave the tap running," she says. "Once, nearly every house in the area made cider. It was a safe drink in the days of unreliable water supplies."

golden sparkle of champagne but not the price tag. For a shilling and sixpence (half the price of a single whisky) Fifties women could escape stout and port-and-lemon for a flavour of the high life. Four years later, Babycham became the first alcoholic drink to be advertised on television, and a new expression entered the post-war lexicon:

I'd love a Babycham.

This new drink had nothing to do with France or grapes, however. Anyone with good enough eyesight to study the label on one of those tiny bottles would have noticed the words 'Genuine Champagne Perry'. Made from fermented pear juice, Babycham was the direct descendant of the brew drunk by early Christian monks and medieval princes.

Jeff Koons eat your heart out. This is proper kitsch, Shepton Mallet style.

But this was a twentieth century version of the ancient beverage. Back in 1906, Bulmers had launched a sparkling Cider de Luxe, which was rebranded as Pomagne during World War One, and, during the hard years that followed, champagne cider became the poor man's bubbly. Clapps of Baltonsborough got in on the act with Avalagne – Champagne of Somerset, then, in 1947, Shepton Mallet cidermaker Francis Showering succeeded in overcoming a host of technical difficulties to mass-produce sparkling perry for the first time.

He wasn't the only cidermaker to do so. Softer and sweeter than cider, perry was preferred by many women. In the mid-50s you might have seen Swindon's answer to Marilyn Monroe – Diana Dors – advertising Bulmers' Golden Godwin, but it was Babycham that captured the popular imagination through revolutionary packaging, advertising and merchandising.

"Babycham was the first drink a woman could order without feeling like a tart or a crone. For dowdy Fifties womanhood, it was a heady sip of the high life..." Philip Norman, Babycham Nights

Not that competitors gave up easily. Bulmer challenged Showerings in court over the legality of 'Babycham' as a trademark, and there were other legal tussles that seem quite hilarious in hindsight but were, at the time, deadly serious. In August 1958 the Court of Chancery granted the Shepton Mallet company an injunction against rival brewers, forbidding them to supply customers who asked for 'Babycham' with a rival drink. Showerings had apparently sent 'agents provocateurs' to order the famous beverage in 500 pubs that didn't sell it...

As the new medium of television spread awareness of the brand around the country, the golden fawn appeared on everything from neon signs to champagne glasses. In the less innocent world of the 1960s, the fawn kept a step ahead with the Babycham Babes beauty contest and TV adverts featuring Patrick Mower on a yacht, but competition from cheap imported wine and spirits pushed the dear little deer out of the spotlight. The 1992 grubbing up of a 120 acre pear orchard at Combe Florey, Somerset, testified to its decline.

You can still buy the foil-topped bottles, though, and, long after the end of the drink's heyday, Babycham-abilia is as popular as ever – search for the brand on eBay and you'll get a thousand results.

Meanwhile, the Showering family's genius for dreaming up new products has made pear cider the cider-type hooch of the moment. The four grandsons of Francis Showering first made their Brothers Pear Cider for revellers at Glastonbury Festival, and, as demand grew, put their vast Shepton Mallet plant to work producing the distinctive alco-pop style bottles.

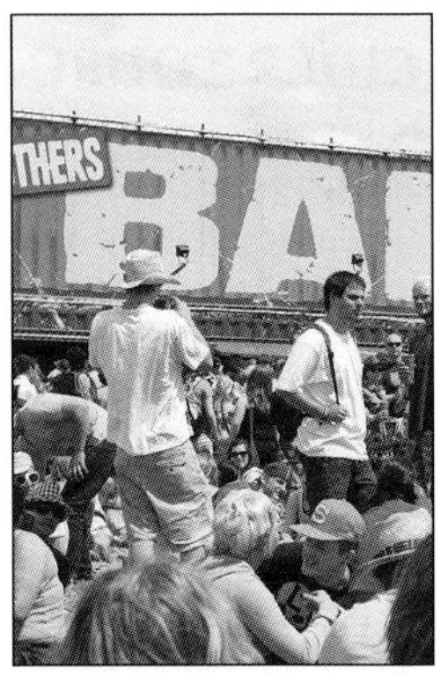

The grandson of Babycham, Brothers Pear Cider is a Glastonbury favourite.

PERRY AND PEAR CIDER

Is there a difference between perry and pear cider? And, if so, what is it? Perry is supposed to be the fermented juice of perry pears, a group of specialised pear varieties that grow best in the Three Counties of Gloucestershire, Herefordshire and Worcestershire. However, it doesn't help us with our definition. Outside the perry-making heartland it's very difficult to get hold of the right pears – Hecks make a fine perry, but sometimes struggle to source fruit. So sometimes dessert pears like Conference are used instead, but the drink is still called perry. Or used to be.

When Brothers launched their first pear-based beverage they called it perry, even though it was made from dessert pears. But a change to pear cider proved popular and, now the Grandson of Babycham has caught on, drinkers are looking for other pear ciders. And rather than try to sell perry to people who want pear cider, producers are changing their labels to fit the new market. Suddenly pear cider is everywhere.

CIDER TOURING

To properly experience the cider of a particular country or region you have to go there. From internet groups you can easily get up-to-date recommendations on places to visit, although we don't suggest using on-line information without checking it first. We've found on numerous occasions that listings are out of date; a pub might win a CAMRA award for cider one year and be Strongbow-only the next.

So what's on offer for the cider tourist? At the very least, the chance to walk into a shop and find real, locally-produced cider. Then there's the opportunity to explore cider country, to walk around orchards and to visit cider farms. You can drink in pubs or restaurants that specialise in cider or wander round museum exhibits, or go to one of the growing number of festivals held in spring, summer and autumn. And then every now and again you'll stumble upon something unexpected, like a cider farm that isn't in the book, or a local cider festival, or a village pub with a field you can camp in.

You can't plan for this kind of adventure, but you can prepare. Be in the right area at the right time and anything can happen.

You'll find all sorts of peculiar equipment if you tour ciderland. This is an ancient scratter at Barrington Court in Somerset.

CAR TROUBLE? TRY CAMPING

Cars and cider don't mix. The strength of artisan ciders is unpredictable and the apple has other powers besides. A half pint can make the world seem just a little strange; the combination of unfamiliar country roads and a confused brain is not a happy one.

So a designated driver is a must. Either that or you find some other means of exploring cider country. Is there a bus going your way? Could you take a train and then walk or ride (carefully)? If you're visiting a particular cider maker you could phone and ask them if there's camping nearby; some Somerset pubs have space for a few tents in a neighbouring field. And cider producers are known to put on their own summer festivals, with camping, music and who knows what else.

B&B is an option too. New Forest Cider is not alone in having rooms within crawling distance of the cider dispensary. Come to think of it, there's a hotel right across the quayside from The Apple cider boat in Bristol. Nowadays you could look up your cidery destination on Google Earth then take a virtual wander in search of the nearest bed.

TOP TIPS FOR ENJOYABLE CIDER TOURING

Allow plenty of time: rushing around busy summer roads trying to visit 20 cidermakers in a day is no fun. Instead, find somewhere good, relax, stay a while...

Be considerate to working cidermakers: it's fun for us to visit cider farms during pressing time, but it might not be great for the people doing the pressing. If in doubt, phone first. Feel free to ask advice, but don't expect people to share their secrets.

Buy some cider: this might seem like unnecessary advice, but if you've enjoyed chatting with a producer, spend some money at the shop. If you don't like the cider, at least buy a jar of chutney.

Don't forget about orchards: the bigger ones are marked on OS maps with a pattern of green crosses. There's nothing quite like standing in the middle of a vast plantation of fruit trees, whatever the time of year.

Look out for seasonal events: spring blossom festivals, summer cider festivals, autumn pressing days, winter wassail.

Spread the word! The cider renaissance is well under way, but it's got a long way to go. Many of the producers featured in this book and other guides rely on visitors for their livelihood. The more people visit, the more cider and perry we'll be able to enjoy.

It's amazing who you bump into at cider stalls. This is HRH at Borough Market in London.

CIDER A TO Z

Apple

This is where it all starts, unless you're making perry. In the UK we're at the northern end of the apple's growing area, and our long mild autumns have given us a fantastic variety of characterful, sugar-rich cider fruit. Apples like Dabinett and Kingston Black are national treasures – or should be.

Barrel

Certain people believe that you shouldn't call a drink 'cider' unless it's been aged in oak barrels. Quite a few others disagree, but the barrel is an integral part of the cidermaking process; most come secondhand from whisky or winemakers and hold 36 gallons. At the other end of the scale are massive vats made of oak staves 3 inches thick, which can hold up to 10,000 gallons; one monster that used to be at Coates in Nailsea was named Adge after the bard of Somerset. It's still working hard at Rich's, just down the M5.

Ciderland

A term coined by countryside writer Walter Raymond in the early 20th century and used more recently by James Crowden for the title of his fantastic, award-winning book. Raymond was talking about Somerset, Crowden about the West Country. But the way things are going the whole country could soon be renamed. Wassail!

Cider Brandy

A spirituous liquor made by distilling cider. French Calvados is such a drink, as is Somerset Cider Brandy. The EU decided recently, however, that 'brandy' can only apply to spirits distilled from wine. In an effort to keep its name Somerset Cider Brandy is endeavouring to achieve PDO status.

Cider House

Traditionally, the barn or shed where cider was made and stored, and where people would gather to drink cider straight from the barrel. More recently it has come to refer to a pub that specialises in cider.

Cidre bouché or bottle-conditioned cider

The next time someone says, 'oh I wish you could get that lovely sweet French cider in this country', tell them, 'You can!'. This bubbly, soft cider is made by keeving, a process which stops the fermentation early and leaves some natural sugar in the cider. It's also lower in alcohol than ciders that have fermented to dryness. Some producers specialise in this method, particularly in Herefordshire, and their cider is every bit as good as its French counterpart. The only reason why the West Country isn't awash in the stuff like Brittany and Normandy is that the French government supports its cider producers and the UK government doesn't.

F

Fermentation (see Yeast)

The process by which sugars are converted to ethanol (alcohol), with carbon dioxide as a potentially explosive by-product. One of the miracles of life.

I

Ice Cider

Cider made from juice that has been frozen to concentrate the sugars. Pioneered in Quebec, where ice wine is all the rage, it has taken off in a big way in New England and is starting to catch on here. Typically, ice cider is strong, sweet – a bit like a really good dessert wine – and fairly pricey.

L

Ladies' Cider:

Back in the day, this is what they called light, sparkly, filtered cider as opposed to proper farmhouse brew. Once it may have been ever so slightly derogatory. Today brands like Thatchers' Katy Rose are big business.

M

Methode Traditionelle

We're not allowed to call the Champagne of cider the Champagne of cider (or even the champagne of Cider), so instead it's the Methode Traditionelle, or Traditional Method. Cider made in this way is fermented in a barrel then bottled and fermented some more, with the addition of champagne yeast and sugar, to give a pale, dry, sparkling drink. It's an elaborate and potentially explosive process which can take eighteen months or more to complete, and which involves freezing the neck of the bottle to get the sediment out. The producer is rewarded by paying a whopping £2 duty per litre – just part of the great UK government cider sell-out.

Mill

The machine that crushes apples so the juice can be pressed out of the pulp. Crushing the apples used to be the hardest part of cidermaking, but today's electric scratters make the job much easier. Some purists still prefer to bash apples in a tub with a heavy piece of wood. Whatever floats your boat...

P

Pear Cider

A post-Magners fad which bears more relation to the alcopops of the 1990s than anything else. Not to be confused with perry, pear cider is a fizzy, sugary drink made from dessert pears, often imported as concentrate and mixed with glucose and water under factory conditions.

Perry

The fermented juice of perry pears, a group of specialised pear varieties that grow best – but not exclusively – in the Three Counties of Gloucestershire, Herefordshire and Worcestershire. Slow Food, the slightly bizarre international group that campaigns for artisanal food products, recently added Three Counties Perry to its Ark of Taste, which is a wonderful tribute to the hard work of local producers in maintaining this ancient drink and the pear varieties used to make it through decades of public indifference. A good perry is hard to beat.

PGI and PDO

Established in 1993, PGI and PDO are designed to protect the identity and authenticity of food and drink products from a particular place. Protected Designation of Origin is the name of an area or place, used as a designation for an agricultural product or a foodstuff, which comes from said place, and whose qualities and character are significantly or exclusively determined by it. The entire manufacturing process has to take place within the determined geographical area. Protected Geographical Indication is similar but less demanding, since manufacture only has to take place partially within the specified area. UK PDOs include Single Gloucester and Blue Stilton cheese, and Cornish Clotted Cream, while PGIs include the Melton Mowbray Pork Pie and the Whitstable Oyster. Herefordshire, Worcestershire and Gloucestershire each have a PGI for cider and for perry, which stipulates that local vintage fruit should be processed in the traditional manner. For producers selling cider and perry in Europe particularly the PGI is a respected mark of quality. Somerset cider doesn't have a PGI. A debate has been going on for years about what 'Somerset cider' ought to mean – well, it's about the juice content, mainly – and so far no agreement has been reached. So at present 'Somerset cider' on a label means about as much as 'Made with English Apples', ie not very much.

O

Orchard

The place where you grow apples, pears, cherries and plums. Traditional orchards of standard trees once covered thousands of acres in every southern county; today the fragments that remain act as unofficial nature reserves, while many cider companies now grow apples in bush orchards, which give much higher yields more quickly. Still, a traditional orchard is a magical place.

Own Brand Strong Dry Cider

Usually sold in large plastic bottles this is the supermarkets' favourite – cheap as chips and easy to transport. A well-known maker of supermarket cider is Aston Manor Brewery of Birmingham, which also owns Knights, the Worcestershire company that makes Duchy Originals cider.

P

Pomace

The 'cake' of solid remains left at the bottom of a press after all the juice has been extracted. Clearing up the pomace after a day's pressing can be a headache, particularly if you live in a city and don't have a bunch of hungry pigs to hand – porkers love pomace. Wondering what to do with the pomace, the Bristol makers at Totterdown Press offered it for collection on the Freecycle website and it was taken within hours by a local farmer.

Pomona

The Roman goddess of orchards has given her name to a kind of book dear to the hearts of cider enthusiasts – an encyclopedia of apple varieties. The most famous, *The Herefordshire Pomona*, was published in the 1880s as a huge two volume affair. You can buy downloads of the pictures from the Marcher Apple Network, which published its own *Welsh Marches Pomona* in 2010. Liz Copas' *Somerset Pomona* is a must for all cider lovers.

Press

A machine designed to get the juice out of apples by applying pressure to the crushed fruit. The Greeks and Romans built fine beam presses for grapes and olives, and these were adapted for apples by Cistercian monks in the middle ages. The classic cider press was made from slabs of oak or elm, with screw threads carved through the solid wood. Crushed apple was built up in straw-wrapped layers to form a cheese, and pressure exerted on it by turning a handle. Most modern cider makers use a hydraulic or belt press, though small-scale hobbyists may use a basket press or manual pack press.

S

Scratter

A device used to pulp or mill the apples before they are pressed. Vigo offers a range of fruit crushers (or scratters) which vary from the Pulpmaster (under £25) to centrifugal mills which cost upwards of £700. The mid-range scratters tend to be hand operated mills. Many small-scale producers also recommend the Fruit Shark which is imported from the Czech Republic (see Listings for details). If you are only making a gallon or so of cider, you could use a kitchen blender to pulp the fruit. In Chester, Mike Houghton's Allotment Cider crew built their own scratter from an old lawnmower engine and a wooden roller studded with screws built into a feed hopper. Ingenious.

Scrumpy

Once, you could hardly drive a hundred yards down a West Country road without seeing a hand-painted sign bearing this magic word, but these days 'Farmhouse Cider' is a more acceptable term. Almost impossible to find unless you happen to be close to a place where it's made – ie the West Country and scattered outposts elsewhere – though you can order online (see Listings). This cider is generally strong, still (or slightly effervescent), and variable. Two barrels of cider made in the same place, at the same time and from the same blend of apples can taste strikingly different. The name may have its origins in the obsolete dialect term "scrimp", meaning a small or withered apple, which also gave rise to the verb "to scrump", meaning to steal fruit At its best scrumpy is a fine drink. At its worst, it isn't.

Single Orchard

Once upon a time each farm made cider from its own orchard, planted with a preferred mix of varieties. Recent interest in orchards has inspired cider companies to do something similar – Gaymers' Newton Vale cider is a good example.

Single Variety Cider

Most cider is made from a blend of apple varieties with complementary qualities – few apples produce a good cider alone. But a Single Variety cider can be something special, drawing on the unique flavour and character of the fruit. Kingston Black is probably the best-known apple of this kind – made into a fine, dry champagne-style cider at Burrow Hill – though Dabinett, Somerset Redstreak, Tremlett's Bitter and Morgan Sweet are also popular. Thatchers has pioneered a line of ciders made from dessert fruit, of which Katy is the most established.

Single Variety Perry

In contrast to cider apples, many common perry pears make excellent single variety perry. Blakeney Red is a classic example. In fact, it is often safer not to blend varieties – or to seek expert advice before you do so – since many perry pears are incompatible.

Terroir

A term coined aeons ago by French winemakers to describe the unique aspects of a place that influence and shape the wine made from it. It seems a bit fancy for cider, but there's no getting away from the fact that certain places are special when it comes to growing cider apples and perry pears. The region south-east of Glastonbury is one, and the area around Kingsbury Episcopi and Martock is another. Particular cider apples thrive on their preferred land, on the right soil and with the right climate, and produce the best cider they are capable of. Plant the same variety in another county and its performance will be markedly different.

White Cider

A favourite among open-air drinkers, white cider makes up for its alcoholic strength by having no other characteristics whatsoever. Presumably it has some relationship to apples, but the main point of white cider is that it attracts a lower rate of duty than beer of a comparable strength, which means it's super-cheap. However, its low tax rate and corresponding appeal to the less well-heeled alcoholic has caught the attention of red tops and politicians, and by the time you read this it may have become extinct. Let's hope so.

Yeast

The more you learn about yeast, the more miraculous this huge family of micro-organisms seems. Yeasts are all around us – some 1500 species have been documented – and they have been used in baking and fermentation for millennia. Wild yeasts grow naturally on the skin of fruit like apples and grapes; when you crush and press apples the yeast is combined with the juice and immediately goes to work, metabolising fruit sugars to produce ethanol and carbon dioxide. Over time a certain strain of yeast will become dominant around the press and other equipment used by a particular cidermaker, and will give the cider a distinctive character. For this reason many craft producers prefer to use only wild yeasts. Others choose to kill off wild yeasts with sulphite and add cultivated yeast. NB Never use baker's yeast!

Q&A ANDREW LEA

CIDER-MAKING GURU FROM THE WITTENHAM HILL CIDER PAGE (WWW.CIDER.ORG.UK)

What got you interested in cider and perry?
Being a student in Bristol in the 1960s – Coronation Tap and all that, plus the excellent Long Ashton bottled cider in the University Refectory. Then following a spell in the tea industry after graduation, I managed to wangle my way into the Long Ashton Research Station to do a PhD and to work on cider-related biochemistry for 13 happy years until the Cider Section was shut down in 1985.

Do you have a treasured memory of a particularly good cider or perry?
My own first keeved (naturally sweet) bottle-conditioned cider. The technique was effectively obsolete so I had no practical experience to draw on until I'd done it for myself. Then I discovered just how good it could be (no bragging!).

How do you account for the recent surge of interest in cider and cidermaking?
Three reasons I think. One is the Magner's effect – cleverly marketed industrial cider which had the effect of making people ask "Just what is this stuff anyway?" Two is the Slow Food movement and the efforts of the likes of Tom Oliver, James Marsden and many others to promote the highest quality of artisan cider that they can. Three is just the cyclical shift of interest that happens over time with most foods and beverages anyway.

Any advice for the novice cidermaker?
Think like a winemaker not a brewer. Check your pH and add sufficient sulphite to do a proper job. When it's finished, keep the air right out. There is nothing 'natural' about cider and it's silly to pretend that there is. Like all wines, cider is a product of man's ingenuity in harnessing the natural world. Don't be frightened to use as much technology as you need to create a superb product. There's no merit in 'muck and magic' for the sake of it.

Do you have a favourite apple variety?
Dabinett, is a well-behaved reliable bittersweet with fine soft tannin. Just needs blending with Broxwood Foxwhelp or maybe Stoke Red which are aromatic bittersharps. All slow fermenters, vintage quality… magic!

Can you tell us about your best and/or worst moment as a cidermaker?
Best – winning my very first First Prize at the Hereford International Competition for my bottle-conditioned cider, and taking a Second at the same time! Worst – throwing away hundreds of litres of tainted cider after a poorly managed keeve – all my own fault but I knew there was no hope of saving it.

What's your most precious bit of cider-related gear?
My copy of Worlidge's *'Vinetum Brittanicum'* (1691), which I bought from a book dealer in New York at a time when the dollar exchange rate made it about half the price it would have been if I'd bought it in London. Otherwise my most precious asset is my own little orchard, planned and planted to my prescription to make a cider that myself and my family enjoy.

What can we do to ensure that orchards are still flourishing in 50 years' time?
Plant or manage your own if you can; keep drinking other people's good cider if you can't.

Anything you'd like to add?
The most surprising thing I learnt in recent years, courtesy of James Crowden, was that there was a flourishing orchard and cider business in the late 17th century in Central Oxford, less than 10 miles from where I now live. Ralph Austen was its owner, and he even sold apple trees to Isaac Newton!

Somerset Ciderland

Can any other area boast such a distinguished tradition of cidermaking as the heart of cider country?

To tourists heading south on Bank Holiday weekends Somerset may be synonymous with motorway jams and cries of 'Are we nearly there yet?', but to the cider drinker this is sacred country. And you don't even have to stray far from the motorway to experience it since those kind road engineers planned the M5 to pass right through the heart of Ciderland. Junctions 22 (Rich's and West Croft) and 26 (Sheppy's) could have been built specially for the thirsty traveller.

In Somerset all roads lead to cider...

Somerset has a distinctive landscape of steep hills and lowlands and an independent spirit. Motorway travellers pass within a few miles of Sedgemoor, site of the 1685 battle that crushed the Monmouth Rebellion and led to the execution or transportation of Somerset people in their hundreds, following the Bloody Assizes of Hanging Judge Jeffreys. Body parts of the executed were displayed prominently in rebel towns and villages, with the worst offenders getting a head or two, and the least an arm or a leg. The independent spirit that drove Monmouth's ragtag army pervades Somerset cider and inspires its champions. Julian Temperley has been fighting Eurocrats and Whitehall bunglers for years, and has long been a thorn in the side of the National Association of Cider Makers. Roger Wilkins has stuck to his guns even longer, refusing to change with the times and becoming a Cider Hero in the process. Old traditions die hard in the land of summer, where Wassail has been celebrated almost continuously for centuries, and where small-scale farm cidermaking has clung on in the face of everything the modern world has thrown at it – tied pubs, government pay-outs for orchard destruction, increases in duty, you name it…

Drive around Somerset and you will still find signs leading you off the main road to farmyard ciderhouses. Nowadays you'll even find new ones as the cider renaissance encourages smallholders and downshifters to sell their wares. The county has had specialist cider companies for two hundred years but no single business has ever succeeded in dominating the county, and as giant companies lose their balance and topple over, or get swallowed up by international corporations, new, smaller businesses take their place. This process has been going on for centuries, and shows no sign of stopping.

The 1920s and 1930s saw Taunton Cider, Coates, Showerings and others struggling for the elusive top dog spot as the farmers kept on making their cider – each one a unique, sometimes challenging product of a particular orchard or village. In the decades after the war the rural workforce shrank, tractors took over from horses and cider barns across the county were converted into houses for the new population of retirees and long-distance commuters. But a few of the old farm presses fell into the right hands, and a few of the old farm orchards were replanted, and the tradition survived.

Good thing too, because there are few places in the world where cider apples grow so well or produce such wonderful cider. Perry pears have never taken off in the same way, but the Somerset varieties documented by Liz Copas in *A Somerset Pomona* are deeply rooted in the county. Some – like Yarlington Mill – were found growing wild, Mother Nature doing her thing in the heart of cider country. Some varieties remain unnamed and even unknown outside a particular orchard. They give particular ciders their unique flavour and feel.

Today's cidermakers are not catering for a thirsty workforce but selling to visitors, pubs or supermarkets. A few are profiled in this section, and more are listed at the back. For a more thorough survey we recommend Alan Stone's *'Somerset Cider Handbook'.*

It may look like a sign directing you to the nearest horse-and-cart emporium, but in reality this means CIDER.

A rescued phone box at Parsonage Farm, home of Parson's Choice cider.

Cider by Bike

We thought long and hard about whether it's a good idea to encourage cider cycling, and decided that if one of our readers drowned in a rhine or got run over by a peat lorry they would at least die happy.

The Moors and Levels are great cycling country, being flat and quiet, although there's a steep little climb up from Westhay to Mudgley and the main roads can be slightly alarming. For best results you could try the following:

1. Book your bike onto a train to Highbridge (the stop north of Bridgwater).
2. Buy the Ordnance Survey map that covers central Somerset (No. 182).
3. Plan a route, bearing in mind that you may not want a long ride later in the day. See Listings for places to visit.
4. Spend a pleasant day lost in the countryside.
5. Remember to go home again, unless you really don't want to.

You can't beat a bike ride around the Moors and Levels, with the odd stop for cider...

As well as selling fine ciders, Perrys has an eccentric museum featuring wicker birds and a collection of animal traps.

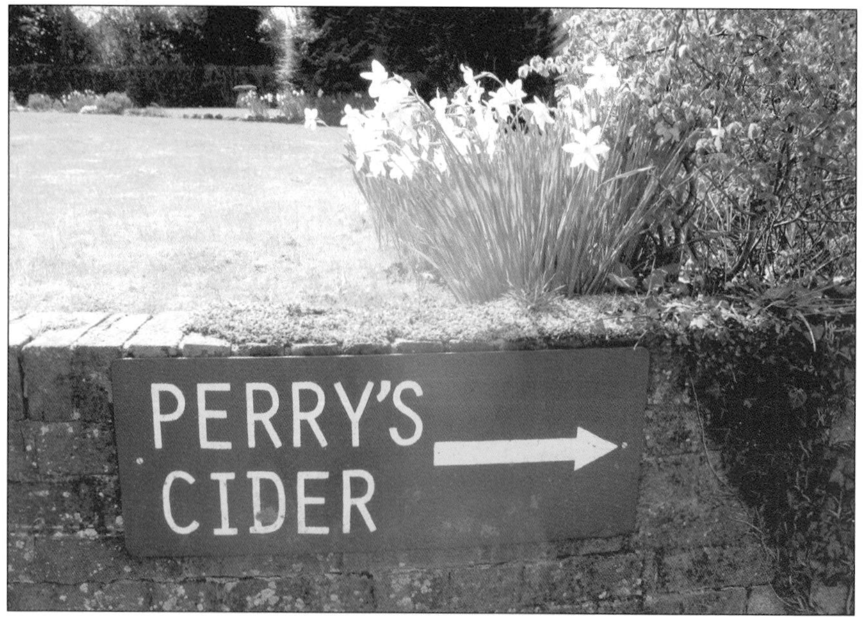

Brent Knoll – Mark - Wedmore

Before the Abbots of Glastonbury supervised the drainage of the Somerset Levels – known locally as the Moors – and the building of flood defences, the flat land crossed by the M5 after its descent from the shoulder of the Mendips would have been fairly damp. You can see today where the ground is higher because that's mostly where the houses are – the houses and the apple trees.

Orchards proliferate on the western slopes of Brent Knoll – which is well worth clambering up if you feel like a break from the motorway – along the low ridge of Mark Causeway and on the steep south-facing hillside rising from Westhay Moor. The apples on this slope are destined for glory at Roger Wilkins' barn at Land's End Farm, Mudgley, while the fruit that grows around Mark and Brent Knoll fills the barrels of Rich's – including Adge Cutler's giant vat – and West Croft Farm respectively.

You could tour these three cider farms in a short jaunt from the motorway. In recent years Wilkins and West Croft have vied for cider farm party capital of Somerset, with the home of Janet's Jungle Juice edging ahead in the Wassail stakes while Rog takes the summer prize with his Harvest-home-type hoe-down.

Serving the holidaymakers of Burnham and Brean, Rich's now offers a fantastic all-round cider experience, with a restaurant and a great little museum.

There have been orchards at Glastonbury Abbey for 1000 years or more. The abbey may be in ruins now, but the apple trees are in prime condition.

Around Glastonbury

There used to be far more orchards than houses in Britain's kookiest town, and if you explore the Tor in autumn you'll see pale apples hanging like lanterns from ancient trees. It's that kind of place. The Abbey has a fine cider orchard and at the Rural Life Museum there are various annual apple-related events, including an Apple Day cider pressing and the obligatory Wassail, and a well-kept orchard complete with sheep, and if you saunter down the road to the Rifleman you can recover from a long walk up the hill with a pint of Wilkins – don't expect to be offered it though, you have to ask.

If you do make it up to the top of the Tor spare a thought for Richard Whiting, the last Abbot of Glastonbury and a venerable churchman of eighty. He was hung, drawn and quartered up there on the orders of Henry VIII, his head being fastened over the gate of the deserted abbey and his limbs put on display at Wells, Bath, Ilchester and Bridgwater. Lovely people, the Tudors.

Below the Tor, to the south, the flat land is covered in trees but those aren't natural woods – this area, around Baltonsborough, West Bradley and the Pennards, is prime orchard country, worth exploring if you're a connoisseur of cider fruit or old-fashioned road signs. Not too many places to actually visit, although Sir Neville Grenville lived at nearby Butleigh Court, and Orchard Pig do their thing in the genteel surroundings of the West Bradley Fruit Farm.

To the east lies Shepton Mallet, where Blackthorn drinkers can go and stare at 11 million barrels of their favourite brew, and closer at hand, to the west, the town of Street – birthplace of many an illustrious cidermaker but best-known as the home of Hecks. Not the worst place to end up after spending an hour or two failing to identify apples.

There are a couple of great campsites within a few miles of Glastonbury and then of course there's the Pilton Festival, as you have to call it round those parts. Someone said there was a bus there, where you can buy cider. Weird.

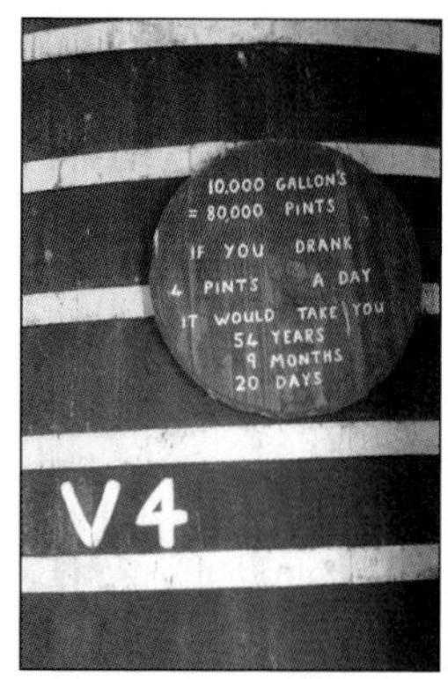

You can't argue with maths like that... One of the giant vats that were rescued from Coates and moved down the motorway to Rich's.

Once the haunt of shotgun-toting ne'erdowells, the Rusty Axe has taken several strides upmarket.

Kingsbury Episcopi and Environs

The pub down the lane from Burrow Hill is called the Rusty Axe, and not too long ago it had a reputation to match its name. These days it's very swish and you can sit outside, have your lunch, and look out for people who are driving round Stembridge in circles trying to find Burrow Hill. The hill itself is like Solsbury in miniature, a conical projection with a single sycamore at the top – you can see it for miles across the flat lands of south Somerset, and from the top (where a swing hangs invitingly from a branch) orchards spread out in all directions.

A couple of miles away the National Trust property of Barrington Court sells cider made from apples grown in the fabulous orchards surrounding the Tudor mansion. It's popular though, so check they have some before making a special journey.

This is great biking country too – you can take the train to Taunton, Yeovil or Crewkerne and explore from there. Settlements and orchards follow the road raised above the floodplain of the River Parrett to Langport; stop at Muchelney to have a nose around the remains of the abbey and admire the ceramics on display at John Leach's pottery. Just before Langport, in Huish Episcopi, stands the famous

Rose and Crown, known as Eli's; in the past they've had camping in the paddock next door, but check before you travel.

Around Taunton

Before finding its way to Glastonbury Festival the Cider Bus spent a few summers at the Somerset County Cricket Ground in Taunton, proof that the county town and its cricket fans like their cider. And no wonder. A couple of miles north of here – so legend has it – the most famous cider apple of modern times was found growing in the village of Kingston St Mary (no prizes for guessing the variety), and just to the west the vicars of Heathfield Rectory once made cider fit for a Queen.

For most of the 20th century Taunton Cider was among the best-known cider companies and it was a sad day when the Norton Fitzwarren factory was demolished.

But don't despair. Sheppy's Cider is not far away, between Taunton and Wellington and only a couple of miles from Junction 26 of the M5, and the Sheppy family have been making cider for the best part of two centuries. With so much holiday traffic passing by their door this isn't so much a cider farm as a cider theme park, with tea room, farm walks, museum, etc. We like the fact that they consider their autumn cider-making tours 'very suitable for all ages'. Children are the future, are they not?

The downside of the motorway is that it encourages everyone to visit the same places and perhaps deters more adventurous explorations, but explore in any direction and you'll find some treasures. Head towards Glastonbury on the A361 and you pass through West Lyng, home of Parson's Choice – an excellent artisan cider made by a father and daughter team and occasionally available at the Orchard Inn in Bristol. They're in the middle of King Alfred's old stamping ground, incidentally, and nearby Athelney and Burrowbridge are worth a visit. Serena de la Hay, sculptor of the M5 Wicker Man, lives nearby.

Alternatively, take the A358 south from Taunton: Ashill Cider near Hatch Beauchamp make a lovely, authentic farmhouse juice, and on the other side of Ilminster, the idyllic village of Dowlish Wake is home to Perry's Cider. The village itself is, as they say, Steeped in History, and was the home of Nile explorer John Hanning Speke. Having

Where else would you find a work of art like this tractor weather vane?

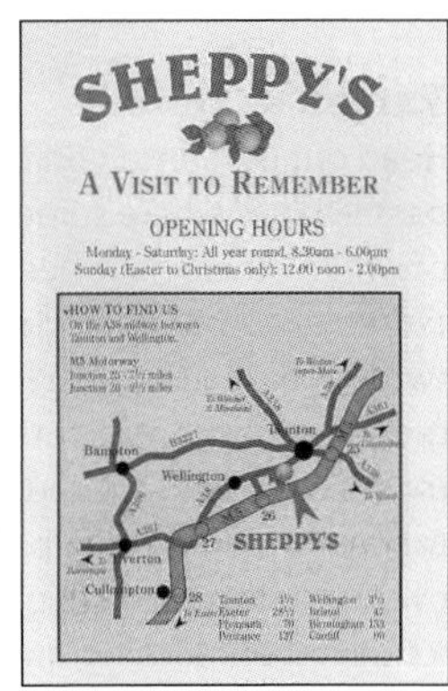

Was the M5 built by ciderheads? Practically every Somerset junction leads you straight to a cider farm, like Sheppy's.

survived the perils of central Africa Speke managed to get himself killed on a hunting expedition in darkest Wiltshire, but that's by the by. The central attraction here is Perry's, where past and present coexist very pleasantly; the museum housed in a 16th century barn is good value (it's free) with unusual exhibits that include a collection of iron hunting traps. The shop and tea room are modern, likewise the cider, which has been rebranded recently and to good effect. In everyday life Perry's isn't that easy to find, so it's well worth the detour to get here.

But now you are here, it's only a hop and a skip to Kingsbury Episcopi. Incidentally, if you want to see a truly amazing cider orchard, stop at Over Stratton, just off the A303, and walk to the south of the village. Stand in the middle of the massed ranks of trees, with the fruit ripening all around, and you'll get a deep sense of what this is all about…

Named after the legendary Parson Thomas Cornish of Heathfield Rectory, Parson's Choice makes excellent use of vintage Somerset fruit.

Parson's Choice

Head out of Taunton on the A361 to Glastonbury and you pass villages where some old family farms are still hanging on while others have been converted for comfortable retirement. Phil Dolding set up shop at Parsonage Farm twenty years ago, while holding down a day job as a groundworks contractor for BT and British Gas, and now makes cider with his daughter, Jeanette. There aren't too many women who put their hands to the press every autumn and we've seen Jeanette hard at work on a November morning, she and her dad silently building cheese after cheese with the rhythm of two people who know each other pretty well.

Jeanette at Parson's Choice hard at work pressing apples. She works with her dad Phil – an unusual example of a father-and-daughter cidermaking team.

The Parson in question is none other than the Rev Thomas Cornish, one of the great characters of Somerset cider history; we're sure the old clergyman would be happy to appear on Phil's labels.

For a good old-fashioned Somerset cider, full-bodied and with the soft tannins of the Taunton Vale, this is near the top of our list. Have a sip before you buy, because you never know quite what a particular barrel will be like until you've tasted it, but we tried this on people who don't normally touch cider with a barge pole and a gallon went in no time. It's all about the fruit, a blend of Kingston Black, Yarlington Mill, Michelin and other vintage varieties – a total of 26 in all. Though Phil has a mechanical harvester he shows true Somerset spirit by refusing to use it, preferring to pick apples up by hand from the four-acre orchard he planted when he started out two decades ago.

Ashill Cider

If you ever find yourself on the A358 travelling between the A303 at Ilminster and the M5 at Taunton, look out for the Cider signs. They lead up and down and around to the village of Ashill, which is only a mile off the main road but seems further. When you've driven in to the farmyard and hooted your horn to attract attention, the Somerset quiet settles around you.

We've been buying cider at Ashill for years and this is part of the pleasure: a moment away from the rush and the racket of traffic. The cider buying process is similarly unhurried and simple. Mrs House will lead you into the cool of an old brick barn, where the cider lies in large oak barrels. Nothing about the place is trying too hard to impress, and the cider has the same straightforward quality. It's got good farmhouse tannins and a robust, earthy flavour.

The House family inherited the cider business along with the small mixed farm when they bought it in 1984; they even inherited a stock of cider, which they began selling right away. As tends to happen with cider and orchards, they found themselves pulled deeper and deeper into the business, and the last time we dropped in were urgently looking for a new orchard to buy.

Of course you could just drive past – time is short, after all. But there aren't too many places like this, where you can taste and buy cider in the quiet of a Somerset afternoon.

Burrow Hill has to be high on the list for any Somerset cider itinerary.

Outspoken and tireless, Julian Temperley is one of the great champions of Somerset cider. Photo by Bill Bradshaw (billbradshaw.co.uk).

Julian Temperley

"You don't choose cidermaking. You fall into it by mistake."

If a journalist wants a quote about the latest Ciderland crisis the first person they call is Julian Temperley, of Pass Vale Farm, Burrow Hill Cider and Somerset Cider Brandy. He usually answers, and invariably has something cogent or mildly provocative to say. Magners may have persuaded a generation to drink cider, but Julian has devoted a lifetime to the goal of changing the way people perceive the drink he considers a closer relation of wine than beer.

AGAINST THE ODDS

JULIAN TEMPERLEY FOUGHT BUREAUCRACY TO RESURRECT SOMERSET CIDER BRANDY

We put up with some strange restrictions on our freedom in this country. Take the distillation of spirits, for instance. Across the Channel everyone and his dog are making moonshine out of pretty much anything that grows. As you read this, old boys in garden sheds from Calais to Kiev are distilling liquor from potatoes and blackcurrants, melons and walnuts, pears and plums. The French make eau de vie, the Germans have schnapps, then you've got Balkan rakia, Romanian tuica, Czech slivovitz and Hungarian palinka,

We have whisky in Scotland, which is strictly controlled and heavily taxed, but also officially sanctioned, but across England and Wales the spirits you're most likely to come across are mass-produced gin and murderous imported vodka. Why? Because it's illegal to make so much as a snifter of distilled spirits without a licence from HM Customs.

The French don't have marvellous brandies and so on because they're somehow better at it than we are, but because our government has spent centuries taxing our every sip and making small-scale production of spirits virtually impossible. French farmers and fruit growers can make a few bob selling fire water to tourists. Guess what? Ours can't.

In Normandy, the Calvados region is famed for the eponymous spirit, a brandy distilled from cider. Calvados is a valuable French export, perhaps not up there with the top wine-based brandies but a significant feature of the Gallic culinary wonderland. Somerset cider can also be made into a fine brandy, but until recently no one had distilled cider legally in the county for centuries.

When, in the mid-1980s, Julian Temperley decided to revive this moribund art he discovered why no one else had bothered for so long. Have a look at the conditions you have to fulfil to get approval for a Rectifier's Licence and you'll have an idea of the hoop-jumping that went on as Julian first ran a museum still at Brympton d'Evercy near Yeovil and then launched Somerset Royal Cider Brandy in 1987, using a pair of alembic stills, nicknamed Josephine and Fifi, that had previously belonged to a Calvados maker. Today you can visit the distillery, which occupes a corner of the farmyard at Burrow Hill, while the cider brandy lies under lock and key in a bonded warehouse.

Julian's aim was to bring together elements of the Calvados tradition with those of Scotch whisky to create a unique Somerset spirit. He had no choice but to aim high; given the rate of duty on spirits and the costs involved – orcharding, cidermaking and distillation with the attendant bottling, marketing, transport, etc – this had to be a product that would compete not only with imported Calvados but also with equivalently priced brandies. To discover whether the venture was successful or not he had to wait years, until the spirit reached full maturity and could be sold at the top price.

The difference in price is striking. At the time of writing a 70cl bottle of Somerset Royal Three Year Old brandy in a nice box costs £22. The same volume of Somerset Ten Year Old will set you back £33. And the top notch Somerset Alchemy Fifteen Year Old is available from the company's online shop for £39. More importantly, perhaps, it's the reputation of Alchemy that must persuade the swanky restaurants and niche stores of the venture's seriousness.

Twenty years on, things were going well. The Telegraph described Alchemy as 'exquisite, smooth, elegant and appley', and the Financial Times was equally happy with the Ten Year Old, refering to 'a raisiny tang lending breadth to the refined apple notes'. Not one to miss an opportunity Julian subsequently managed to secure a number of oak casks that had been rescued when the MSC Napoli came to grief in Lyme Bay in January 2007 – they were, apparently, protected from the sea by a load of Zulu bibles. These barrels were filled with Ten Year

Old cider brandy, which was then bottled for Christmas under the name 'Shipwreck'.

Then came a bizarre and potentially disastrous turn of events. The European Commission decided to rewrite the 197 pages of regulations which define all the spirits produced in the region. The Commission intended to keep the words 'cider brandy', which are in the current regulations, but five wine making states objected, namely France, Spain, Germany, Italy and Greece. Defra was consulted, but made no objection; nor did the Ministry even mention the issue to UK distillers. So the words 'cider brandy' were dropped, meaning that it would, after a lapse of a year so, be illegal to use them. At the time of writing, Somerset Cider Brandy is technically illegal.

In response the company applied for Protected Geographical Indication (PGI) status, which was granted in 2009 subject to a 6 month consultation period. The day before this ended and the PGI came into force, complaints were received from three countries, and the whole thing was put on hold again. PGI status was finally granted in February 2012; to celebrate, Damien Hirst designed a new label for the tipple known in Spain as el 'british brandy de manzana'.

In the meantime, judges at Radio 4's 2009 Food and Farming Awards awarded Julian Temperley their Special Award for Somerset Cider Brandy.

"It is, in the end, an award for Somerset's cider tradition," he said, "Because without the generations of cidermakers in the past and orchardists, we wouldn't have the knowledge base to be able to introduce such a fine brandy in the south west."

For Julian there's personal satisfaction in having overcome the obstacles placed in his path. But there's a practical reason why people should go out and buy a bottle of Somerset Cider Brandy This is, after all, the spirit of Somerset orchards – the concentrated essence of the Somerset cider apples grown by the company on standard trees in local, traditional orchards. Not long ago the company bought a seventy-acre orchard at Over Stratton, near Crewkerne, which would otherwise have been grubbed up. In the ordinary countryside, traditional orchards are oases for wildlife, particularly birds (see Orchards section). The RSPB should be buying up Somerset Cider Brandy by the barrel.

In the flat landscape Burrow Hill stands like a miniature version of Solsbury Hill. There's a swing hanging from that tree, incidentally.

Among his favourite possessions are copies of the 19th century Herefordshire Pomona and the cidermaker's bible – John Worlidge's *Vinetum Britannicum* of 1676. The former is a massive, richly decorated two-volume tome, the latter a tiny, shabby-looking book that includes the first mention of cider brandy. Written during cider's Golden Age, it inspired Julian to try and invent a new one.

Good cider was made at Pass Vale Farm before Julian arrived. He inherited the terroir – the unique combination of soil, geography and climate that gives a special quality to varieties grown in a particular place – and made the most of it, winning awards for Burrow Hill Cider throughout the 1970s and exploiting any and every marketing opportunity – from Somerset County Cricket Club to Glastonbury Festival. Quality was always paramount, and at the core of Julian's cidermaking philosophy remains the simple principle that good cider comes from the juice of vintage varieties – he grows around 40 – fermented and matured in oak.

The cider barn at Pass Vale Farm.

Somerset Cider Brandy's two stills, Josefine and Fifi, once belonged to a Calvados maker in Normandy.

Having established his reputation as a good cidermaker and outspoken champion of the Somerset cider tradition, Julian set about dragging the industry upmarket. establishing the first legal cider distillery in more than a century (see previous page) and joining a select few makers of Methode Traditionelle (champagne-style) cider.

Critics have been impressed both by the Kingston Black bottle-fermented cider and by Somerset Cider Brandy, not to mention Julian's version of Pommeau, the aperitif Pomona, in which cider brandy is blended with apple juice. High-end products make more money, which means the company has been able to invest in orchards, a new belt press and a permanent staff.

But despite the enthusiasm of press and public, and despite the obvious benefits in terms of rural employment, wildlife conservation and cultural diversity, Julian has had to fight every step of the way. On the one hand you have HM Customs and Excise, which has made the distillation of spirits into a bureaucratic nightmare, and on the other the rule-makers of the European Union, who seem to take a personal delight in tormenting Julian.

First the UK government caved into the demands of EU wine makers for a crippling tax hike on champagne-style cider, encouraging the import of cheap, industrially-produced cava and prosecco at the expense of artisan cider and perry. Then, more recently, a rewrite of the EU rules on spirits saw 'cider brandy' erased as a legal product – UK bureaucrats failed to prevent it, or even to tell anyone what was going on.

Through all this Julian has somehow remained positive and upbeat, rarely restrained in his opinions but always keen to point out that Somerset cider is about a county and a culture, not just a few individuals.

What started out as a hobby has become a cider success story for Neil McDonald (left) and Andrew Quinlan of Orchard Pig.

The Orchard Pig

Andrew Quinlan was drawn to cidermaking by a liking for Normandy cider. Scrumpy is definitely not his thing. In 2003 he tried his hand at making a barrel, much as many of us have, filtering his cider to remove what he describes rather eloquently as 'the furry bits'. Enjoying the result, he made more the following year, and even more the year after.

By 2006 he had his friend Neil McDonald working alongside him and, still as a hobby, made more than 20,000 bottles of cider. At this point they sat down to put together a business plan, then hired Blue Marlin of Bath to work on the brand. The name 'The Orchard Pig' refers to the Gloucester Old Spots Andrew keeps as a hobby, and it fits their need for something quirky, memorable and different. No doubt Andrew, a former Marine with experience in sales and marketing, was also aware of the selling power of that word 'orchard'.

The new business had several things going for it. Magners had got people interested in cider to the extent

All Aboard!

Somerset Cider Bus Cider plays on the fame of the blue Leyland bus that has become a Glastonbury Festival landmark, and it marks the arrival of the next generation of Temperleys. We already have fashion designer Alice and photographer Matilda. The Cider Bus Cider is Edward's baby. Like father like son? Let's hope so. The cider is certainly a recognisable Burrow Hill product, lightly carbonated but – praise the lord! – not too sweet. CAMRA might add it to their list of Unreal Ciders, but you can taste the tannins.

First came the bus of the cider... now here comes the cider of the bus.

that they would pay a decent price for a bottled product. Neil came from a farming background and had expertise in orchard management, which he has put to exemplary use with the West Country Ground Force. And they were making cider in West Bradley, Somerset, within easy reach of scores of orchards planted with the finest cider apples in the world.

For much of the 20th century the firm of Clapps had made fine bottled ciders just along the road in Baltonsborough, building on the fine work done by Sir Neville Grenville at nearby Butleigh Court. Clapps were famous in the 1920s for their champagne-style cider, which they called Avalagne. Almost a century later The Orchard Pig is rapidly achieving a similar success with its appeal to up-market drinkers and its consistently high quality. The cider is not made Normandy-style, by keeving, but is filtered, sweetened with sugar when necessary, carbonated and pasteurised. Andrew is up-front about his methods and doesn't touch saccharin. The Orchard Pig cider slides down very nicely.

Curiously, Andrew doesn't see too much future growth in bottled ciders. Market research has shown that most pub-goers choose their drink at the bar, by looking along the taps, so if you want to sell a lot of cider your name has to be on a tap. Ergo, you sell cider in kegs, which is what The Orchard Pig will be doing a lot more from now on.

Andrew may have started out making cider that he liked, but now he's doing what any good businessman would do – giving the public what they want.

The area around West Bradley where Orchard Pig is based is top cider apple country.

More than a few gallons of cider have been served from Rog's barrels. You can have Dry or Sweet. Mix them together and you have Medium.

Roger Wilkins

Other cidermakers can count royalty among their fans, but who's had a public thumbs-up from Joe Strummer and Johnnie Rotten? Who else but Somerset's punk cidermaker, who has steadfastly done his own thing for four decades and is now spoken of in awed terms by cider fans the world over. Ask any cider tourist for their top five world destinations and Mudgley will be on the list. The otherwise unremarkable village has appeared in countless newspapers and magazines, has been filmed several times and has even been namechecked by indie stars Reef.

No doubt Roger's grandfather would enjoy the attention, though he would be horrified by the decline in farmhouse cider sales since his death in the late 1960s. Somerset pubs that used to sell gallons of local cider every day now sell virtually none, thanks to changing tastes and the iron grip of the breweries, and it would take an impossible number of cider pilgrims to make up for the loss of all those hardened local drinkers.

While other makers have expanded massively (Thatchers) or developed new markets (Burrow Hill) Roger has kept on pressing apples, fermenting the juice and selling his cider at proper farmhouse prices. The increasing reliance on 'farm gate' sales means that the cider barn and famous Lounge Bar are a-buzz with customers and locals, even in the dead of winter, and in the summer the place is packed with happy ciderheads clutching their half-pint mugs of Dry, Medium or Sweet.

The man himself is a living testament to the health-giving power of cider. By his own admission he started on his journey to cider stardom when he was six, and as a young man drank eight pints a day while running a farm as well as making and selling 50,000 gallons of cider a year. Not long ago he cut down to four (though presumably he's allowed a couple extra for his Wassail and Harvest festivals),

It's rumoured that this wall painting at Land's End Farm is by the world-famous street artist Banksy. It probably isn't, though the parachuting cows and rats are familiar Banksy images.

Rog Wilkins at home in the cider barn at Land's End Farm. Picture by Stephen Morris.

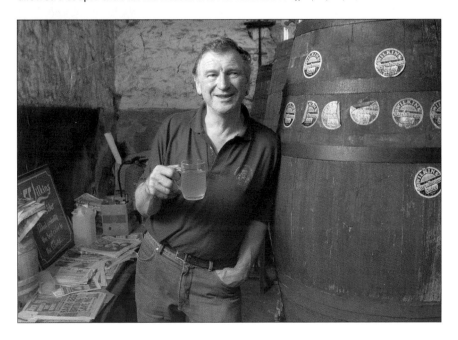

which seems pretty reasonable. Then again, he's not sitting in front of a computer all day but running around after cattle and doing all the physical work associated with cidermaking on a medium scale.

In the autumn you'll find him in the orchards above the farm picking up apples by hand, or down in the barn working the press. As anyone who has attempted to squeeze the juice out of an apple will know, this is hard, physical labour. At Wilkins the apples are loaded onto a conveyor, which takes them up to a mill; the crushed pomace is funnelled down to the bed of the hydraulic press, where it is built up in layers in the old way. Roger and his assistant build cheese after cheese in this way, for months, as farmers and farmworkers used to all over the county, year after year. And when he's not doing that he's dashing about, looking after his customers and sharing his thoughts on the topics of the day. He's continually astonished, even now, by the price of houses in the village, and can't understand why so few people produce anything these days. He wasn't a big fan of Mr Blair.

What some other Somerset cidermakers find hard to understand is why people love Wilkins so much. Everyone else is rushing about trying to be as modern and stylish as possible, and here he is, still pressing the same old fruit in the same old way, adding a pinch of saccharin to make the Sweet but otherwise making no concession to changing tastes. To the unwary his Dry can come as a shock. It's pretty sharp, with some hefty tannins, and we've seen the odd novice wince at the first gulp. But to the initiated it goes down like orange juice.

It's not easy to find Wilkins outside his immediate neighbourhood, and if you've made it as far as Wedmore you might as well just go to the farm. There was a famous incident when Rog asked for a pint of his own cider at a local pub and was charged rather more than he expected, so don't expect to find his cider too often. The Rifleman in Glastonbury has a barrel tucked out of sight, and the Bird in Hand in Westhay is another option. He's also on the Ciderpunk list and has cider distributed to festivals by John Hallam, the bearded cider impresario. The Cotham Porter Stores in Bristol supposedly has Wilkins, although there wasn't any to be seen last time we went.

Let's face it. What you really want to do is drive down

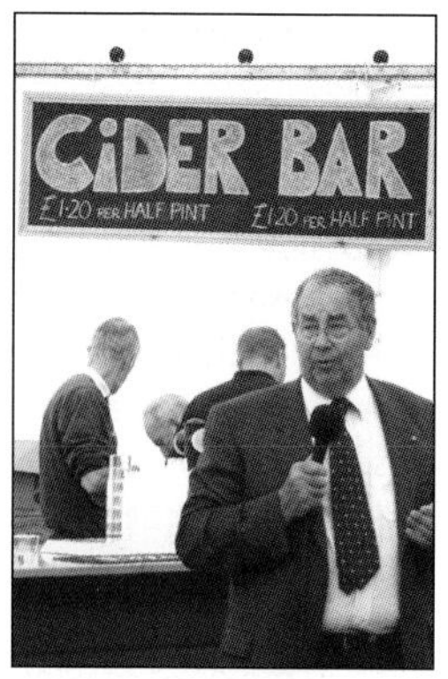

An expert in his field, John Thatcher can often be found among the judges at cider competitions. Here he is doing his bit at the Bath and West.

The scale of cidermaking at Myrtle Farm has changed a bit in recent years, but the principles remain the same.

that seemingly endless lane to Land's End Farm, park up and dodge through to the Lounge Bar, to receive a brimming mug from Roger himself.

Expect to leave with a gallon. If you want it to keep, decant it into clean plastic bottles, filled right to the brim and sealed tight.

Even in black and white you can sense the warm, carrotty glow of Cheddar Valley.

Thatchers

It's a bit tricky, this one. When we were planning The Naked Guide to Cider we realised we needed some 'inward investment' to keep the cover price down and a bit of help with marketing, so we approached Martin Thatcher, who agreed to sponsor the book. We should have written this profile before he said yes, and locked it in a safe until the book was ready to go to print, but we didn't. So we're probably biased. Oh well.

Anyway, if you live in Bristol or the Southwest and you like cider, the chances are you consume Thatchers on a fairly regular basis, either carrot-orange Cheddar Valley (a personal favourite), dry, flavoursome Traditional, the more delicate Gold, or the queen of lady's ciders, Thatchers Rosé. Under the leadership of Martin Thatcher the company has been remarkably innovative while continuing to make and sell good, straightforward cider. Despite expansion into the up-market bottled cider sector, the company still sells more than half its cider in draught form, through pubs and shops, and at the Sandford HQ.

Martin Thatcher's great grandfather started making cider in 1904.

Martin's great-grandfather was apprenticed as a carpenter but abandoned the trade after being asked to prepare a suicide for the coffin. He went into farming instead, and began making cider in 1904 as part of the general business of running a farm. By the 1960s John Thatcher was running Myrtle Farm and making the cider, and over the next thirty years he turned Thatchers into a regional favourite. He was – and still is – a huge supporter of cidermaking in Somerset and of the industry in general, having been involved for years with the National Association of Cider Makers; he was given their Fred Beech Award for services to the industry in recognition of his efforts to get orchards included in the Single Payment System in 2004/5. By this time Martin Thatcher was running the company, taking the traditional Somerset producer into new markets with new products and new varieties, and investing heavily in the Sandford site. While the old farm buildings have been converted into a shop and other facilities, a modern factory built where the cowsheds once stood can process 25,000 tonnes of fruit a day; the new Bucher presses still squeeze apple juice through cloth like the old pack press, but so efficiently that the pomace extruded at the end of the process is bone dry and almost odourless.

In orchards behind the mill, apples are grown along wires to form a hedgerow, part of a continuous process of research into varieties and growing techniques. Thatchers is closely involved with the NACM's pomological tests, and has at any one time 500 varieties growing on an experimental basis in its exhibition orchard. This is the sort of work that used to be conducted at Long Ashton – you could even see it as a descendant of the farmer's nursery of gribbles – and it has already given us new varieties like Gilly, Lizzie and Angela, as well as Prince William. Not for the first time, the future is growing down a Somerset lane.

For the romantic who loves old orchards and quaint cider barns this operation may seem a bit, well, modern, but how else can a family firm compete with the corporate giants? As it is, Thatchers employs 90 people directly, buys fruit from numerous growers, and has an influence that spreads much further across Somerset and beyond; if you win a cider competition there's a decent chance that John Thatcher will be among the judges, while we know of at least one community cidermaking venture that has benefited from Martin's help and advice, not to mention a certain publishing project…

So we're biased, but with good reason.

Cidermakers have been persuading women to drink cider for more than a century...

Quality control is paramount at the Thatchers cider farm in Sandford. Somerset

THATCHERS KATY – ONE FOR THE LADIES

When factory production of cider began at the end of Victoria's reign it became possible for the first time to control sweetness, flavour, alcoholic strength and sparkle. With pasteurisation and bottling it wasn't necessary to make cider that was loaded with tannins to help it keep. Nor would you lose alcoholic strength if you wanted to make a cider sweeter.

Soon the term 'lady's cider' came into use, to describe light, filtered ciders that no farm labourer worth his salt would dream of quaffing from his owl or firkin. In the 1950s

Bulmers made a concerted effort to promote cider as a light, refreshing, non-fattening drink, targeting women specifically in its advertising, and the Hereford company held on to this market with its unrivalled Woodpecker until the end of the century.

Then Thatchers came up with a cunning plan. Suppose you were to create a cider that was aimed at women not just in its branding and marketing, but in the choice of fruit used to make it. Katy, aka the rather more dangerous-sounding Katja, is an eating apple With a Girl's Name, which the Somerset company rather brilliantly chose as the basis for a light, dry, effervescent cider. Then there's the more colourful version. Made from Katy apples, Thatchers Rosé offers a light, summery alternative to pink wine – for centuries cider makers have tried to persuade the British public that cider should be drunk like wine, not like beer, and it looks as though Thatchers have succeeded.

But this breakthrough drink was apparently created more by accident than by design.

Says Martin, "What actually happened is that whilst we were discussing the ongoing problem of Katy cider coming out slightly pink, someone had a Eureka moment and said 'Why don't we make it pink?' We then spent a lot of time and energy making it as pink as possible! The pink pigment comes from apple skin, and it's about how we press and deal with the mash."

Is this the ultimate Lady's Cider?

Morris dancers at the Thatchers Wassail celebration.

MY CIDER STORY

NEIL WORLEY FROM WORLEY'S CIDER, IN THE VILLAGE OF DEAN, NEAR SHEPTON MALLET

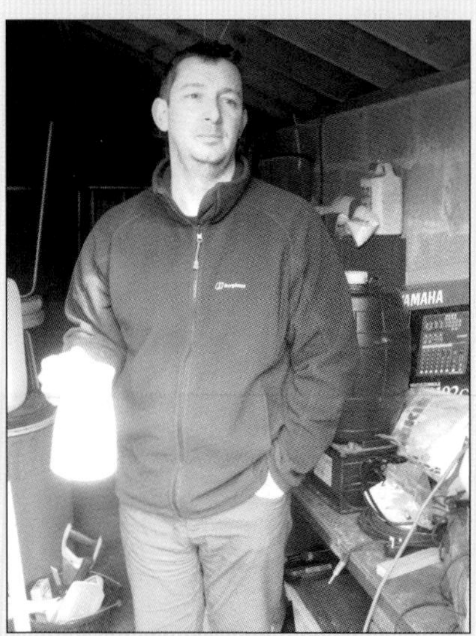

Neil Worley adopted an unusual approach to cidermaking by not pressing the apples himself.

We're a small operation, pressing around six tonnes of apples in 2009. It's pretty much a one-man band at the moment, with a bit of help from friends and family to pick up the crop at harvest time.

Unusually, my interest in cider making was sparked by a trip to the Asturias region of Northern Spain in 2002. Like many of the provinces in Spain, Asturias has its own unique language and cultural heritage, including a tradition in making a still, dry cider with a very distinct flavour. There's also an established etiquette to how the cider is poured and drunk: pour a small amount from a bottle held high above your head into a glass held down by your knees, and knock it back in one gulp. Woe betide anyone who doesn't abide by it.

Having developed an interest in drinks production during the real ale revolution of the 1980s, this exciting and exotic Asturian cider culture immediately captured my imagination. I know it may seem strange, but not having grown up in a cider-making region, I had no idea that similar local cider production cultures existed in some regions of England and Wales. I thought cider was that sharp, fizzy stuff you could buy in pubs.

On sharing my new-found passion for cider when back in the UK, it soon became apparent that I'd been missing out on a venerable and exciting tradition on my own doorstep. It included all the elements to draw me in: an active mythology, inaccessible and unmapped locations, a cast of colourful characters, and best of all an exciting, slightly dangerous, almost illegal air about it. I was soon immersed.

A year or two after that we moved to a hamlet near Shepton Mallet, which is the home of some of the big industrial cider makers. As far as I could make out the place was awash with cider enthusiasts. In terms of my cider education, it couldn't have been a better move.

One of our first visits was to Roy Trott's marvellous old cider barn on the Pilton road. A fantastic character and renowned local maker, Roy turned every cider-buying trip into an hour of storytelling, simultaneously celebrating and bemoaning the passing of the golden age of cider.

At Roy's knee I soon discovered where most of the apples were grown, and learned that the crop of many older cider orchards were left to rot on the ground with nobody interested in picking them up. An outrage, I thought. With righteous indignation burning bright, I vowed to do justice to as many of those unused cider apples on our doorstep as possible by making my own cider. Although I hadn't at that stage realised what bloody hard graft it is to pick them up by hand!

Having a young family and a 'real' job as well, we weren't blessed with the luxury of heaps of spare time (or cash). So right from the start we decided not to buy our own press, but rely instead on getting a professional with a decent mill and press to do that labour- and time-intensive part of the job. I spent my cider-making time selecting the best apples I could find, organising their movements between orchard, press and fermenting room, monitoring the process and cleaning, cleaning, cleaning...

Neatly sidestepping the hard work of harvest time, the very first batch of cider I made was a bit of a cheat. I bought 50 gallons of juice from Roger Wilkins' famous press and fermented a batch for consumption at my 40th birthday party. The cider was lovely, but suffered from the classic rookie mistake of tipping a bit of sugar into the juice to 'make it keep better'. Even at 10.5% it didn't last anything like as long as I'd envisioned, and there were a lot of very sore heads the day after that party!

The following year, from a contact supplied by Roy Trott, I sourced our own apples for the first time from Major Rands in West Pennard. The Major's military bearing ensured a regular supply of very clean and perfectly ripe apples from a variety of excellent vintage cultivars. We made five separate pressings, yielding 450 gallons of juice, and set about the fermentation in great hope.

Visiting the Cider and Orcharding tent at the Royal Bath & West Show the previous year had precipitated in me an almost uncontrollable surge of excitement. Although I'd decided there and then to enter the competition the following year, when it came around I was nervous as hell. After days of siphoning, tasting and selecting the best two gallons of dry farmhouse cider from the previous year's production, I nervously dropped them off at the judge's bench. I can honestly say I nearly fell over when I discovered we'd won First Prize in the Dry Farmhouse category. And in only our second year of making.

Our approach is traditional, but not dogmatically so. I've had apples pressed by both hydraulic rack-and-cloth and modern belt presses. We've tried adding yeast (once – didn't like it), using sulphite before and/or after fermentation and leaving it out entirely. We've ended up usually adding the minimum effective quantity of sulphite after fermentation only. We feel not adding sulphite at all is a bit like leaving your car keys in the ignition while you go shopping – you might get away with it, but it's a bit of a risk.

None of our equipment is very high-tech; we test acidity with pH papers, and use a basic hydrometer to test sugar levels in juice and to monitor fermentation. We use plastic containers for fermentation as they are so much easier to keep clean than oak barrels. Though we do have a few oak barrels and try to age all our finished cider through them at some stage before consumption.

The one truly indispensable piece of equipment we have is a good pump. Before that investment was made I could frequently be seen on autumn afternoons, filling my food-grade bucket with juice from a barrel on a trailer, legging it into the garage, climbing a stepladder and pouring it into the fermenting vessel. It was like a scene from It's A Knockout – never again!

In my opinion, it doesn't take that much to make decent cider: the right apples to create a well-balanced juice, cleanliness and a bit of patience. Having said that, if you want to improve your cider – and perhaps more importantly, be able to repeat it – you need to taste other people's cider, ask questions, keep good records and try new blends and techniques.

Last year we tried the Breton technique of keeving for the first time. Using an almost entirely Dabinett juice, we've ended up with a naturally medium cider with a specific gravity of round 1012. Very pleasing for a first effort.

In general, though, we try to make a cider that appeals. Our approach is to make cider people will enjoy, rather than making what we think people ought to drink using arcane techniques and apple varieties for the sake of it.

We believe the secret to making great cider is to understand what people want to drink, and then having the ability to find the apples and processes that will deliver it. It's as easy as that!

To keep in touch with Worley's Cider or to locate stockists, check out the Facebook page: Worley's Cider.

Bristol: The Cider City

Leave your car at home and set off on foot to wander the streets of cider's capital city...

Among British cities none can rival Bristol for its cider consumption. This is the merry battleground where Thatchers and Gaymers vie for the hearts and tastebuds of thousands, as the city's highly trained barstaff greet new customers with the eternal question, 'Fatch or Forn?'. We might have a laid-back reputation, but where else would the population get so riled up by a cider maker's efforts to keep up with the times that it launches a campaign of Facebook protest and billboard vandalism? Black is back. No, it really is.

We're lucky enough to have several of the country's best cider pubs, only two of which are dangerously close to the docks. But you can walk into any number of Bristol pubs and find cider made by some of the world's best producers, and we're talking authentic old boozers, not outposts of some monotonous chain. So here's a highly subjective list of our favourites – sorry if we've left your local out:

We thought the drinkers had mutinied and sailed The Apple away, but she was just off having her bottom scrubbed...

Coronation Tap

The most famous cider pub in the city, the CoriTap has fans all over the world and a dedicated clientele of Bristol University students and music lovers who squeeze themselves into the Tardis-like wood-panelled bar to enjoy a pint of Thatchers. Landlady Jan has a motherly attitude towards the youngsters, ensuring that their cider consumption doesn't get too out of hand, although it doesn't take too many halves of Exhibition (8%) to raise the spirits quite considerably. The term 'Corried' is now to be found in the Urban Dictionary and it doesn't mean, 'how you feel after a nice cup of tea and an episode of your favourite northern soap'.

Celebrity sightings at the Clifton watering hole are common. Jan's visitor's book strains under the weight of the famous names that have supped at the CoriTap (see box), and there is even a rumour (are we allowed to say this?) that Princess Anne's chauffeur/bodyguard took her there on the way home from an official visit to Bristol when she was a teenager, to wait for the traffic to die down. Either that or she was thirsty.

The CoriTap has also more recently carved a niche for itself as one of the city's more intimate live music venues winning awards along the way. It plays host to some of the finest musicians from Bristol and beyond and holds an annual cider and music festival, the CoriFEST, attracting hundreds from far and wide.

The Apple

Cider… on a boat! Somehow this doesn't seem altogether wise, but the authorities have thoughtfully put a notice up near the deck-level bar warning revellers against swimming in the harbour. The Apple now seems a bit of a fixture in the Bristol cider scene, but when it opened in 2006 the idea of a bar devoted pretty much exclusively to cider was radical enough to win the place all manner of awards.

On summer weekends the top deck is heaving, as is the quayside itself, and if you want to sample the whole gamut of apple- and pear- based beverages there are few better places to do it. Where else could you follow a fine Normandy-style cider with the worst in Scandinavian fruit-flavoured medicine? But in the middle are a good range of solid standbys. There's even a strong cider not unlike the Cori's Exhibition. On our last visit the draught ciders were a bit on the sweet side, but perhaps it was just the weather.

Bristol Cider Shop

Quite possibly the world's finest purveyor of cider, the Bristol Cider Shop stocks over 80 varieties of cider and perry, from draught classics like Hecks and Burrow Hill to

They've been Corried

Alison Moyet
Amanda Redman
Bob Gwillam
Brian Blessed
Daniel Day Lewis
Ewan Blair (competed in the CoriQuiz, but did he win?)
Gareth Chilcott
Greta Scacchi
Ian Kelsey
Jed Pitman
Jonathan Kerrigan
Justin Lee Collins
Kylie Minogue
"Lou Carpenter" (Neighbours – must have come in character)
Lucy Benjamin
Massive Attack
Miriam Margolyes
Nick Knowles
Nick Moran
Peter O'Toole
Richard Burton
Russell Osman
Shellie Conn
Vincenzo Pelligrini

the latest prize-winning bottle-conditioned delights – all have a 100% juice content and are made within 50 miles of Bristol by small independent producers. If you make the short but mildly demanding ascent of Christmas Steps, you can be sure of a friendly welcome and the chance to try a draught cider or two; your hosts will do their best to make sure you leave with a cider to suit your taste.

They also sell some rather nice cider mugs, T-shirts and books, including this one. In fact, we feel slightly responsible for the existence of this remarkable cider emporium, since Peter and Nick took the plunge after coming along to the launch of the first edition of *The Naked Guide to Cider* in October 2010. As Peter explains, they decided to drive around and buy a load of cider, reasoning that if they couldn't sell it, they'd have to drink it. The rest, as they say, is history.

Stuart Marshall at The Orchard, CAMRA's top cider pub in 2009. Picture by Sean Busby.

Orchard Inn

If you ever get dragged along to the ss Great Britain against your will, don't despair. Just smile and nod until everyone's busy studying rust and then leg it. Out the door. Up Gas Ferry Road. Down the alley to the right, and along the back of David Abels' shipyard. And there, across the road, stands the Orchard.

Literally, it's one minute from Brunel to Bristol's best pub selection of authentic farmhouse cider. They've been selling Thatchers for years, but nowadays you'll also find ciders here that are sold nowhere else other than the farm they're made on – like Ashill Cider from the foot of the Blackdowns, or south Devon's Brimblecombe, which is still made using a stone mill and a horse. Apparently there are cider lovers who attempt to drink their way down the blackboard, starting at the top and ending at the bottom. We should point out that this is not very sensible, unless you live within crawling distance of the bar.

The pub itself is as real and straightforward as its ciders. Good food at lunchtime, proper cheese and onion rolls, and regulars who aren't necessarily that happy about the pub winning the CAMRA award for Top Cider Pub in 2009. Aardman may have their new offices round the corner but this isn't Harbourside, this is the last remnant of the working docks.

Surrey Vaults

Used to be the Bristol Cider House and although it isn't completely dedicated to cider, there is still a decent selection of craft ciders.

The Stable

The Stable, which has five other bars in the West Country, is a modern Harbourside bar/restaurant dedicated to pizza, pies and lots of craft cider. The winning formula persuaded Fullers to buy a large chunk of the company in 2014.

Nova Scotia

Not strictly a cider pub but it would be churlish to leave out this wonderful old dockside inn, best enjoyed when the sun is shining on the quayside. In such circumstances a pint of Thatchers Traditional goes down quite nicely. You could always take the ferry into town and have another pint at the Old Duke, another fine pub that brings cider and jazz together – in a mellow moood.

Cotham Porter Stores

Walking in is a bit like entering the front room of a strange, rather dysfunctional family, mostly men who are no longer in the full bloom of youth. Thatchers again the cider of choice, drunk with a slice by the proper old boys, though you may find Moles Black Rat or another guest. The outdoor toilets have a genuine cider house ambience, and there's a cricket team if you're feeling sporty.

Apple Tree

When the suits at Gaymers wonder whether or not to continue making Taunton Traditional, this thought must cross their minds – if we take away their Traditional, what will the Apple Tree's regulars do? This one room Bedminster pub, now painted an orange brighter than a pint of Cheddar Valley and decorated with a strange constellation of apples, has a character and clientele all its own. In the winter it seems quiet, but on summer weekends music blasts out of the covered outdoor area in an onslaught against the Methodist Chapel opposite. That outdoor area – definitely not a garden and no, don't take the kids – must have been put together by the designer who did Roger Wilkins' Lounge Bar.

When they cleared the Bedminster slums after the war they left the Apple Tree behind - city planners showing good sense for once.

MY CIDER STORY

SEAN BUSBY CO-FOUNDER OF BRISTOL CIDER OUTFIT THE TOTTERDOWN PRESS...

Pressing day at the Totterdown Press. Some of us are working quite hard...

An urban chapel to the apple, the mighty Totterdown Press was founded in 2007 by partners in cider Richard Jones and myself, Sean Busby. Situated in the heart of south Bristol's Victorian terraces, this small but perfectly formed small-scale cider making outfit proves that you don't have to live in the sticks to produce good clean cider.

Cider has played a significant role in the lives of many in these parts, my own being no exception.

The romantic bit

Having grown up in Somerset and living on a farm from the age of 12, the influence of this traditional drink was never far away... about 15 paces actually, in the old stone barn adjacent to our kitchen. Here sat three enormous wooden barrels, an ominous presence in the gloom of the "cellar".

It was my stepfather who introduced me to the wonders of what was in these barrels, and I fondly remember times spent sharing a jug or two with him and friends who had spent hot hours hauling hay bales and forking silage, before retiring for refreshment.

A friend came to help with silage making one day, I had to go to the local college to learn something, but this mate was at the farm all day helping the men. At some point during the afternoon they took him to visit a local "character" who had a smallholding further down on the moor. This was one of the old timers, his accent so broad it was tricky to understand him... and he made his own cider, some of it remarkably clear. And my friend thought he could drink. Maybe he was 18. An amusing scenario for those with a little more experience. By the time I got home from college, they'd brought him back to the farm, and he was, to say the least, a little tired and emotional. He had odd eyes, one out the back door and one up the chimney so to speak. My mother made us all tea, and he poured the gravy on his pudding.

As the inevitable teenage years drifted by, my friends and I were well placed to sample many different ciders, and if things were a little rough we commonly would drink "scri and vi", that classic combination of cider and Vimto, designed to make the more difficult pints a bit smoother. When it came to visiting mates who'd gone off to University, we'd fill up one of those collapsible camping water containers, complete with tap. And hence the Screech Cube was born, sneaked in to Student Union bars in Hatfield, Kingston-Upon-Thames and Liverpool I recall seeing it being passed over heads at several discos.

But there comes a point in time when one's attitude to consuming this magical brew changes, and I now fully appreciate just how good a drink a properly made cider can be. It was time to turn from imbiber to producer, but not actually stop the imbibing completely you understand.

The practical bit

So, in 2007 we embarked on our first venture as part-time cider makers. A modest basket press was purchased through eBay, and on April Fools day we drove to Wales to collect it.

This was followed by the purchase of a scratter, again an eBay find. This time we headed to Hampshire to part with our cash. The eBay pics led me to believe it was a sizeable beast, but I was mistaken. We got the thing home and spent a frustrating ten minutes in Richard's kitchen trying in vain to push one apple through it. No go. We duly returned it and got a refund. It was time to buy a Fruit Shark, sourced from a woman called Vicky who imports them from the Czech Republic. It's essentially a powerful electric shredder for fruit. And it works.

A source of apples (apple source) was needed, and fortunately being in the south west and with local contacts getting cider apples didn't prove to be a difficulty.

So, we have apples, scratter, press, fermenting bins and associated gubbins. Our set-up enables us to produce about 30 gallons over the course of maybe two days, short November days that is. Time is always against us, and if we had more of it then we could up our volume. The apples are collected from the orchards and kept in hessian sacks until we have an opportunity to scrat and press. They may sit like this for three or four weeks, but this seems to do them no harm.

Firstly all equipment is given a thorough sterilising and rinsing, a golden rule to adhere to. Tipping the apples into a dustbin with holes in the base means we can wash them through easily (pressure washer very useful), and then it's a case of sorting them by hand as they're fed in to the Fruit Shark, chucking the rotten ones as we go. The pulp from the Shark is put into the basket press and the juice is squeezed into a bucket which is transferred to the fermenting bin (fill the bugger right up mind, to the very top). We reckon 20lb of fruit will give you about one gallon of juice, maybe a bit less. We choose not to add proprietary yeast, preferring to let the naturally occurring forms do their thing, and after three years we've not had one batch fail to ferment.

Then it's a case of leaving the bins to themselves in the garage, giving them a little warmth and security against the coldest nights, maybe sit them on some polystyrene, wrap a blanket 'round them. And then go indoors and have Christmas. And wait.

Use a hydrometer to check on the fermentation progress, compare the readings to those taken on the day of pressing at the fresh juice stage. We like a dry cider, so no sweetener is added and fermentation is left to finish naturally (about mid April). We then rack into clean bins. Left for a further three weeks or so we syphon it into five-gallon plastic barrels. These are kept in a cool dark place and we can then fill bottles/hip flasks/jam jars etc as required. A valve on the barrel lid means a squirt of CO_2 can be injected occasionally to stop air from spoiling the drink.

That's it really. Fundamentally it's just apple juice and time. Or as one woman said to me, "Really? You put thyme in it?"

Sean Busby does his bit for the local cricket team – drinking all their cider.

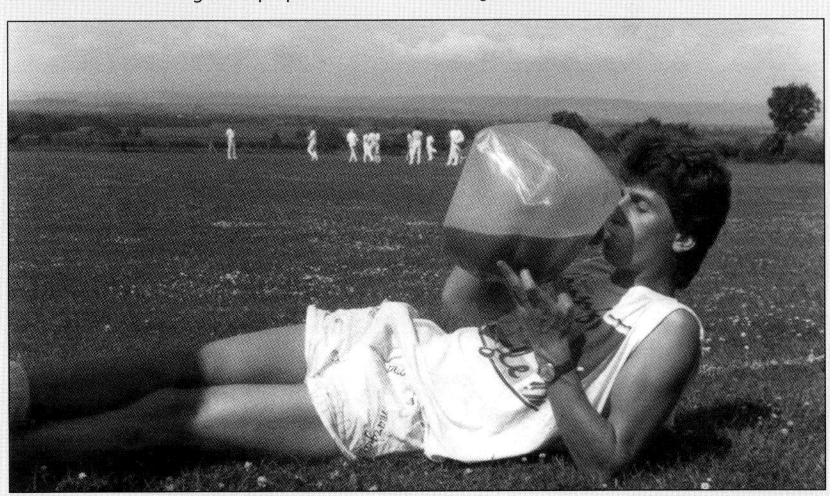

Three Counties

Herefordshire, Gloucestershire, Worcestershire: The ancestral home of upmarket cider and perry...

It may not seem fair to lump together Herefordshire, Gloucestershire and Worcestershire. After all, each of the Three Counties has a separate PGI for its cider and perry – whereas Somerset doesn't.

What, more than anything else, makes it necessary to talk about the counties as a single area is the perry pear, a tree which is found almost exclusively within their borders. Probably 95% of perry pear trees grow here – within sight of May Hill, as legend has it – and the identity of perry as a product of the Three Counties has been recognised by no less an organisation than Slow Food. Any old pie vendor can get a PGI if they don't mind doing the paperwork but a Slow Food Presidio is Special (in the Sawdays sense of the word).

Gathering Apples at Severn Cider in Gloucestershire.

People have tried growing perry pears elsewhere – Long Ashton Research Station conducted a long and thorough experiment in the subject but most of the trees they planted in orchards outside the Three Counties either succumbed to disease or failed to bear fruit, which suggests a deep connection between tree and landscape. These days you do find perry pears elsewhere – Matthew Wilson has an orchard near Robertsbridge in East Sussex – but the true home of perry lies west of the Cotswolds.

The extreme longevity of these trees, coupled with their size, makes them a defining feature of the landscape and villages of the region; they even play the role taken by oak, lime or horse chestnut in other areas, making up avenues (look out for one on your left after you cross the M50 heading towards Dymock on the B4215) or marking boundaries. Their skeletal winter appearance adds to the gothic quality of a region abounding in crumbling farmhouses, ancient timber-framed cottages, and dark barns of corrugated iron.

For the last 130 years one cider company has dominated production and orchard management in the area around Hereford, defining with its policies the apple varieties we now associate with the county. Bulmers Norman, a carefully selected import from France, is everywhere. Orchards are beautifully maintained and tend to be larger and more obviously commercial than the typical Somerset farm orchard. It is mostly thanks to Bulmers that Herefordshire has not lost as much of its orchard coverage as Devon (which lost Whiteways) or Gloucestershire. Hopefully the company's new owners will stick with English apples.

Let's face it. For many people around the UK and across the world, cider means Strongbow – Magners and Blackthorn are niche products by comparison. Yet alongside the Hereford giant, the Three Counties boasts small producers who make the finest cider and perry in

The Big Apple Blossomtime festival at Putley Village Hall – definitely worth a visit.

Loading up the bags of apples ready for scratting and pressing at Severn Cider.

the world, using vintage apples like Foxwhelp and Hagloe Crab and perry pears like Moorcroft (aka Malvern Hills) and Flakey Bark.

Simon Day from Once Upon a Tree at the Putley Big Apple event.

Chepstow to Gloucester

Between the Forest of Dean and the wide loops of the tidal Severn the A48 runs through country that was once covered in fruit trees. Orchards of plum, pear and apple trees crowded down to the bank of the river, where barges and trows moored to load up fruit bound for the Midlands and South Wales. When the railway came along it was used to carry vast quantities of fruit, particularly the Blaisdon plum and Blakeney Red pear. During World War I this most useful of pears was eaten, made into perry and, strange as it may seem, used to dye army uniforms khaki.

A trip north from Chepstow is well worth the bridge toll. The road takes you through Lydney and into the pages of a Gloucestershire Pomona (it hasn't been written yet, but Charles Martell has posted hundreds of fruit varieties on the website of the Gloucestershire Orchard Group, see Listings). As you approach Blakeney a sign to the right offers you Hagloe, birthplace of the excellent Hagloe Crab cider apple, and another points you in the direction of Awre.

One word of advice – have a look at the tide tables before setting out to this village on the bank of the Severn, as the surrounding lanes disappear periodically under water. Awre (pronounced 'arrr') is home to the Red Hart Inn, which does a fine Sunday lunch, and to Severn Cider. Otherwise carry on along the A48 to Newnham-on-Severn, where the Railway Inn has a frightening selection of ciders and perries – forty or fifty when we last visited – many of them local and otherwise hard to come by. Landlord Dave will help you choose a good one.

Where are we? Oh yes, Newnham. So let's carry on through Westbury-on-Severn (very posh over here, you'll notice) and Chaxhill. A couple of miles further on, stop at the Severn Bore pub on the right. You could of course arrange to do this when the Bore is due to come along, though you might have to fight for parking with a score of surfers. The pub's all right, but if you have an interest in orchards you'll want to set off back along the riverbank footpath (ie downstream). Go in September and you'll see what looks like a forest from a fairy tale, tangled with brambles and elder and with apples hanging here and there.

This orchard is the last remnant of a vast enterprise and it is a treasure trove of varieties, many of which exist nowhere else. It should be protected and there's a good chance it will be.

We're almost in Gloucester now, so you can go round the ring road and back along the other side of the river – Days Cottage is just to the east of the city though you'll find their cider and perry at Bristol and Stroud farmer's markets. You could take a detour to Slad and toast Laurie Lee at the Woolpack… Alternatively, don't stop when you get to Gloucester but keeping going, west on the A40 and then north, towards Newent, Dymock, Much Marcle…

The Big Apple at Putley. Everyone likes apples.

Much Marcle and Putley

This is another route out of the Pomona, with every town and village recalled in the name of a famous cider apple, perry pear or plum. In the 17th century the Golden Age of Cyder unfurled its banner over this region, and you have to wonder how many of the grand old houses were built on the proceeds of the press. Perry pears are everywhere, standing alone in the fields like a remnant of some primeval forest, or marshalled into an avenue.

Running north to south, the Marcle Ridge offers the orchards of this mini-region protection from the prevailing westerly winds; sunshine, soft rains, good soil and human perseverance have made this a centre of cider and perry. A glance at the Ordnance Survey map (No. 149) shows a landscape covered in the tiny green crosses that signify orchard or vineyard, as it has been for more than three centuries. Come to think of it, a perry pear can live that long.

Made infamous for a time by mass murderer Fred West, Much Marcle is a bastion of independence. Long past the official retirement age Jean Nowell made cider and perry single-handed at Lyne Down Farm, regularly pressing a ton of fruit a day and winning awards left, right and centre. Jean was a founder member of the Big Apple Association, which has been celebrating the apples and cider of the Marcle Ridge since 1989, and she also set James Marsden of Gregg's Pit on the path to righteousness. Whatever it was she taught him, he has become the most tantalising producer of top-quality cider and perry, sticking to the no-duty limit and enjoying the frenzy of perry lovers desperate to get their hands on a bottle.

The orchards of Gregg's Pit stand on a hilltop overlooking the village, which is all red brick and green trees apart from a row of giant stainless steel cylinders. Closer inspection reveals that these storage tanks belong to Westons, the family-owned company that was founded eight years before Bulmers (and don't you forget it) and has so far avoided being swallowed up by the Hereford behemoth. Founder Henry Weston was inspired by local MP, Mr C W Radcliffe Cooke, who lived just down the road in a grand old place called Hellens; you can look round for a small fee and help to press perry pears, some of them harvested from the 300 year old avenue leading up to the house, during the Big Apple weekend.

James Marsden of Gregg's Pit talks to visitors at the Big Apple Blossomtime festival, Putley.

Westons has got the visitor experience thing to a T, with dray horse rides, works tours and a restaurant. You can also buy cider by the pallet-load, but you can buy cider anywhere; you have to visit The Bounds, with its 17th century farmhouse and 21st century cider factory to get a sense of where the cider comes from.

But don't go home just yet. Head north a few miles (via the lanes if you've got a map) and have a look at Putley, a village with more orchards than is strictly fair and lots of footpaths to explore. The Big Apple holds cider and perry trials at the village hall, just along the road from Dragon Orchard – a pioneering example of Community Supported Agriculture.

Definitely not cidermaking on a small scale – the Bulmers factory in Hereford is BIG.

Hereford and Environs

Let's get this out of the way first. Bulmers is massive. The factory looks like a petro-chemical works and there's no shop or other reason to visit. We went to have a look, though, and walked around the fenced perimeter of the factory to admire the giant storage tanks and immense pipes snaking from one building to the next, not to mention the rows of Heineken lorries and stacks of kegs. Worth it, just to see what Big Cider really looks like.

What you're supposed to do as a cider tourist is visit the Cider Museum down the road, tucked in behind a supermarket. Housed in the old Bulmers works, the museum may not be a fantastic day out for all the family but it is intriguing, with cider antiquities – a Victorian travelling press – and cider apples (in season) arranged on the boardroom table. Downstairs you're reminded once again that this kind of cidermaking is an industrial operation, with rooms full of bottling equipment and other stuff left behind when the company moved down the road.

This is also the home of the Offa's Dyke Distillery, established after a lengthy struggle by Bertram Bulmer, though we're not sure how much actual distilling is going on there these days. The cider brandy still tastes good, however, and the shop also sells cider and perry from local producers like Olivers.

Which gives us an excuse to leave Hereford and head north-east, towards Bromyard. We're going to Ocle Pychard, which you can get to on the main road, but if you have time go by the back lanes and explore this landscape of hills, orchards and grand old farmhouses. Olivers is only open on Saturdays, but if you've drunk Tom's perry you'll know it's worth waiting for the weekend.

Simon Day has put his experience as a wine maker to good use: this ice cider is made from Blenheim Orange apples.

Herefordshire Cider by Bike

We don't need to worry about encouraging cider cycling in the Three Counties as the local authority already does it. We would advise caution, though, particularly where it's

Ice cider

Put Magners out of your mind: ice cider involves taking ice out of cider rather than putting it in. It's all the rage in Quebec and New England but at the time of writing the only home-grown ice cider is a 2009 Blenheim Orange made by Once Upon a Tree.

Ice wine was known to the Romans and became a big hit in Canada during the 1990s. At its most basic, the technique involves leaving grapes to freeze on the vine and then pressing them frozen; with a proportion of the water content trapped as ice, the resulting juice is high in sugar, giving a strong, sweet wine. For a while now cidermakers in Quebec have been doing the same thing with apples, and consumers as far south as New York seem willing to pay pretty good prices for the faddish drink.

Harvesting and pressing frozen apples is not much fun, neither is it very practical in Herefordshire, so Simon Day's approach was to choose a late, easily-stored, characterful apple – the Blenheim Orange – press it, and then freeze the juice at a local ice cream factory. He then allowed the juice to thaw gradually, releasing a thick apple syrup that gradually became thinner and paler. At the appropriate moment he removed the remaining ice, which was almost pure water and virtually tasteless, then left the super-sweet juice to ferment until the alcohol level was 7.5% – he was aiming for 8% but erred on the side of caution.

The result? Quite unlike any other cider, the Blenheim Orange we tried bore some relation to a proper dessert wine, only with a dazzling apple flavour. It isn't cheap but it is both unique and delicious.

busy – wide lorries and narrow roads can make riding a bike uncomfortable. You can download directions from the Herefordshire Cider Route webpages (see Listings) for two routes:

Ledbury – takes you on a 20-mile jaunt from Ledbury station to Much Marcle and Putley, mostly by quiet lanes. A perfect way to enjoy The Big Apple weekends, although getting to Ledbury in the first place might pose a bit of a challenge; the journey from Bristol takes three hours.

Pembridge – takes you from… your car, which you have conveniently parked in Pembridge, on a slightly less sensible 19-mile journey around beautiful but mostly cider-free countryside. Tempting just to drive to Dunkertons.

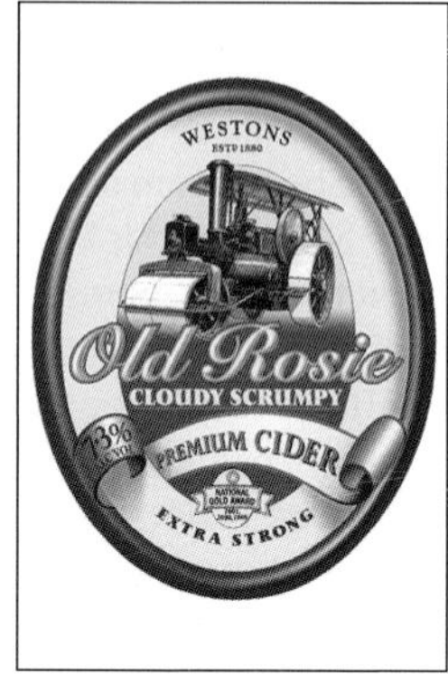

A lifelong favourite for many cider drinkers, Old Rosie is named, rather bizarrely, after a steamroller.

Westons

There are strange parallels between the cider industries of Somerset and Herefordshire, with one giant company in each county, numerous smaller producers and one large family-owned business in between. Both Thatchers and Westons are over a century old, and both have succeeded in retaining their old customers while simultaneously drawing in new ones with exciting brands and great marketing.

Past and present coexist at The Bounds, home of Westons cider for more than a century.

While Thatchers is unashamedly modern in outlook, making the most of its computer-controlled plant with a constant stream of new brands, Westons is still considered by many to be a traditional cider maker. If a pub advertises its prowess in the cider department it probably sells products from one or other of these companies, and often both. The fridge at Ye Olde Cider Bar in Newton Abbot is choc-a-bloc with Thatchers; ask for scrumpy, meanwhile, and you'll get Weston's Old Rosie.

This easy-drinking, much-loved cider is named after a steamroller, with just a hint of Laurie Lee. To have survived so long in the dangerous middle ground of the cider industry, Westons has always been brand-savvy. And when Henry Weston fell into cidermaking back in 1880, he established another important principle – that the company's cider should always be made to the highest standards. Rigorous hygiene combined with strict control of fruit quality gave Westons the reputation it still has today; the list of vintage and apple and perry pear varieties on the company's website is impressive by any standards.

A visit to Bounds Farm is one of the essential rites for the cider pilgrim, not so much for the activities on offer or even the excellent Scrumpy House restaurant, as for the place itself. The 17th century farmhouse is still there, and a fine old building it is too. Henry Weston's original press and stone mill are there too. And then behind the house, massive and shiny, stand the huge new storage tanks. Nowhere else can you better appreciate the continuity between the Golden Age of Cyder and the 21st century – and the differences between those days and these.

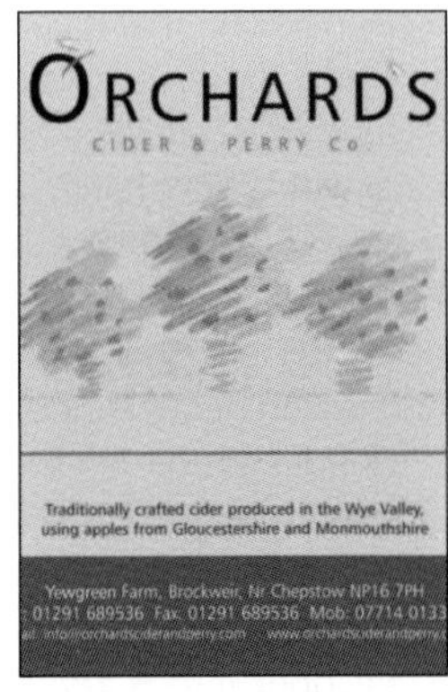

Keith Orchard uses a mix of Somerset and local Forest of Dean varieties to create clean, crisp ciders and perries.

Keith Orchard

Growing up in Backwell, Somerset, Keith Orchard learnt a lot about cider. In the 1960s, when he was a youngster, the biggest name in the area was Coates, while Thatchers was one of several local cider farms. Thirty years later only Thatchers was left. To Keith, who now makes cider and perry in Brockweir in the Wye valley, the preservation of varieties and tradition is an important motivation.

When he first moved to the area he planted Backwell Red, his old local cider apple, in the orchard beside his house, giving his blended Wye Valley cider perhaps a hint of north Somerset. It's sharper and fresher than some, with a clean flavour that is partly down to the apples and partly to Keith's fondness for stainless steel. His cider barn housed a wonderful collection of old steel fermentation tanks, each with a front hatch fastened on with big shiny bolts - they looked the sort of thing you'd travel in to explore the bottom of the ocean. When we visited in April you could put your ear to the side of a tank and hear the cider sizzling and fizzing gently inside.

Keith has now left the old farm and makes his excellent cider and perry in the village instead, but not before making a mark on the place. When he found the farm it was semi-derelict, with woodland scrub growing right up to the door. It took a while to find the old orchard below the house, never mind clear the monster brambles, but the excavations uncovered some beautiful old trees including a perry pear that seems to be unique to the place. There are other perry pears growing along the boundary wall, as well as walnut, plum and dessert apple and pear trees.

You can still find stone mills and press bases around the Three Counties – this one is at Gregg's Pit.

It's a beautiful area, and unique in many ways. The common land covering the hill between Brockweir and St Briavels was enclosed as long as ago as the 17th century, often by the commoners themselves, and even now the patchwork of tiny farms, intersected by a maze of narrow lanes, remains very different from the rest of Gloucestershire. Smallholders were making a living from cider apples – Redstreak and Forest Styre – three hundred years ago, and the old perry pears in the orchard have survived from that age. They've lasted better than many of the cottages, which were abandoned when the more successful farmers gradually took over their neighbours' land.

Along with the trees themselves, old stone mills and the stone bases of presses also survive – there were several outside Keith's old cider barn, while James Marsden uses a stone base up at Gregg's Pit. The ones outside Keith's old place are made of gritstone and were once carved in great numbers straight from the rock in numerous small quarries; we've heard from various sources the story that you can see these stones, half-carved, sticking out of the rock at one or other quarry, but whether this is true or not remains to be seen. You're more likely to find one built into the wall of a stone shed or cottage, proof that recycling is nothing new…

So Keith may use modern gear to make his fresh,

Frank Naish

Photographed by
Neil Phillips
www.orchardeye.com

Frank Naish
was 85 years old when Neil Phillips spent a day with him. He had been involved in cidermaking since he was a child helping his father, Robert, gather and press the autumn harvest from the family orchards at Piltown Farm, West Pennard, near Glastonbury where the trees have never been treated with chemical fertilizers or pest-killers. Frank passed away in 2013 aged 89.

3280

distinctive cider and perry – regular prize winners at CAMRA, the Bath and West and elsewhere - but he's doing his bit to keep the old culture and varieties alive. Recent plantings include Pig's Snout and Old Josie, and he's closely involved with the countywide search for old varieties. He found one of these, a Gloucestershire apple called Welsh Druid, growing down in the village, but the owner cut it down before anyone could propagate it. Wild yeasts he considers a part of what makes a cider or perry unique but has found that they can only be trusted to work on a relatively small batch – 100 gallons might be left to its own devices, while 1000 gallons gets a dose of cultivated yeast.

His advice to novice cidermakers is to be aware just how physically demanding – and dirty – the business of pressing fruit can be. He started out on Vigo's biggest hand-operated press, but after spending all day filling a 45 gallon drum upgraded pretty quickly. When people come to help him press he warns them not to wear clothes they value. Apple juice stains hard.

Tom Bull of Severn Cider loading his pick-up during apple harvest.

Local artist Steve Hyslop makes the prints used to label Severn Cider – note May Hill in the background.

Severn Cider

Severn Cider is aptly named, though it used to be called Severn Sider Cider, which was even better. The purpose-built shed where the apples are pressed and fermented is only a couple of hundred yards from the west bank of the Severn, in the village of Awre, and the cider and perry made by Tom Bull and his father Nick reflects the unique geography and history of the place.

The Severn is to cider and perry what the Gironde is to wine. In each riverside parish subtle differences in soil and climate have created varieties and variants that you won't find anywhere else, some of them famous three centuries ago. The parish of Awre occupies a wedge of land that juts into the estuary, forcing the wide waters into the narrow channel of the river, and during high tides the narrow lanes around Awre can disappear under water. This is the birthplace of the Hagloe Crab and the home of fine perry pears: Blakeney Red, called Red Pear in these parts, and a related variety covered in thorns which is known, appropriately, as Thorn. This shouldn't be confused with the other, more widespread Thorn, but how could it not be?

A thriving perry and cider industry grew up, using

mills cut from sandstone and millstone grit quarried in the parish, and taking advantage of the river's tides for transport, but declined in the era of factory production. So Severn Cider has revived an old and venerable tradition, producing ciders in particular that are dry, full-flavoured and distinctive. Nick is proud of the varieties they use. 'Charles Martell doesn't know about this one,' he says of a particular rare fruit.

Tom works at the quarry nearby but in the autumn he has a team of pickers out collecting apples and pears from old traditional orchards at Chaxhill and other local villages, and if you're driving along the A48 in October you might see his pick-up truck going slowly along with a ton of apples on the back, stacked in sacks and strapped tightly down. Tom's operation is small-scale at the moment but ambitious; when we visited he was on the look-out for a big hydraulic press to replace the Voran they use at the moment, and he'd just acquired a huge new container that looks like the fuel tank of a 1950s space rocket. The cider barn is new and so is the Cellar, where you can learn about cidermaking, and taste and buy cider. At the moment Severn Cider seems like a place where men work and make cider and drink cider – let's hope it stays like that.

Tom Oliver is a champion of Three Counties Perry, and the only maker to use the extremely rare variety Coppy.

Find your way to Ocle Pychard on a Saturday, visit Oliver's, and try out the most expensive farm toilet in Britain.

Tom Oliver

When Tom Oliver was growing up at Moorhouse Farm, near the Herefordshire village of Ocle Pychard ('oak-le pie-chard') his father warned him that the farming life they knew was changing fast. Back then the 300-acre farm specialised in growing hops – Tom's grandfather grubbed up cider orchards after World War I to make way for the more profitable crop – with a substantial workforce employed full-time or on a seasonal basis. But the combination of disease and cheap imports put paid to the hop business; when we visited the farm the huge, fantastically complicated hop-processing machine was about to be dismantled and taken away for scrap.

Like many other small mixed farms – the farms that give our countryside its intimate character – this one faces an uncertain future. With misguided environmentalists attacking livestock as a source of carbon emissions, and supermarkets pushing prices ever lower, the family farm could soon be extinct. The government tells farmers everything will be fine if they diversify, then clobbers them with taxes and pointless regulations.

While his brother defies the stranglehold of bureaucracy to raise Hereford cattle for beef, Tom divides his time between the music industry – he is, among other things, tour manager of The Proclaimers – and the business of making cider and perry. A love of music took him away from farming as a young man; a love of perry brought him back. He did his homework, spending time with an old farmer who made perry on autumn Sundays as part of the yearly round, and learning from pioneers like Kevin Minchew and the Dunkertons. In 1999 he began making cider and perry commercially and within five years he had won the prestigious Arthur Davies Cup at the Royal Bath and West Show. He won it again in 2009, just for good measure.

Like Julian Temperley, Tom recognised early on that fine cider and perry need to be appreciated as the wine of the West, and that perry in particular has unique qualities relating to variety and place. He played an important role in the founding of the Slow Food Presidio for Three Counties Perry, and continues to extol the virtues of this venerable drink to anyone who will listen. Recently he has started selling on a one-off basis to retailers in the USA, and is excited by the possibilities of this untapped market. Closer to home, a visitor's centre is gradually taking shape, including a brand new toilet – what with the drains and soakaway Tom reckons this must be the most expensive farm toilet in the country.

When you compare this to the visitor-friendly cider farms of Westons and Sheppys, you appreciate that Olivers remains a small-scale artisan operation, a beguiling mix of art and industry. Tom has his favourite perry pear varieties, among them Gin, Butt, Oldfield, Blakeney Red and the almost-legendary Coppy, which had become so rare when Tom started production that only one mature tree remained standing. The fruit comes in from thirty different growers, and from it he makes exquisite still perries, both single varieties and his Three Counties blend ('as debonair as a Savile Row suit' according to Matthew Fort), and delicious keeved perries in the Normandy style – foaming and full-bodied with a delicate but richly textured flavour. Perfect for a summer wedding, or a winter wedding for that

You can't keep a good man down... Tom Oliver won the Arthur Davies Cup at the Bath & West for the second time in 2009.

Loaded magazine on Olivers Dabinett (Sept 09)

"There's no place for corks or wine bottles in Ciderland I tell thee. I skinned my paw on this bastard, and it tasted like horse sweat anyway. So undrinkable I had more just to check."

It says something about Tom that this is one of his favourite reviews…

matter.

So far Tom has resisted going into the distillation business, although there is a still in Normandy with his name on it and he has researched the subject with habitual thoroughness. What his researches suggest is that perry is not suited to distillation by itself; he has his eye on a Calvados called Domfront, which contains both apples and pears. How long before we're all drinking Ocle Pychard Perry Brandy?

The orchard at Gregg's Pit, a resolutely small-scale producer that specializes in excellence.

Gregg's Pit

If you ever think you're too busy to make cider or perry, go along to Gregg's Pit in Much Marcle during one of The Big Apple weekends. As Director Marine for Natural England, James Marsden has onerous responsibilities, yet he finds time to make perries and ciders that have won him the top prize in The Big Apple Cider and Perry Trials almost every year for more than a decade.

Perched on a hilltop overlooking Much Marcle, Gregg's Pit is named after a flooded marl pit surrounded by aged perry pears, one of which is unique to the orchard and bears its name. When James found the old cottage it was in a terrible condition, dilapidated and overgrown, but two decades have wrought a complete transformation. The orchards are beautifully kept, while the cider and perry operation – which James and his partner Helen Woodman

Since the 17th century the Three Counties have been covered in orchards. More survive in the region today than anywhere else in Britain.

keep resolutely to a craft scale – is confined to a neat, purpose-built outbuilding. Well, it's a shed, but a shed with a difference. This is no repository of old bikes and broken lawnmowers, this is a state-of-the-art craft cider works that incorporates the best of the old (a venerable stone press base) with the best of the new (stainless steel fermentation vessels with tops that are lowered automatically to the level of the cider inside).

The shed epitomises James's approach to the business, which is clean, stylish and well organised. He likes the cattle out of his orchard six weeks before harvest, at which point the grass should be a little less than 2 inches long. He draws up a chart in the summer that shows which trees should be ready to harvest when, and plans the season's pressing around this schedule. Fruit is then tested daily so that it is collected and pressed at exactly the right moment.

This level of care is perhaps only possible on a small scale, and it partly explains why James wins so many prizes. But efficiency alone is not enough. He has what all the good perry makers (in particular) have – a passion for his craft and a sense, developed over more than a decade, of what makes a cider or perry just right.

If you want to see, incidentally, just what attention to detail means, take a look at the Greggs Pit website - www.greggs-pit.co.uk. Better still, go along during the Big Apple autumn weekend, and see for yourself. And if you see a bottle of James's perry, buy it. The stuff sells fast.

Dave Kaspar of Days Cottage: these old, unsprayed orchards are home to little owls, bats and many other species.

Days Cottage

Viewers of the Channel 4 TV show River Cottage might remember seeing the intrepid Hugh Fearnley-Whittingstall bombarded by falling perry pears. He was the guest of Dave Kaspar and Helen Brent-Smith, makers of apple juice, cider and perry at Days Cottage in Brookthorpe, just to the east of Gloucester.

Their story should be a warning to anyone who is thinking about buying or planting an orchard. Twenty years ago Dave and Helen moved to the cottage, on the farm owned for centuries by Helen's family, intending to downshift a bit. In the nearest field was an orchard of standard trees, planted in 1912 with the aid of a government grant, and the first autumn, as the fruit started falling from the trees, they decided to press some for juice.

And that was it. They were hooked.

Each year they pressed more fruit, making cider and perry as well as apple juice, and becoming one of the first stallholders at the Bristol farmer's market when it was launched in 1998 – you can also find them at the market in Stroud. At the same time their fascination for local varieties and the culture of orcharding drew them into the Gloucestershire Orchard Group, which had been set up to conserve, promote and celebrate traditional orchards in the county.

Subsequently Dave and Helen have planted hundreds of apple trees, 160 of which form the Gloucestershire Museum Orchard of local varieties. Through GOG they have also set up an orchard skills centre at Days Cottage, which offers courses in pruning and propagation, the aim being to train the next generation of enthusiasts to care for orchards and graft or bud their favourite varieties themselves. The centre is based in a yurt placed just outside the range of fruit falling from a mammoth Yellow Huffcap, and there's an open canvas-roofed structure for warmer weather; a training orchard and nursery complete the picture. You can visit on Apple Day and take a walk around the orchards, including a fantastically old but still productive orchard of apples and giant perry pears, one of which has the business end of a pitchfork wedged into the trunk. Most odd.

A giant perry pear overshadows the new Orchard Skills Centre at Days Cottage.

Dragon Orchard

Norman and Ann Stanier moved back to Putley in 1993, to take over the long-established fruit farm run by Norman's parents. It was a great idea in principle, but in practice the dominance of supermarkets and the explosion in cheap imports made small-scale fruit growing a tricky proposition. What the couple did have was an excellent orchard in a wonderful location, and they hit on the idea of launching a cropsharers' scheme – a form of Community Supported Agriculture.

In other European countries, and in the United States, CSA has been adopted by farms struggling to survive in a climate of low food prices and high land values that encourage the sale of farmland for housing. The idea is that people invest in a farm and take a share of the crop, and with Dragon Orchard they also get something less tangible but equally precious – a share of the orchard experience.

So you pay an annual subscription and in return receive lots of cooking and eating apples, apple juice, cider and perry. You also have the opportunity to visit Dragon Orchard for one weekend each season, enjoy a meal, tour the orchard and the village and generally soak up the atmosphere. Alternatively you can sponsor a tree, which is a cheaper alternative that still includes an invitation to visit this delightful spot a couple of times a year.

Having said that, anyone can visit the shop at Dragon Orchard, where you can buy cider, perry and juice from Once Upon a Tree. Anyone interested in orcharding – and its future – should go and see how a fruit-grower and cider maker can work in tandem, creating world-class drinks and offering people an intimate connection with a delightful place.

Dave and Helen's approach to cider and perry production combines simplicity with a willingness to experiment. We've been buying their cider at the Bristol farmers' market for years, and enjoy the robust, fairly sharp blend. Recently the perry, particularly the Blakeney Red, has been very good, a soft, delicious, cloudy drink which goes down alarmingly well. Helen has great respect for the perry pear, which is capable of playing tricks even on the experienced maker.

She cites an instance in which two (brand new) barrels of juice, pressed from the same pears one day apart, behaved completely differently. One cleared to make a fine clear perry that was ready before Christmas. The other refused to clear and took a couple of months more to ferment down to that delectable perry sweetness.

One thing she has found, though, is that their ciders and perries have become increasingly consistent over time, as the wild yeasts in the cider barn find their equilibrium. This happened more quickly with the ciders, while the perries took longer to settle. While most of their cider is blended, they make single variety ciders when there's a glut of particular apples, or when they discover a new technique. We recently tried a Brown Snout cider which was tangy, sherry dry and coloured a fabulous rusty pink. This was achieved, Helen says, by crushing beetroot with the apples – a technique learned, like much of their art, from a local old-timer.

Gathering apples for cidermaking at Once Upon a Tree.

Once Upon a Tree

One of the goals of craft cider pioneers has been to drag cider upmarket, away from the 3 litre plastic bottle and the cheap pub pint. Back in the 17th century, so the story goes, fine ciders and perries rivalled wine both in quality and price, and if we want a thriving 21st industry we need products that do the same.

Enter Simon Day, whose father Tom was winemaker at the Three Choirs Vineyard near Newent. Simon grew up among vines and, despite the best efforts of his parents to dissuade him, followed his father into the industry, working in the US, New Zealand and Australia. Back in the UK, he was briefly involved with winemaking in Surrey and Kent, before working with La Mare Vineyards in Jersey.

Like so many others, Simon didn't really plan on

becoming a cidermaker. He came back to Herefordshire to take over his late father's consultancy business, Vine and Wine, and moved to Putley, where he could hardly fail to notice the vast orchards that spread out in all directions from the village. Once he saw how good the fruit was, he decided to have a go at making some cider.

With a background in wine, his approach is rather different from most. The first year he fermented each variety separately – as winemakers do with grapes – to see what contribution each could make. He also tried a variety of yeasts. As he continues to experiment he's always looking for the best balance and fruit expression possible with the raw materials at his disposal; he's less interested in what people have done in the past with particular varieties than in an apple's potential in a given year.

In 2009 he made the cider equivalent of a white burgundy, using Michelin, an apple not generally noted for its suitability as a single variety. He entered this new invention in the Single Variety class at the Hereford International Cider and Perry Competition for which, bizarrely, no prize was awarded.

Unusually for a maker who wants to link cider and wine, he is wary of applying the concept of terroir to orchards. Whereas the grape harvest from a particular vineyard tends to be fairly consistent in terms of quality and flavour, apple harvests can vary wildly. Ciders made from apples harvested in the same orchard on consecutive years may have little in common; the Dabinett he made in 2008 was markedly different from the same cider the previous year.

Once Upon a Tree's Putley Gold and Marcle Ridge blends are consistent, but customers are by now aware that other blends and single variety ciders – and perries – are products of a particular year. So if you come across an award-winner like their 2011 Dabinett cider, Carpenter's Croft bottle-fermented cider or Priggles Perry, grab it while you can.

Cider designed to compete with wine, produced by Once Upon a Tree.

MY CIDER STORY

NEIL PHILLIPS, THE SCRUMPING PROJECT, OLDLAND COMMON, SOUTH GLOUCESTERSHIRE

“ In the familiar surroundings of Rhybridge Farm's apple orchard, Britain's oldest cider maker, Frank Naish, is showing me a tree that he planted from a pip nearly eighty years ago. Groaning under the weight of its gorgeous red fruit, I wondered if Frank had given this particular variety a name? "Well," Frank paused, and then simply said, "they're just called Ours." It was a beautiful day, and I was in good company. ”

During my career as a West Country based photographer, I have had the pleasure of working for numerous cider producers – from small, artisan farmers like Roger Wilkins to larger companies such as Gaymers and Thatchers. These visits gave me the opportunity to see behind the scenes, hear some fantastic tales from people like Frank Naish, and sample the odd glass of alcoholic apple juice. I quickly developed a fascination with the ancient craft of cidermaking, with all its rituals, myths and superstitions. It was during a trip to Hecks Cider Farm in Street that I stumbled on some locals unloading sacks of apples from the back of their cars…

As the group carefully poured the apples into larger containers, I was told by one enthusiast that this was an annual event – not only great fun "for all the family", but also a unique and interesting way to bring the wider community together. She explained that one weekend every late autumn was set aside to go out and collect all the unwanted apples in the area. The produce would then be gathered and pressed to make cider. I sensed a real buzz about what they were doing that day, and it inspired me try something similar where I live in Oldland Common.

I discussed the idea with friends and neighbours who have an interest in (drinking)

Members of the Scrumping Project at their pressing day at Grimsbury Farm in South Glos.

cider and, with Tim Bishop as my chief ally, the Scrumping Project was born.

Early on, the group was very fortunate to apply for and win a community grant from South Gloucestershire Council which is keen to protect and promote local orchards. This fund allowed us to purchase materials and cover other vital costs. The Friends of Grimsbury Farm gave us the use of their all-important press. Although I had witnessed cider production first-hand and knew a little about the drink's subtle and sometimes not-so-subtle taste, I still set about seeking advice from some of the experts I had met over the years. Fortunately, being cidermakers, whether market leaders or independent farmers, they were only too happy to share their knowledge with a fellow enthusiast, and I began to learn the techniques and understand the fine art of turning apples into alcohol – albeit on a relatively small scale.

The aim of the Scrumping Project is to make an artisan or craft cider utilising many of the traditional practices I have heard and read about. Around South Gloucestershire, like many places I suspect, autumn brings countless trees surrounded by fallers. As far as I can tell, these perfectly good apples are going to waste. Therefore, the project uses fruit from unused and forgotten orchards. We have been lucky to obtain apples from some much-loved orchards too where a wide selection of cider apples are grown and cared for by people who really know their fruit. This means we are using good-quality bitter, sweet and sharp varieties. We also attended a number of local events to promote the Scrumping Project and link up with like-minded people who have their own apple trees and want to see them put to good use.

In October, like our Street counterparts, the Scrumping Project organises a weekend of exploiting the natural resources on its doorstep – mums and dads, grandparents, teens, and toddlers all mucked in to collect around a ton of apples. The produce was pressed and the waiting began…

No one involved in the Scrumping Project has ever made cider before and it was a nerve-wracking time. We kept the process as simple and organic as we could but because it was the project's first year we were cautious, using sulphites and adding yeast to all but one of our fermentation barrels.

A purpose built hydraulic press is a good option for producers looking to increase output.

In January we sampled the fruits of our labour and named the result Forgotten Fruit. Described as "clean and fresh tasting", we launched the cider with a celebratory drink at Willsbridge Mill Wassail. We have also thanked those farmers and growers who let us roam their orchards by donating them a bottle each. It has proved a hit among the local cider-drinking community, and we also entered it at the Royal Bath and West Show. Hopefully, the Scrumping Project will continue to grow as we experiment with different apple combinations, and get more people involved.

Pictures coutresy of Orchard Eye. For further details of the Scrumping Project go to www.orchardeye.com.

Tasting Notes

Devon and Cornwall

Cider is making a big comeback in the deep Southwest, not that it ever really went away.

We thought 'scrumpy' had been banished from the cidermaker's lexicon until we motored past the Wellington Monument, heading for Devon. Somerset people are notoriously snooty about cider made anywhere west of the Blackdowns, and we were curious to find out whether this was prejudice based on the flagons of Cripplecock you find alongside the pasties in Cornish service stations, or an example of inter-county rivalry. It's only half an hour from Taunton to Exeter on the M5, so the cider can't be that different, can it? Then again, a half-hour drive takes you from perry-loving west Gloucestershire to the beery world of the Cotswolds, so anything is possible…

Ye Olde Cider Bar, Newton Abbot, where the cider revival has been going on a bit longer than elsewhere – a century or more.

Until the late 1980s one name dominated the Devon cider scene. Whiteways Cyder was set up not long after Bulmers and Westons, by Henry Whiteway, a farmer in the village of Whimple. Good products and fantastic marketing turned the company into one of the 20th century's great cider success stories, to the extent that operations moved to a London HQ; Whiteways ciders were shipped around the world and if you happen to visit the Caribbean you'll find the company's non-alcoholic Cydrax and Peardrax still being made under licence in Trinidad and Tobago.

Victor Lewis-Smith described Peardrax as 'a foul, resinous, cloying, sweet beverage', but to Trinidadians it is a national treasure. They might not be aware that royalties from each sale go to Gaymer – now C&C – which owns various Whiteways brands after a furious half-century of takeovers that saw the Whimple factory close in 1989. As in Norton Fitzwarren and Long Ashton a vibrant enterprise has been replaced by housing, while commercial cidermaking is concentrated in a couple of giant, highly-automated factories. That's progress.

The closure of Whiteways left Devon cider in a forlorn state, and in 2000 Common Ground reported that the county had lost 90% of its traditional orchards in less than 40 years. A similar rate of loss was experienced in Cornwall, particularly in the fruit-rich Tamar Valley, as farm workers abandoned the land and cheap imports replaced home-grown fruit.

However, a revival is now in full swing, and south Devon now offers the cider tourist a quite remarkable range of cider-related experiences. Including scrumpy.

Ye Olde Cider Bar in ye olde days, when cider was drawn straight from the barrel.

Ye Olde Cider Bar, Newton Abbot

If you like cider and you're in Devon you absolutely have to visit Ye Olde Cider Bar. To pass it by would be a crime. Owned for the past forty years by Richard Knibbs, the place has been going for a lot longer; photos show drinkers back in the 1930s helping themselves from barrels in the old ciderhouse manner.

A truck heads out with another consignment of cyder. Nothing remains of the Whiteways factory today – except the orchard nearby.

How is this drinking den different from a thousand characterful old pubs? First up, the only beverages available are ciders and fruit wines, and there's a pretty decent selection of both. Not craft ciders particularly – though Parson's Choice was the guest when we visited – but Westons, Thatchers and larger-scale local producers, like the Winkleigh Cider Co. One or two are an acquired taste. At 8% Wiscombe Suicider is pretty lethal and it has more than a whiff of vinegar about it. Some regulars will drink nothing else.

And this is, first and foremost, a local ciderhouse. On Saturday nights, so manager Hannah told us, the youth of Newton Abbot fills the place to bursting point, but during the week the regulars hold sway. Even when they're not around, they have a presence. Above the bar hangs a double row of cider mugs, some two-handled in the old style, others with the owner's name written on the base. A row hanging over the heads of the drinkers is for regulars, Hannah explains, 'who are no longer with us.' These lost friends are also remembered in photographs lining the long, narrow room leading back towards the garden, some a century old. They show members of the Long Bar Cork Club, which has been meeting on Sundays for at least a hundred years.

The LBCC remains a club for men only, but the bar itself has become generally less chauvinistic over the years; women used to be served halves only, and we can think of a few cider fans who would take exception to that kind of injustice.

Until recently Ye Olde Cider Bar was a temptation to students at Seale-Hayne Agricultural College, and one or two spent rather more time at the bar than they did on their studies. All the better for us; when it comes to cidermaking you can't beat good hands-on experience.

Cidermaking has deep roots in Devon, and recently a renaissance has started in the south of the county.

Good to see a cider company doing its bit to promote road safety...

Tom Oliver on Ye Olde Cider Bar

"Both me and Andy Atkinson from Cornish Orchards, both being old Seale Haynians, if there is such a word, probably helped acquire our taste for cider and hence cider making, while students at the Cider Bar. I used to enjoy the afternoon session particularly. For a while there was a small indie record shop run by Shane Walters called Speed Records just round the corner so I would go in there to listen to some of the latest releases and then dive into the cider bar. From what I can recall I loved the simplicity of cider drinking and the chat and the low price!"

When they closed the college, did they realise how many future cidermakers the world would be without?

Brimblecombe

When you set off on a cider quest you never quite know what's going to happen, and we certainly didn't expect Brimblecombe. Not that this small producer on the edge of Dartmoor is a secret – it's been written up by CAMRA – but nothing can prepare you for the reality of a 14th century cider barn and its unique products. If you want to get a sense of what it was like to make and drink cider two or three hundred years ago, then this is the place to find out. Other cider companies might have a museum on site but Brimblecombe has the museum built in.

Where to start? The barn itself is medieval, a long cob building tucked against the side of a narrow valley just east of Dunsford. The thatched roof has long gone, replaced by the farmer's favourite roofing material, corrugated iron, but the interior can't have changed much in centuries. The remains of a stone mill are set into the floor near the entrance and then you come to the massive old press which stands in the gloom like an altar to Pomona – some of the ironwork is believed to date back 400 years. On Saturdays at pressing time two tons of crushed apples are shovelled onto layers of straw and built into the mother of all cheeses – not a job for the faint-hearted – and the juice slowly squeezed out as the press is tightened one turn at a time.

The juice is piped straight into barrels in the cider barn, which is about six feet below the level of the press bed, and you could not find a better place to ferment and store cider. Cool and gloomy, it's the perfect environment for a long, slow fermentation, with wild yeasts that have had several centuries to get properly established.

So what's the cider like? The young cider (we visited in May after a cold winter) is clean and bright, having been thoroughly filtered by the straw. Bizarrely, it also smells of straw and has a soft, grassy sweetness that also derives from this method of pressing. This might not suit every taste but you're unlikely to experience this ancient flavour at your local pub – unless you're lucky enough to live near the Orchard. As the cider matures the straw flavour fades; in 2010 the 2008 vintage was pleasantly dry, while the

Life moves fairly slowly at Brimblecombe, where the cider is made and stored in a 14th century cob barn.

A common sight at small cider farms. If you don't toot you might end up sitting for a long time, waiting for something to happen.

cider from a barrel dated 2006 was more of an acquired taste, acetic though not painfully so. Maggie, who manages the place on behalf of owner Ron Barter, pointed out that their cider is naturally not very strong – rarely much more than 6%. An expression of Dartmoor's murky microclimate? Some cidermakers would love it if their cider came out at that sort of strength, if only because pubs are more likely to take it.

The previous owner, incidentally, used to sell his cider to Whiteways, for blending. Or that's the story, at least. If you want to find out all about it go and visit on a Saturday in November (call first to confirm and for directions), watch the pressing and listen to some tales…

Nick Pring of Green Valley Cyder. Uses vats that came from Whiteways.

Green Valley Cyder

And don't forget the 'y'! Whiteways made CYDER and Green Valley is a scion of the great old company. When the machinations of Big Cider forced the Whimple works to close, Chris Coles, Nick Pring and other former employees – faithful employees of many years' standing – got together to set up a new business. Quite legitimately they rescued equipment from the factory, including large oak vats that had to be dismantled and then reassembled at the new site between Exeter and Topsham.

Ah, the good old days, when men wore hats and women stayed home to make the dinner...

So Green Valley (which takes its name from the wide vale of the River Clyst) started its life like graftwood taken from a dying tree, and to the casual observer it does resemble a miniature version of a proper cider factory. The space it occupies is tiny, but into it are squeezed vats and tanks, shiny steel pipes and a profusion of hoses. When we visited, Nick and crew were wrestling bulging bags of cider into boxes in preparation for the Devon County Show, and bottling the first of their Vintage Cyder from 2009. A slow fermentation over a long, cold winter had given them their best ever, Nick reckoned.

At first Green Valley may be tricky to find, but not because it's hidden down a Devon lane. This cider factory is concealed behind the biggest farm shop you're likely to see this side of California – the Darts Farm Shop. We found the cider by chance, wandering past a deli counter offering Cornish Yarg with Wild Garlic and some outrageously good pork pies. Walk past the cheese, turn a corner and there it is: 10,000 gallons of delicious Devon cider. And they don't just make cyder. Green Valley also sells the best selection of cider you'll find in that part of the world, a range of bottled ciders from Cornish Orchards, Heron Valley, Sandford Orchards and Newton Court as well as Sheppys and Burrow Hill. There are prize winners galore and some fine bottle-fermented and conditioned ciders. Kid in a candy store?

So what about Green Valley's cyder? It won CAMRA gold in 2008, but the first sip of the scrumpy – to a Somerset palate – seemed a bit sweet. No, not sweet, soft – soft tannins and not too much acidity. Delicious but an altogether different experience from drinking, say, Wilkins. You can see why Somerset judges don't favour traditional Devon ciders, but you can also see why the people that matter (that's us) enjoy them. It's cyder. It's scrumpy. It's a different world 30 miles down the M5.

The press at Brimblecombe, where the apples are pressed through straw. The resulting cider is uniquely delicious.

Cornish cider is also undergoing a renaissance. Cornish Orchards is particularly good.

Elsewhere in Devon and Cornwall

Once again, we recommend '*Ciderland*' for James Crowden's excellent investigations into the Devon and Cornwall cidermaking renaissance. In both counties there are fine producers at work, some well established, others just starting out. What can we say? Get out there. Ask around. Visit the makers. You'll find some of the best in the Listings section.

MY CIDER STORY

JEZ HOWAT OF WWW.146CIDER.COM AND A FOUNDER OF WWW.CIDERWORKSHOP.COM

I am currently a hobbyist cider maker, although I have commercial aspirations. I am registered as exempt with Customs and Excise and am going through the process of setting up a business model in order to sell locally in Southampton. I have been making cider since 2005 starting with just a few litres and doubling up year on year to 850 litres in 2009. My 2010 plans are to increase this to 1200 litres.

My website is 146Cider – I have been involved in web-based forums since starting to make cider – they are great places to learn and share worries and triumphs. When I first started making, I joined an online community which was immensely helpful. In 2009, a few things happened which caused some of those people who had offered such expertise to leave and so I chased them down and together we formed The Cider Workshop (www.ciderworkshop.com). Those people, who I now have the pleasure of running the Workshop with include Andrew Lea, Ray Blockley (of Hucknell Cider Company), Mark Shirley (of Rockingham Forest Cider), Dick Dunn (of Talisman Cider in the USA and also editor of the Cider Digest) and Roy Bailey (of Lambourne Valley Cider). This forum has flourished with such people at the helm, and is a vibrant community of helpful and friendly people – exactly the sort of community that could help budding cider makers.

The Cider Workshop was initially a creation of necessity, as the 'old platform' had collapsed. I created a website to run alongside it, which utilised existing resources, such as Andrew Lea's Wittenham Hill Cider Portal – possibly the most useful cider resource available online. We have started to build bridges with the likes of the National Association of Cider Makers, who occasionally set out the official line on various topics. Now, it has a life of its own and whilst there are other similar things in 'ciderspace', I believe the Workshop is one of the more inclusive and welcoming portals.

Entering competitions is a good way to compare your cider with the efforts of other craft makers.

I used to enjoy a pint or three of Magners which got me interested in cider and had been talking to a colleague about his university fermentations of cider. At the time my 6-month old daughter had been diagnosed with a very harsh form of muscular dystrophy and had spent a worrying time in hospital. It was around September time and I thought I would have a go at cidermaking. So I bought a small Vigo press off eBay and milled the apples in a blender. This made my first 25 gallons. The apples came from local roadsides and round the back of a church, so it made a pretty thin cider, and it was a bit oxidised too. However, it was nice enough for me to think I should try again. I joined an online web forum and asked lots of questions. The second year I made 50 litres, but this time I was better prepared and had the support of a number of other cidermakers through the web community. I guess cider making was initially a way 'out' of the business of daily life... there is nothing so calming as the process of washing, milling and pressing. I guess that's why I have doubled quantities every year for the last five years.

I have a fairly exclusive relationship with a friend who owns a few acres of orchard near me. Stephen Hayes (Fruitwise) sells heritage apples and doesn't have a use for his windfalls. I am very lucky that he also has a small cider apple orchard, so I can collect as many apples as drop for my main blend.

I use a wide variety of apples, although I like to keep a track of them. My favourites are Tremletts Bitter, Yarlington Mill and Harry Masters Jersey (all cider apples), but also I am very keen on Egremont Russet and Orleans Reinette – both very good eaters.

In 2009 I took over an allotment plot and planted six trees to provide me with some extra apples. However, as I have access to pretty much all the main varieties I could want, I have planted some rarer varieties.

My aim is to produce a cider that is representative of the season as a whole, therefore the process starts in early September, with a visit to my friend's orchard. This is also picking time for them because they sell their heritage fruit (that is their business, my cider is really a by-product of this). I work for them picking in order to get their windfalls – all very credible dessert and culinary apples.

As the season progresses, the cider apples come good, starting usually with the Tremletts – these are a highly tannic apple that will spice up the fairly weak cider at this early stage. As we go into October, the Egremonts, Ashmeads and Reinettes are ready for pressing, adding aromatic dessert flavours to the blend – the Yarlingtons and HMJs then add further bittersweet.

My aim is to achieve a 50 per cent dessert, 40 per cent cider apple and 10 per cent culinary blend. However, the trick is in ensuring that you have the best ingredients available. Treat them gently and you can't go too far wrong. I hope that I produce a Hampshire style of cider. It's pretty much half way between a western and an eastern style. Last year I also made an experimental single variety Egremont Russet cider (only a gallon), which I was very impressed with.

Technically, its all about cleaning. Before the season, everything gets washed, sterilised and the work area gets prepared – setting up a workflow within the cidermaking area is really important when you're working on your own. As the apples start to arrive, storage space becomes equally important. I try to store a maximum of 200kg of apples at a time – both because its hard to press more than that without a lot of hard work, but also because it is simple to check the boxes while the apples waiting to be pressed.

I can press 40kg at a time – on a good Saturday, with no other commitments, I can achieve four pressings in a day (the magical 200kg). From this, I will expect a yield of 120 litres of cider. Because this is a hobby, most of the pressing gets done in the evening – I might start a pressing at lunchtime and leave it until the end of my working day. Then I clear the press and get one more in for the evening. Every year my equipment list gets longer – the weakest link in the process being upgraded or replaced. Last year it was the mill. I now have a Vares Fruit Shark – an electric mill that is both popular with fellow cider makers and incredibly efficient at its job. This has saved hours in pressing. I have also invested in two Spiedel 300 litre tanks – which in reality hold 350 litres of juice. The pressed juice is shocked with Sodium Metabisulphite (I still use Camden Tablets as I know where I am with them), and left to ferment.

I use a home-made rack and cloth press. My father in-law made a steel frame, based on plans made available by Ray Blockley of the Hucknall Cider Company. I then built a base from a spare piece of kitchen worktop and frames out of beech wood specially ordered. They were probably the most expensive part of the press but are absolutely worth it. The cloths are Ikea net curtains.

I perform what Andrew Lea refers to as a 'directed natural fermentation'. This means that the cider is shocked with Sodium Metabisulphite and then left for nature to take its course. This results in a much slower starting fermentation, and a longer fermentation period. Patience (ironically, as Magners would say) is the backbone of cider making. Patience and having good friends who really know how to make cider.

The Dorset Cider Revival

The county's craft makers are producing some excellent ciders as Dorset stages a comeback

Dorset has never rivalled its neighbour Somerset in cidermaking, but in 1796 there were 10,000 acres of orchards in the county and numerous farms where cider was made. However, in the aftermath of World War II both the cider industry and the orchards that sustained it very nearly disappeared as government grants helped farmers transform large areas of the countryside into a giant wheat factory.

Across much of the county virtually nothing is left, but in the south-west, in the hill country that runs uninterrupted into neighbouring Somerset, there are still some substantial orchards. Rupert Best of Hincknowle, near Melplash, sends 1000 tonnes of cider apples to Shepton Mallet each year and also runs the The Royal Bath and West Show's excellent Cider and Orchards Pavilion. Elsewhere in Dorset, fragments of orchard survived the onslaught of industrial agriculture, along with a few small cidermaking ventures.

The region south and east of Crewkerne is good cider apple country and the scene of a remarkable renaissance that has given us at least two award-winning craft cidermakers, a cult cider festival, numerous community cidermaking clubs and the most significant new ciderhouse outside Bristol. There's no doubt about it: in this part of Dorset, cider is a force for good.

Nick Poole with his trophy after returning from Normandy where he took a first prize in the Concours de Cidre with his bottle-conditioned cider.

Nick Poole And Powerstock

"Every cidermaker should do a keeved cider," says Nick Poole, Dorset craft producer and founder of the Powerstock Festival. "I always keeve half mine, so I always have a sweet cider to blend."

It's an unusual approach in an industry which tends to rely on saccharin and sucralose, but then Nick is an unusual cidermaker. Not so long ago he entered his dry Normandy-style cider in a local competition and won, which wouldn't have been anything to write home about had the locals in questions not responded to his victory by flinging their berets in the air and crying 'Sacre bleu!' Yes, Nick beat the French at their own game and now focuses his modest output on keeved cider – 1000 bottles at the latest pressing.

Rose Grant pressing apples to make her Dorset cider.

Rose Grant – Ciderland's Top Blogger

If you want a really good insight into the craft producer's life we recommend working your way through Rose Grant's blog, The Cidermaking Year (www.ciderbyrosie.co.uk). Every trial and joy is described in her brisk, chatty style; for people planning to take the leap from hobbyist to commercial maker, the wisdom of her experience will be invaluable. Rose started making cider at her home near Blandford in the early 1990s, gradually using her own fruit as the trees in her small orchard gained maturity. In 2003 she introduced herself to the online cider group ukcider and a couple of years later she began writing her blog, initially for publication on the ukcider site and later for her own. At the time she expressed the hope that:

"The page could be of value to aspiring cider producers, especially if like me, they are gearing up from cider as a hobby to small scale commercial production. I am happy to share my woes and joys along the way if it helps other people to get into the production of real cider."

A fine cidermaker and Bath & West supreme champion, Rose Grant is also a prodigious blogger.

Subsequently she has taken her readers along every step of the journey that has taken her to victory at the Bath and West (Supreme Champion 2009) and into the pages of James Crowden's '*Ciderland*'. A born blogger, she manages to make the most tedious chore sound strangely gripping, and her enthusiasm for all things cider-related is infectious. Rose also has fairly firm opinions – strange, that, in a cidermaker. Her views on oak barrels are diametrically opposed to those of certain other opinionated producers…

And the cider itself? You can get it at pubs in her part of the world – the Square and Compass and the Stable, to name a couple. The last we tried was fairly sharp and deliciously fresh, more like a Devon cider than a Somerset. By coincidence, it seems that Dorset cider may have traditionally been more like its Devon cousin, though with most of the trees gone it's hard to say for sure.

The Square and Compass near Swanage: One of the country's finest cider houses.

The Lost Varieties Of Dorset

That we know anything at all about the history of Dorset cider is down to research undertaken in the last few years by Nick Poole and Liz Copas, who lives near Crewkerne and bravely crossed the border to go apple-hunting.

The pair spent two seasons driving all over, examining fruit and talking to farmers who tended to tell them the same story: we used to have a big orchard for cidermaking but the government paid us to grub it up in the 1970s. The result of this hard work is that 400 trees will be planted, with 25 rare local varieties, including King's Favourite and Golden Ball. Visit Dorset Cider (www.dorsetcider.com) for further details.

Return Of The Cider House

Dorset gives a fascinating insight into what can happen when cider-mania takes root, with a number of cider clubs springing up in villages. In Powerstock, a village that has no school or shop, the cider club has become an important focus of community life, with members meeting once a month for lunch in an old barn. Could the ciderhouse become the unofficial village parliament once again?

At the same time, pubs in west Dorset are becoming some of the best in the country for cider drinkers. The Square and Compass has been drawing the crowds for a century, and now offer Cider by Rosie, landlord Charlie Newman's own cider, and plenty of guests. The Castle Inn in West Lulworth has a decent range and regular cider events, and there's also the Mill House Cider Museum on the way to Dorchester. And in Bridport the Bull Hotel now has the Stable, where you can enjoy Dorset pizzas washed down with Dorset cider. Isn't that what they call fusion?

MY CIDER STORY

PENNY WHATMOOR FROM MILL HOUSE CIDER MUSEUM, OWERMOIGNE, DORSET

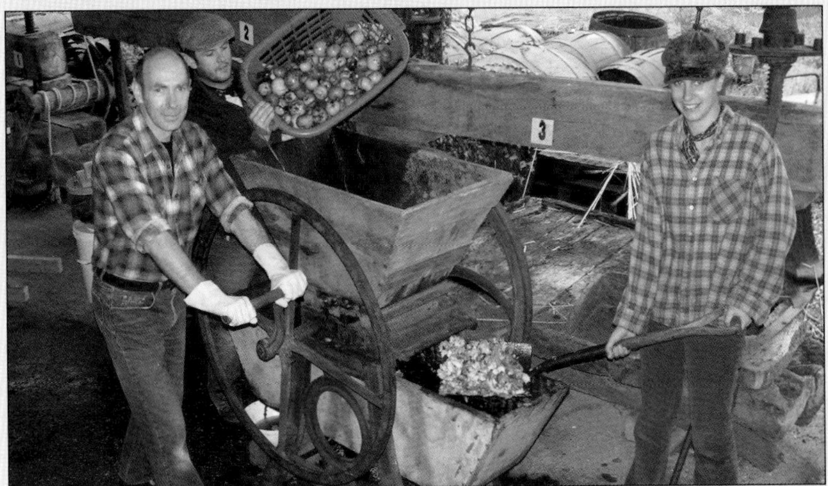

Making cider the old way at the Mill House Cider Museum.

The Cider Museum was started by my father Derek Whatmoor and his brothers in the early 1980s. They had a farmer friend who owned an antique shop. He acquired an antique cider mill and press, and the brothers decided to buy it. They bought in a small amount of apples and made about 20 gallons of traditional cider, which turned out to be very nice. The next year they bought a larger amount of apples, some hessian cloths and wooden formers and made a larger quantity of cider. Over the years they made more and sold it to the public, buying in bottles, and wooden barrels from Eldridge Pope Brewery in Dorchester. For better advertising, they wanted to put up some brown and white signs on the local main roads. To do this, they had to be considered a museum, so they went around Dorset, Somerset, Wiltshire and Devon collecting unwanted and interesting cidermaking equipment and memorabilia.

Traditional farm cider was made and sold successfully for over ten years. In the early 90s due to staffing level changes, costs (and two replacement hips) the conclusion was reached that it was not really cost effective to make larger amounts of cider on the antique equipment any longer. The museum has over 42 cider mills and presses, a video display showing the antique equipment in use, and displays on the different aspects of making cider, so it was decided to buy in and retail a selection of farm ciders.

So for the last six years I have been running the cider museum and we have demonstration days in October, where the Cider Making Team (staff and four or five friends) dress in traditional clothing to show people how cider used to be made.

We source apples from many different places. There are a few orchards around the museum with Kingston Blacks, Bramleys and other eating and cooking apples. We usually have a trailer load of cider apples from Burrow Hill in Somerset as well – so a complete mix of apples that varies from year to year.

We use a hand-driven scatter mill – the rinsed apples are just tipped in through the top hopper and it produces a rough pulp. We use a traditional Dorset press, acquired from a farm in Shipton Gorge, dating from the early 19th century. We now use long thatching straw to make the cheese to follow the traditional method. Modern combine straw is too short. This makes an impressive spectacle for the public and the straw can also be easily disposed of afterwards – rather than emptying and washing out cloths. The straw and pressed pomace was an important feed for the farm animals over the winter.

The juice is then poured into traditional wooden barrels – we have used ex-rum barrels, and brandy barrels which give a slightly different essence to the cider. I have never felt the need to add yeast – it always starts working within a week with the natural yeasts. We make sure the barrels are completely full to expel air, and rest the bung over the top loosely. Over the next few months we keep the barrels topped up with apple juice, under a lean-to roof beside the museum. As fermentation completes, I taste regularly to see when it needs racking off – traditionally when the first cuckoo is heard.

As we use such a variety of apples, this traditional farm cider tastes different every time – but it is still, smooth, dry and generally appreciated by everyone who drinks it. I think a great cider can be made very naturally and simply. We also hire out the equipment in the autumn for people to bring their own apples and then take the juice home. Because some people bring small amounts of apples, I bought in a Vigo basket press a few years ago because the antique press needs a large quantity of apples to work well. Some villages get together and bring trailer loads of apples, producing over 100 gallons of juice at a time.

In April everyone who brought their own apples in the autumn to make cider is invited back for a Best Cider competition, discussions and tastings. It is very interesting to sample all the very different styles of cider, and for people to talk about their different methods of making it.

With more interest in using natural ingredients and home production we have seen a great resurgence of small-scale cider making in the last few years. This traditional art will not be lost and continue long into the future.

For more about the Mill House Cider Museum, visit www.millhousecider.com

Pressing through straw is laborious but produces a lovely cider.

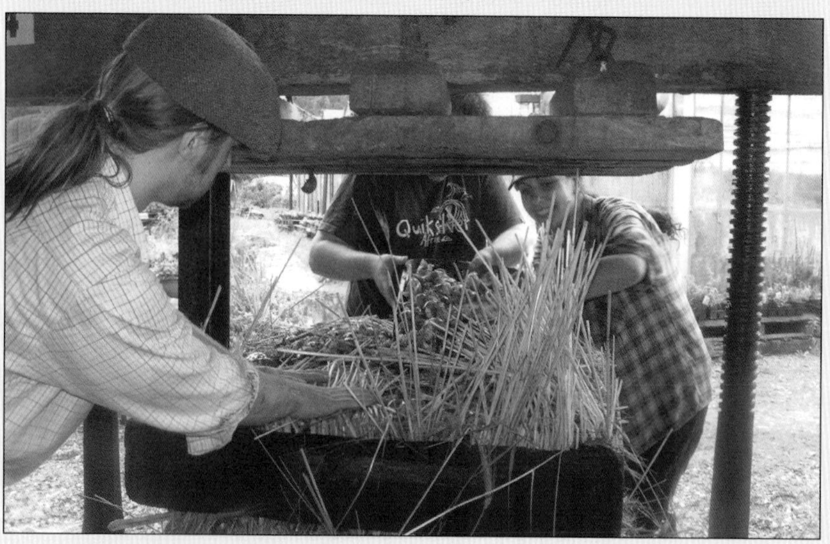

Tasting Notes

Eastern Counties

The apples may be different from what the rest of the country use, but the cider tastes good...

Travel east from London and you'll find a cider tradition quite different from that of the West Country, but just as ancient – and as fiercely championed by its makers (and drinkers). By long tradition, producers in Sussex, Kent and East Anglia use cookers and eaters, rather than specialised cider varieties, to make their cider. Why is this? One reason is perhaps that fruit growers in the region enjoyed a lucrative trade supplying table and culinary fruit to the capital, and made cider more as a by-product than by design. Farmhouse cider was as much an everyday part of life in this fruit-rich region as it was in the West Country, but the orchard economy was destroyed almost overnight when Golden Delicious arrived from France – like the Normans a millennium before – to be followed by container ships loaded with cheap fruit from sunnier climes.

First harvest your apples.

To a cider lover from western parts this business of making cider from cookers and eaters might seem a bit odd, although Thatchers has achieved wonders with Katy and also makes a good Cox single variety. You'll also find the odd Bramley slipped in to a West Country cider that needs some extra acidity.

But the Eastern Counties tradition is a proud one, in which varieties well known in the kitchen are given a new role. Bramley is often a base, with Worcester, Cox or Russets blended with it to suit the maker's taste. Introduced as a pollinator in the 1960s, Crispin is a gargantuan apple that finds its way into the region's ciders. There are plenty of drinkers who prefer the fresh, crisp, low-tannin ciders of the east, which is no doubt why Aspalls and Merrydown do quite well for themselves.

Collecting windfalls in the orchards of Kent.

KENT – CIDER IN THE GARDEN OF ENGLAND

Things are looking up for cider-drinking Londoners. While the capital's pubs are looking beyond Magners and increasingly stocking Westons, Aspalls, Thatchers, Biddendens, etc, there are increasing opportunities for cider fans to get out in the countryside, visit producers and drink some good craft cider. And people are making the most of it.

Twenty years ago cidermaking in Kent was mostly going on under the radar, but after Biddenden started producing as an extension of its winemaking activities small-scale outfits began springing up all over the county. Today there are about 15 producers and many welcome visitors on tours and tastings, or to help out at pressing time. Recommended stopping-off points include:

The National Fruit Collection, Brogdale

If you're interested in fruit, cidermaking or culinary history then this mother of all mother orchards is a place you have

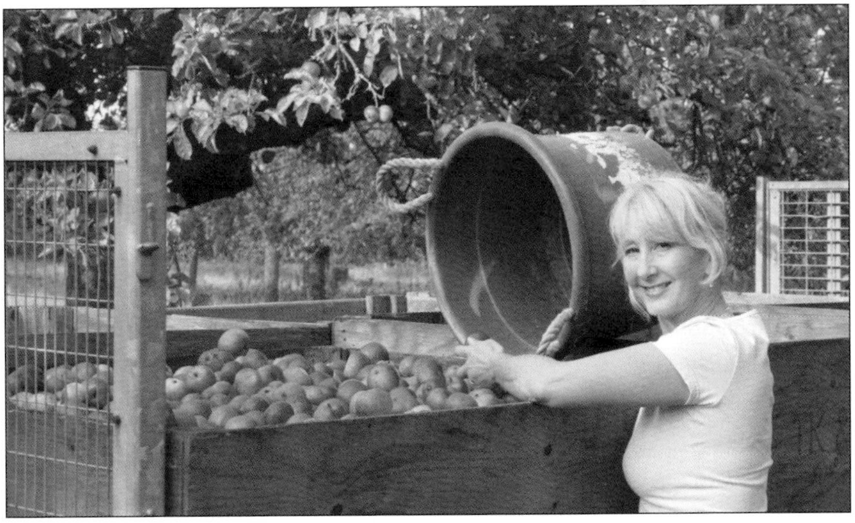

No matter what sort of apples you use, harvesting by hand means craft cider makers only use the finest fruit.

to see. With over 4000 varieties of apple, pear, plum, cherry and nut, Brogdale Farm offers visitors the chance to taste the apple varieties Henry VIII would have eaten, the nuts Columbus would have carried to America, and the varieties of plum the Victorians loved so much.

If you can't make it there in person, have a look at '*The New Book of Apples*' by Joan Morgan and Alison Richards, which is based on their research into the 2000 apple varieties at this living museum.

The apples from Hawkins Rough orchard are brought back to the yard.

Badgers Hill (Canterbury)

Badgers Hill is a fruit farm and cidery (a term common in Kent, though not one we use in the West Country, unless we're describing someone who imbibes excessively, as in 'look at 'e, 'e's all zoidery'). One of the first to revive the Kentish cider tradition 20-odd years ago, which they did mostly because they'd been shafted by the supermarkets and couldn't sell their fruit any more. Grey cloud… silver lining. Badgers Hill specialises in cider made from Cox's Orange Pippins, and also sells sandwiches and barrel-based crafts.

Biddenden Vineyard (Ashford, Kent)

Deep in the garden of England, Biddenden is the county's oldest commercial vineyard, which may explain why its cider is so powerful. The oak-aged Special Reserve has an ABV of 13.5%, which puts it up there with a good red wine. Also look out for Monk's Delight, which is made from Kentish cider, honey and spices and designed to be served hot. The shop and café are open daily and you can sign up for a vineyard tour if you fancy it.

Rough Old Wife

"She may be rough but by god she tastes good."

What can you say? It may be a name that's hard to ignore, but Rough Old Wife cider is also rooted in the place where it is made. If you don't believe us, pop along to Hawkins Rough Orchard, in Old Wives Lees, near Canterbury and see for yourself. Then again, they could have called it Hawkins Lees Cider, couldn't they?

The partners in crime in this case – how often does a cidermaking venture grow out of a couple of mates thinking how nice it would be to make a barrel? – are

Simon Reed and Andy Maclean. They started out in 2004 and have doubled production each year since, so that they are now nicely poised just below the 1500 gallon mark. Simon puts this steady rise in demand down to a sort of secondary fermentation of the Magners effect: the Irish company attracted everyone's attention and reminded people that they weren't 13 any more and could drink cider without making themselves sick, and for a couple of years people were happy to drink the stuff. Then they started looking around for something more interesting.

"It's similar to what happened with real ale," Simon reckons. "There were a handful of microbreweries 30 years ago. Now there are 120. And right now we're in an early stage of the appreciation of real cider."

That's the spirit! The Magners Moment wasn't a freak peak but the start of a long-term revival. The question is, where does a small producer like Rough Old Wife go from here?

For Simon it's about creating an identity for the cider which can withstand the annual variations in fruit quality that make consistency so hard to achieve. To this end he uses wild yeasts (as most Kentish producers apparently do) and ferments each year's cider in oak barrels from the same Scottish distillery. So whatever the variations in the juice, the flavour and character imparted by its environment should be similar. It's a neat idea, and should help Simon achieve his aim of creating a distinctive brand equivalent to the Chateau quality of a French wine. Chateau Rough anyone?

Like many of his West Country colleagues, Simon believes there should be a legal definition of full-juice, real cider, which he would call 'cyder'. We're not going to get started on that definition business again, but most readers will agree that he has a point. If you disagree, well, you can go along to Rough Old Wife HQ and have a chat. Go in the autumn and you can help with the cidermaking while you're at it; apparently Londoners are heading that way in increasing numbers, like the hop pickers of old, though more for fun than out of economic necessity.

It's easier to pulp dessert and cooking apples than the smaller and harder cider apple.

SUSSEX – MERRYDOWN COUNTRY

This may not be a county many associate with cidermaking, yet Sussex is home to one of the biggest cider and perry emporia going. It's also where Merrydown started out, and if you enjoy a drop you may well consider this the cidermaking capital of the world. Set up after World War II, the company made wine-strength cider – or apple wine – which proved hugely popular in austerity Britain. This wine was always promoted as something quite different from West Country ciders, made with champagne yeast and with 'apples that are good enough to eat' rather than nasty old bittersweets. Unfortunately for Merrydown, it had to endure the same tax regime as its western rivals, and the 1975 Budget did for wine-strength cider with a 103% rise in duty. So apple wine became vintage cider, with an ABV reduced from 13% to 8.5%, but after a successful period in the 1980s the business struggled. Refinancing in 1998 was followed, in 2005, by the company's sale to SHS, owner of WKD. The new proprietor has so far resisted the urge to rename the cider MDN.

Meanwhile, back in Sussex, the craft cider revival has taken hold. If there are any old cidermaking concerns around these parts, they're keeping pretty quiet, but there are plenty of up-and-coming producers, not to mention one massive cider and perry emporium…

Once the apples have been scratted, it's time to load up the cider press.

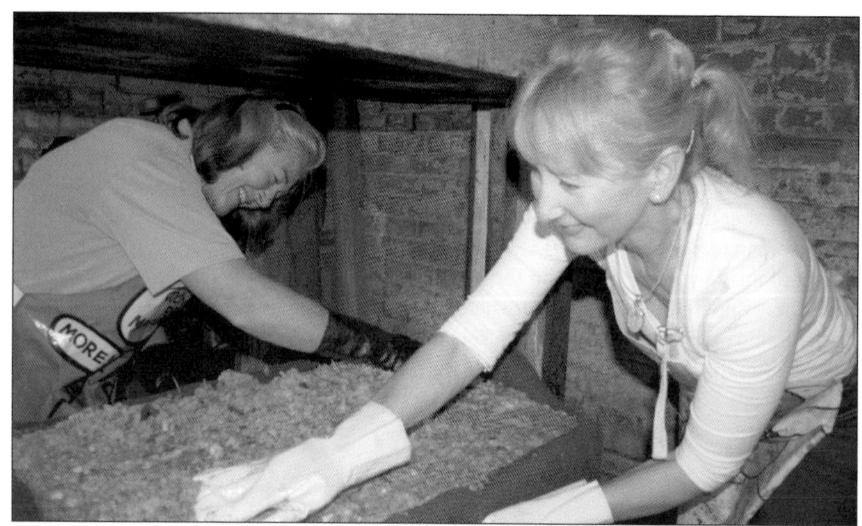

Making the cheese for pressing at Rough Old Wife in Kent.

Sedlescombe Organic Vineyard (Robertsbridge, E Sussex)

What do you do with a 10 acre farm on a well-drained, south-facing hillside, in 1979? Start a vineyard. This kind of diversification is one of the few benefits of the global agricultural revolution that has had such a dire effect on UK farming, and today Roy Cook makes and sells both wine and cider. The apples come from an orchard across the road. The farm shop is set in an old hay barn and offers English wines, country wines and fruit juices, as well as cider and gifts – why not go along between Easter and Christmas and see for yourself?

There are many variations on the press theme but most of the bigger ones are either screw or hydraulic.

The National Collection of Cider and Perry

When we asked Rod Marsh why on earth the National Collection of Cider and Perry is based at a farm in Sussex he had a good answer. It's neutral territory. Imagine something similar in Hereford or Somerset and you'd no doubt have a bias in favour of local producers (as you do at the museum in Hereford, come to think of it). Middle Farm is aptly named, lying as it does between the great West Country cider lands and the Eastern Counties of Kent and Suffolk; the 100 draught ciders and perries on offer represent the best of both traditions.

When John and Vivian Pile moved to the farm in 1960 they quickly realised that the poor soil was not going to support them. Looking for ways to diversify, they began selling milk and other produce from the back door and over the next 20 years built up a successful farm shop. In 1981 John was in Somerset buying butter and cheese on a route which took him past Sheppys and Perrys; so he bought a barrel of each along with ciders from a couple of Devon producers and took them back to sell in Sussex.

So successful was this new venture that, two years later, John applied to Companies House for the shop to become the National Collection of Cider and Perry, little knowing that the process would take three years. For one thing, he had to prove that his venture had pre-eminence in its field – difficult when there is no field to be pre-eminent in. But eventually he convinced the authorities that this collection was both national in scope and unique in its variety, and now Middle Farm offers cider lovers in London and the

South a taste of the West.

Rod now manages the collection, as well as making his own Pookhill Cider from locally sourced fruit. Readers in the West Country might be surprised to know that bittersharps and bittersweets can be found in Sussex, as can perry pears. Matthew Wilson of Robertsbridge in East Sussex is a third generation fruit farmer who now makes perry from his own vintage pears – you'd need pretty good ears to hear the church bells of Dymock from there…

Rod is not alone in crediting Magners for the recent surge of interest in cider and perry, but he reckons the famous orchard adverts started a renaissance which is now evolving. Drinkers have tried the sweet stuff over ice and now want to see what else is out there; they might go for a gentler draught cider like Janet's Jungle Juice then, as their palate develops, move on to the classic dry ciders that Rod himself favours.

'Somerset is the spiritual home of cider,' he told us, 'Particularly what I call the golden triangle.'

Roughly covering the area between Shepton Mallet in the east, Martock in the south and Wedmore in the west, this is the region we keep coming back to – the heartland. Wilkins is a favourite with Rod – 'a gentleman' is how he describes Roger – but the cidermaker he tries to emulate with his own pressing is Frank Naish of West Pennard. To make a cider like Frank's seems a pretty good life ambition.

'Cider is part of the fabric of this country,' Rod says. 'It's our oldest national drink. We're at the northernmost limit of apple-growing which means we have a brilliantly long ripening season, and this gives our cider apples their distinctive qualities.'

The National Cider and Perry Collection is a celebration of this great tradition – a museum where you can drink the exhibits.

Some producers like to store their cider in oak whisky barrels. Others prefer not to mix the flavours.

EAST ANGLIA

Over the past forty year no region in the UK has lost more orchards than East Anglia. Commercial fruit-growing and farmhouse orcharding were central to the region's economy for centuries and in the Victorian age some of the greatest nurserymen plied their trade to the north and east of London. Fruit imported from the Empire was a challenge, but it was the birth of the European

Community and competition from French growers that destroyed an industry and a culture almost overnight. In terms of cider, East Anglia has a curious history, with two hugely successful companies based within a few miles of one another. Today only one is left, but the national craft revival has its success stories here too, with both traditional eastern ciders and West Country ciders being made and enjoyed. It might come as a surprise to know that the now-legendary Leave Our Cider Alone Facebook group, which made headlines in the spring of 2010 by gaining 50,000 members in no time at all, was launched by a man from Holt, in Norfolk.

"It was just to raise awareness that this was happening, as loads of people won't be checking the budget," Jono Reed told his local paper. It seemed to work pretty well, didn't it?

Andy Maclean with the end product from Rough Old Wife after all that harvesting, scratting, pressing and waiting...

A Short History Of Gaymer

Cider isn't supposed to be served with a head on it, is it? That's what we thought until we encountered Addlestones, the peculiar draught cider that comes in a glass so massive you can barely lift it off the table. Anyway, Addlestones is made by Gaymer Cider Company, which is now owned by C&C, parent company of Magners, and which also makes Blackthorn and sundry other ciders at its Shepton Mallet factory. But Gaymer did not start out as a Somerset company but as part of a localised Norfolk cider industry. In 1845 White's Directory stated that "orchards are numerous in Norfolk, especially on the south side of the county, where many of the farmers make cider for their own consumption, and some little for sale."

Twenty miles south-west of Norwich, the village of Banham (which lies on good clay soil) was home to several cidermakers at the time, including two national award winners – Routs and Gaymer. The latter had started production around 1770, but on a small scale, and it wasn't until the later 19th century that William Gaymer took hold of the business and turned it into an eastern rival to HP Bulmer. His father, also William, used to deliver cider to Cambridge colleges in his horse and cart, but the younger Gaymer had bigger ambitions.

His early experiences of cidermaking weren't all positive however. When he was nine he came home from school to find two labourers operating his father's stone mill. Immediately he took over from a lad who was hoeing apples into the path of the runner, but slipped and fell into the mill. His right hand was caught between two cogs and his thumb ripped off.

Undeterred, the younger William grew up to transform the business. In 1870 he came across a hydraulic press for the first time and, ignoring his father's protests, bought it. Great care was taken in orchard management and in the selection of fruit – with Ribston Pippin the knock-out variety that helped Gaymer's ciders win numerous late Victorian cider competitions. In 1896 the company moved to Attleborough and a factory with its own railway siding, and William took full advantage of the transport infrastructure by supplying cider to railway companies as well as clubs, military messes and the House of Commons. By the 1920s the company was exporting its dry Gaysec, sweet Gayflag and special Olde English ciders world-wide from offices on Hackney Road in London, and when William died in 1936, aged 94, he left behind a thriving business.

It did not outlast him long. In 1961 Showerings was busily building up a cider and perry empire on the proceeds of Babycham, and launched a take-over bid. Surprisingly, production continued in Norfolk until 1995, by which time Matthew Clark plc had taken over Showerings; like Taunton Cider and Whiteway of Devon, Gaymer saw its factory closed and production moved to Shepton Mallet.

Barrels of cider waiting to be collected at the Gaymers factory.

Aspall, Cider Survivor

Aspall Cyder is a fascinating institution, a cider company that is still going strong after almost 300 years. Established by Clement Chevallier in 1728 the business is still in the family, with the current management team of Barry and Henry Chevallier representing the 8th generation. If you've read many of the company histories in this book you'll appreciate that this is quite an achievement.

It might have been a different story. Clement originally tried to plant vines but they failed, so he brought apple trees from Jersey and did what many thirsty landowners have done before and since – made cider as a substitute for wine. The succeeding generations continued the tradition without necessarily relying on it; the Rev John Chevallier (1774–1846) discovered a new strain of barley which went

Aspall Cyder: established in 1728 and still in the Chevallier family in 2010.

on to be cultivated across Britain and abroad, Temple Chevallier (1794-1873) was a professor of astronomy and mathematics and JB Chevallier (1857-1940) won a double-first at Cambridge and played in four FA Cup finals for the Old Etonians... He also changed the spelling of his favourite tipple to 'cyder', while also making it stronger and selling it bottled, with a wired-down cork.

By 1970, however, cidermaking at Aspall Hall was at a low ebb, and when John Chevallier (1933-present) left the Navy and returned to the family home, he decided to follow new avenues, producing apple juice and vinegar. This proved a shrewd choice, since the emerging health food shops and supermarkets offered outlets for these new products. With breweries taking over pubs left, right and centre, it was much harder to sell cider, and this part of the business laid low for the rest of the century.

But when Henry and Barry joined the business in 1993 they went back to the family's roots, redesigning and recrafting the cider just in time for the current revival. With a fresh, crisp taste and packaging that reminds people of the Golden Age of Cyder, they got everything right, and their appeal to high-end hedonists has seen Aspall products served on cruise ships and at posh festivals. Clement is probably watching from on high, approving and perhaps a little thirsty...

Henry Chevallier is the eighth generation of his family to run the Aspall business.

THE CIDER REVIVAL IN EAST ANGLIA

It isn't exactly buzzing with cider action over there, but you'll find a few small producers dotted around the region:

Whin Hill Cider, Wells-next-the-Sea

Unusually, this is a Norfolk craft cidermaker, based in Wells-next-the-Sea, that makes cider and perry using West Country vintage fruit grown in its own local orchard. Ten acres of cider apple trees and 150-plus perry pear trees provide plenty of raw material in a low-intensity environment which is half-way between an old traditional orchard and a modern bush orchard. If you're in north Norfolk look out for the shop/bar beside a car park in the centre of Wells (it isn't a very big place).

The Cider Shed, Norwich

Norwich is a city with more top-notch pubs than most, and

one of the best is the Fat Cat, which is hidden away down a back street to the north-east of the city centre. The Fat Cat also has a microbrewery, which shares a site with a venture set up in 2005 but with much older roots: the Cider Shed.

This is a story that should inspire up-and-coming producers. Ryan Burnard started making cider in 1987, following the age-old principle of setting up shop in a tried and tested location. In his case the orchards surrounding Banham – those that helped Gaymer win so many Victorian prizes – provided the fruit for a range of highly individual ciders. In the past he's made and sold Bees Knees, which is sweetened with honey and Bejan Beauty Rum Cask, which is made in Barbadian rum casks.

Seizing the marketing opportunities on offer he started selling cider opposite Banham Zoo, a local tourist attraction, eventually opening a proper bar. But the lure of the bright lights was too great so the Cider Shed upped sticks and moved. The newish venue looks like a shed from the outside but on the inside it's less like a shed and more like an American microbrewery. The Monty's Bone Dry is named after the pub dog, in case you were wondering.

Gaymer can trace its roots back to the village of Banham near Norwich in the 1770s.

Crone's Organic Cider, Kenninghall, Norfolk

Organic cider pioneers Robbie and Jane Crone started pressing apples for juice and cider in 1984, and since then they have carved out a niche for themselves as small-scale producers with a whole-hearted commitment to orchards and wildlife. Specialist off-licences and organic wholesalers provide a market, and the Soil Association has rewarded their efforts with numerous awards.

Q&A JAMES CROWDEN

AUTHOR WHOSE BOOKS INCLUDE *CIDER: THE FORGOTTEN MIRACLE* AND *CIDERLAND*

What got you interested in cider and perry to begin with?
Cider at thrashing time on the South Devon cliff tops near Dartmouth circa 1958, sheep shearing time at Meavy on the edge of Dartmoor about 1960 and as a lunchtime beverage at a remote farm in the Tamar Valley.

Do you have a treasured memory of a particularly good cider or perry?
One of James Marsden's Kingston Black ciders a year or two ago and one of Alex Hill's bottle-fermented sparkling perries aged for 14 years. Smokey and apricoty. And of course Julian Temperley's Cider Brandy

Do you have a favourite variety?
Kingston Black and Dabinett for farmhouse cider – high tannins chunky, heavy-duty... Bordeaux equivalent. Acquired taste.

If you could drink cider in any time or place, where would it be?
In the garden after sheep shearing or haymaking when your throat is parched and you are in need of refreshment. Cider's the original antidote to hard physical work.

How do you account for the recent surge of interest in cider and cidermaking?
Historical basis and our rich cider heritage spelt out and made accessible. It's also linked in to real food and drink, Slow Food and the concept of terroir. Better cider being made: ie not just rat's piss from a dirty farmyard or mass-produced cider of dubious origins and provenance.

Better advertising. Even Magners got young women and men drinking cider rather than lager though how much Magners cider comes from Irish apples is very open to debate. For three years the orchards featured in their TV adverts were shot in New Zealand... How Irish is that? But it worked.

Do you have any advice for the novice cidermaker?
Develop a palate, work out what is good what will sell and learn the common faults with cidermaking and storing cider. Steer clear of concentrate and dessert apples. Develop your own flavours from apples close to home and then when you know what you want plant an orchard with the varieties you want so that it matures before you retire. Start young.

Can you tell us about your best and/or worst moment as a cidermaker?
Best moment: going home after seven weeks of night shift.
Worst moment: when everything is wet for weeks and there's a cold wind in the cider house.

What's your most precious bit of cider-related gear?
Original copy of Worlidge 1678

What can we do to ensure that orchards are still flourishing in 50 years' time?
Make sure that more people drink cider and that they appreciate where it comes from. Start cider academies in Primary schools.

Any suggestions for ways of sorting out the duty problem?
Define cider far more carefully by origins of fruit, methods of manufacture, juice content etc and percentages of cider apples versus dessert apples and accurate labelling enforced by the FSA on the use of glucose syrup, colourings etc. Heavily tax white cider and ciders made with glucose syrup and which have a juice content of below 50%.

Anything you'd like to add?
Keep drinking the cider and perry of course.

Wales: Land of My Cider

Perhaps the most amazing cider renaissance has taken place in Wales.

Orchard country is no respecter of borders. Cider apples and perry pears grow just as well in the eastern part of Wales as they do in the Three Counties, and the past quarter century has seen a tremendous revival in cider and perry making in the principality. Since 1999 Cymdeithas Perai a Seidr Cymru – otherwise known as the Welsh Perry and Cider Society – has been hard at work, its mission to 'encourage a greater appreciation of these natural craft drinks, spearhead a new era of orchard planting and promote Welsh perry and cider as an indigenous alternative to wine.'

Welsh cider and perry are competing successfully with English products.

The story of Welsh cider is not so different to the English version, with cider truck (see History section) being an integral part of agricultural life in Monmouthshire and Radnorshire as it was across the border. The main difference is that no commercial cidermakers set up shop on the Welsh side to compete with Bulmers, Westons and the rest, so when farm cidermaking died out after World War II orchard owners either sent their fruit to Herefordshire or grubbed out the trees. Cider continued to be made on a small scale, of course, but it wasn't until the 1980s that craft producers began making Welsh cider for the enjoyment of a wider public.

In 1999 Dave Matthews and Alan Golding decided to have a go at cidermaking and found they had the knack. But having set up Seidr Dai, the Cardiff-based producers wanted to do more. They saw the merit of cidermakers' associations but also appreciated that in Wales a body was also needed that would promote the consumption of cider, something along the lines of CAMRA. So they formed Cymdeithas Perai a Seidr Cymru, using the internet to overcome the obstacles posed by the geography of Wales and allow producers in all parts of the mountainous land to share stories and information.

With an annual festival and the publicity generated by high-profile prize winners (Seidr Dai won Best Perry at CAMRA in 2006), the Welsh renaissance has gone from strength to strength, with numerous craft producers up and running and at least one company challenging the English in pubs as far away as London…

Andrew Gronow of Gwynt y Ddraig grew up in Churchill, Somerset. It's just possible he had a glass of Thatchers now and again…

Ralph's

One of these pioneers was Ralph Owen, who was making cider back in the 1970s when he was farm manager on Bertram Bulmer's estate on the island of Anglesey. The cider was made from fruit picked in Radnorshire on an annual pilgrimage that became a permanent move in 1986 when Ralph took over Old Badlands Farm and began farming for himself.

Farming naturally included cidermaking, and Ralph quickly established himself as a craft producer with a fascination for traditional methods. Today all his fruit is pressed on a Victorian oak beam screw press or vintage hydraulic machine, and Old Badlands also boasts a horse-powered stone mill that was brought from another farm and reassembled on site. Judging by the awards Ralph has won over the past few years, this equipment evidently does the job.

A Welsh Pomona

(with thanks to Dave Matthews)

Among the well-known commercial varieties grown in Welsh orchards are some rare local varieties that have been discovered and preserved in the Museum Orchard in Monmouthshire:

Broom Apple – mild bittersweet found near Raglan.

Twyn-y-Sheriff – another mild bittersweet from a farm of the same name, also near Raglan.

Frederick – more common Monmouthshire sharp, said to make a good single variety cider

Berllanderi Green – perry pear from Raglan, where a solitary tree was found, said to make a good, rounded perry.

Chapman's Orange – perry pear from Cardiff area, also from a single tree, gives a rich, orange-coloured perry.

The Ciderhouse at the farm has become one of the places the true cider fan has to visit, but you might also come across Ralph or his son James on tour with a travelling scratter and press dating from the 1880s – the Cider Museum in Hereford is a regular port of call.

Ralphs has been at the forefront of the cider revival, using traditional methods and some fabulous old gear.

Gwynt y Ddraig

One of the intriguing questions about the current cider revival is this. If the industry was in such a poor state in different parts of the country before the renaissance, how did today's craft producers get the cidermaking bug? Where, for example, did Gwynt y Ddraig cidermaker Andrew Gronow get his inspiration? He and his uncle Bill George set out on the road to cider success in 2001, when they made a few barrels for fun, but what got them started?

It turns out that Andrew spent his formative years in the 1980s living within staggering distance of a certain north Somerset cider farm, where he and his mates amused themselves by shooting pigeons off the farmer's cabbages. In those days John Thatcher was still very much a farmer-cidermaker, selling his cider from the barrel as smaller Somerset producers still do today. Living in

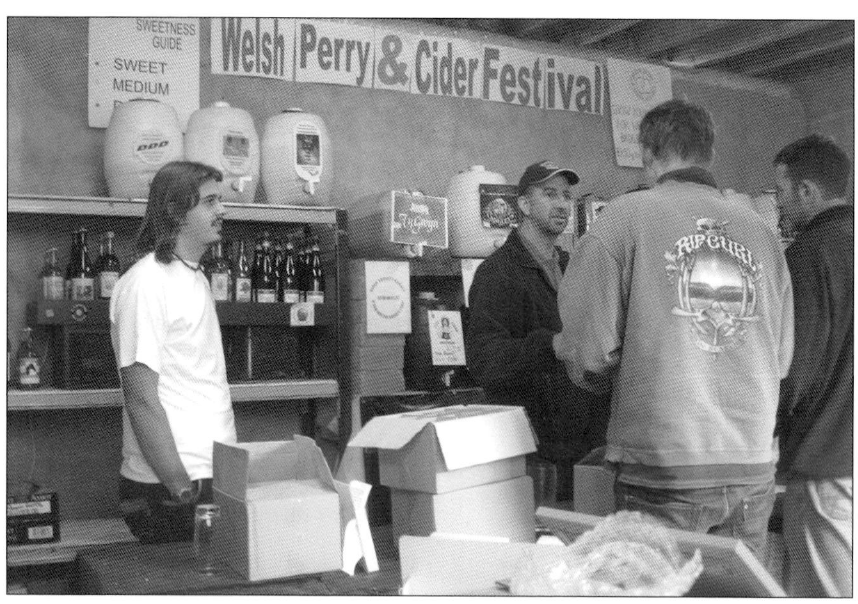

The Welsh Perry and Cider Festival goes from strength to strength.

Churchill, Andrew learnt about cider the best way, drinking Thatchers and exploring pubs and other cider farms in the surrounding villages.

"We used to go for the roughest stuff," he says now, with just a hint of pride.

Leaving Somerset, and with school and college behind him, Andrew spent some time working in Australia before coming back to Wales. He was running a welding business, while his uncle was a civil engineer, when they decided to gather up some apples and make their first batch of cider. The first time around they used any old fruit, pressing in the traditional manner and fermenting the juice in old oak casks. Having enjoyed the results they decided to take more care with the fruit the following year, and quickly developed several good, distinctive blends. Raised on Thatchers, Hecks, Wilkins and Rich's, Andrew knew a proper cider when he tasted one, so it's no surprise that his ciders have found a following not just in South Wales but in Bristol and the Midlands.

In 2004 Gwynt y Ddraig enjoyed its first success at the CAMRA awards, which set the fledgling company up nicely for the great surge in cider drinking that was about to burst over the country. Successive prizes – including Overall Champion at Hereford in 2010 – have brought Black Dragon, Orchard Gold and other products to the public's attention, and Andrew is keen to credit CAMRA in particular for its work in spreading the word.

"Without all the competitions, the public wouldn't be aware of ciders around the UK, so hats off to them."

With a distinctive logo and memorable brands, Gwynt y Ddraig has caught on, which raises a problem familiar to craft cidermakers. How do you achieve the consistency that consumers demand? Andrew's answer is that consistent quality is vital, but that flavour does tend to vary a little from batch to batch. Sometimes people will get in touch to ask why a bottle of a particular cider tasted different from a previous one – they're happy to learn that natural variations are part and parcel of a traditional approach to cidermaking. Besides, Andrew is an enthusiast.

"I love cider," he says. "It's good for you, isn't it?"

Ralphs has won more than its share of awards, as these mugs testify.

Q&A DAVE MATTHEWS

CO-FOUNDER OF THE AWARD-WINNING CARDIFF-BASED CRAFT CIDER OUTFIT, SEIDR DAI

Dave Matthews: one of the founders of the Welsh Cider and Perry Society.

What was it that first got you interested in cider and perry?
I grew up in Gloucestershire in the village of Gotherington, and the local village cidermaker was Tilley's. Later, I met local producer Kevin Minchew, who introduced me to perry.

Do you have a memory of a particularly good cider or perry?
The best I've ever tasted was a Green Huffcap Perry made by Jean Nowell of Lyne Down Cider, back in the late 1990s. She remains the best cider and perry maker I've ever come across.

Do you have a favourite apple or pear variety and why?
I love the Frederick cider apple, a Monmouthshire variety. It's incredibly sharp, good for blending. I have too many favourite pear varieties to mention.

If you could drink cider in any time or place, where would it be?
In the cellar at Broome Farm, Ross-on-Wye.

How do you account for the recent surge of interest in cider and cidermaking?
Two reasons. There are a lot of people doing a lot of cider festivals, which is giving good publicity. Also, people are really interested in having something local and natural.

Do you have any advice for the novice cidermaker?
Keep everything clean and airtight, and only use ripe fruit.

Can you tell us about your best and/or worst moment as a cidermaker?
The best was winning any of the three of my Welsh titles, or CAMRA Gold for Perry in 2006. I'm lucky enough never to have had a worst moment.

What's your most precious bit of cider-related gear?
Probably my old twin-screw wooden press from the late nineteenth century.

What can we do to ensure that orchards are still flourishing in 50 years' time?
Increase the demand for craft cider and perry.

Any suggestions for ways of sorting out the duty problem?
Slash the duty on champagne cider and perry. Impose minimum pricing to stop the supermarkets selling at low prices. Introduce a sliding scale of duty, with none to pay up until 7000 litres.

Tasting Notes

Cider in The North

These days the frontiers of Ciderland stretch as far north as Scotland...

Wherever you can grow apples – or buy them, for that matter – you can make cider. We've found people making cider in Cheshire, Yorkshire and even (perish the thought) north of the border in Scotland. Cider apples may be hard to come by, but there's no problem getting hold of old whisky barrels in those parts.

So if you're reading this in a flat in Newcastle and thinking that life really isn't fair for a would-be cidermaker in a northern city, this is for you...

Brother Rainer the cidermaking monk at Ampleforth Abbey. Who said drinking cider is habit forming?

Cheshire Cider

It's always good to hear about a small-scale cider operation beating the local breweries in competitions, and in 2009 Cheshire Cider saw off the beer makers to win Best Beverage at the Fine Foods NW Awards, with judges refering to a 'nice freshly elegant flavour'.

The cider is pretty straightforward. Dessert and culinary apples from the orchards of Eddisbury fruit farm are washed and crushed, and the juice fermented.

"Our cider," they warn, "Is served flat, and may be cloudy." Sounds pretty good to us.

21st Century Cider Monks

Henry VIII must be rolling in his grave. Not only are there Catholic monasteries thriving on English soil, but at least two of them are known for their quality of their cider

Just outside Gloucester, Prinknash (pronounced 'Prinish') Abbey has an ancient history and enviable reputation for its cider and perry, but unfortunately all their production is currently for Brothers only (no, not those Brothers).

And far to the north-east, at Ampleforth Abbey, Brother Rainer has made the news in recent years both for the quality of the cider he makes from fruit grown in the abbey's orchard – and this is in Yorkshire, don't forget – and for teaming up with Julian Temperley to produce an Ampleforth Cider Brandy. The first batch was ready in 2006, but remained secret until 2008, when journalists had a field day with puns about 'spirits'.

It's likely that monks were experimenting with distillation before the Dissolution of the Monasteries – probably at Glastonbury, using cider as a base. Almost five hundred years later, a monastery is selling cider brandy. They're tenacious people, monks.

The present orchard contains 2000 trees and more than 40 varieties of apples, including Ribston Pippin, the oldest variety grown at Ampleforth and originating from a tree grown locally at Ribston Hall in the 17th century – this was the apple that made Gaymer's cider such a success in Victoria's reign. You can buy cider and cider brandy from the monastery shop.

From plot to (pint) pot. It's amazing what you can get from an allotment (see next page).

Cider With Thistles

The odds on Peter Stuart ever becoming a cidermaker were not high. Living in East Lothian the chances of him even drinking a glass of farmhouse cider were slim, but shortly before getting married Peter went to help a friend with lambing and in the process met a cidermaker, who offered him a barrel of Somerset cider for the wedding party.

The cider was evidently a success, because two years later, in 2008, Peter was making his own, having spent time learning the craft in Herefordshire. Looking for fruit, he pitched up at Belhaven Fruit Farm and there enjoyed a fortuitous encounter with farmer Ian Rennie. He knew a good idea when he heard one, and the pair launched Thistly Cross Cider, using as much Scottish fruit as they could get and supplementing it with apples from other sources. Local strawberries find their way into Thistly Cross Red, and the company also makes an unusual cider with ginger. Look out for these treats in the Edinburgh area…

Peter Stuart raises a glass of Thistly Cross from East Lothian.

MY CIDER STORY

MIKE HOUGHTON FROM CHESTER ON THE SUCCESS OF ALLOTMENT CIDER

I suppose it all started when I got an allotment in September 2006. Half the allotments on the site were abandoned and it was very overgrown. Not being able to grow anything on my allotment that first year I turned to food for free in the shape of blackberries and rose hips on the abandoned plots. I discovered a couple of apple trees and thought – "I'll make some cider!" I bought *Real Cider Making on a Small Scale* by Michael J. Pooley and John Lomax and set about it.

A mate of mine (we play in the local Samba Band) brought round a couple of old demijohns and a Boots wine making fruit press. I tipped out the couple of buckets of apples I'd got from the allotment and began picking out the bruised ones and wondering should I core them before slicing them and putting them into the food processor... We got a couple of demijohns of juice that we sealed with air locks and waited for the bubbles to appear. Sure enough it fermented and by Christmas I had my first taste of Allotment Cider and was hooked.

Over the summer of 2007 I built a cider press, proudly carving an apple in the top. We use a Clarke 4-ton bottle jack to power it. In October I went to the 'Apple Day' at Erdigg (a local National Trust property) where I got the allotment apples identified (Charles Ross, James Greave and Golden Delicious) but more importantly saw a demonstration by Ralph's Cider & Perry of Presteigne. It was a revelation.

The equipment

Cider making that year was on the allotment which meant no electricity. I'd bought a Vigo 'Pulpmaster' (bucket with an electric drill powered chopper) which was useless with a battery-powered drill. I resorted to using a petrol engine strimmer lowered into a waste bin full of apples which not only pulped the apples but also spread apple pulp generously over the allotment. The cider press though worked well (a joint split under pressure but a few extra coach bolts sorted it). I'd collected

The Allotment Cider team built their own press to make use of a surfeit of apples.

a pile of 18.5-litre empty water containers from a contact at the local council offices which worked well with an air lock in the top. Over the year I'd collected lots of empty beer bottles which were washed and de-labeled and spent hours bottling the cider that Christmas.

In 2008 a friend from the allotment built a scratter from an old lawnmower engine which he attached to a wooden roller studded with screws built into a feed hopper. That October I got a lot of apples (unknown varieties) from a friend of a friend and we produced something like eight water containers of apple juice. The hardest part this year was the bottling – it's a fiddly messy job, makes a complete mess of the kitchen and most of my friends are doing something else that day. As a consequence some of the containers didn't get bottled and slowly turned to cider vinegar over the summer. Still a few herbs from the allotment, a bit more bottling and labelling and I had lots of herb vinegar to give as Christmas presents.

By 2009 I felt I was really getting the hang of it. My best discovery was the Vigo 5 litre Bag in a Box which made bottling redundant. I didn't have the huge glut of apples like the previous year so I don't think this year's cider is going to last.

The process

Apples are collected from wherever I can. Allotment apple trees (with permission), friends' donations or road and path-side apple trees. I really need to find somebody with an old orchard in their back garden who would be willing for me to collect all their windfalls. I never wash the apples and include some which are up to half brown. The odd twig and worm go in and as it says on the labels – organic but not necessarily vegetarian. I was bought two cider apple trees for my 60th birthday in 2009, a Kingston Black and a Black Dabinett so look forward to using these in a few years time.

The scratter works well. The metal shaft on wood bearing got too hot the first year and had to be modified with a metal plate. A lid and feed tube were added to reduce 'splashback'. This year I intend to spruce it up with a coat of paint and line the hopper to stop the apple pulp sticking. We hang the scratter over a plastic dustbin to collect the pulp and have to give it a vigorous shake every now and then to clear the pulp. The pull cord starter on the engine is broken so we're reluctant to stop it once we've got it going.

The press is the enjoyable bit. If I was starting again I'd design the joints differently and the 'retaining wall' round the collection tray needs to be deeper (we have to stop pressing to allow the juice to clear). The first time I used some lace curtain fabric to wrap the 'cheeses' but this tore under pressure. I've now got some hessian sacking which works fine – wash it first or else the cider will taste of sack and it does fray at the edges which adds to the rustic look.

The water containers are great fermenting vessels – light to store, not too heavy when filled and reuseable. I had to reduce and drill large corks (bought from www.the-art-of-brewing.co.uk) to fit. I start the fermentation process in my cider shed on the allotment and bring them home when it starts to get too frosty. I syphon the cider off before Christmas being careful not to suck up too much of the sediment at the bottom.

The Bag in a Box system works really well for storage. You can get the tap out when the bag is empty so they should be reuseable. The cardboard boxes are a bit flimsy and I have ended up making a couple of boxes out of plywood which look better. I notice Vigo do a 15 litre Manucube which I might try this year.

The cider

I never add anything to the apple juice. The press and scratter get hosed down at the end of cider making and the water containers, bottles and other bits get a good wash in warm water and washing up liquid followed by a rinse before I use them. I like the idea of it being 'chemical-free' as I sometimes get an allergic reaction to the sulphites in manufactures' beers and ciders. The final product is flat, dry and about 7 or 8% alcohol by volume. When drunk at Christmas it tastes fresh and appley and develops a true cider flavour over the summer. I've never been able to keep it for longer (I do give a lot away). The fermentation process is stopped by the time I bottle or bag the cider but I have tried adding half a teaspoon of sugar to some. This has led to a couple of bottles bursting and one of my bags blowing up like a balloon – fortunately not bursting, imagine the mess that would make. Perhaps I should put the word out for friends to collect empty champagne bottles.

The future

I need to find a reliable source of free windfalls, Now I've got a trailer collecting them isn't a problem. I am getting in touch with the local Transition Group and other allotmenteers to ask for contributions.

I have tried fermenting pear juice (we have a pear tree right outside our front gate) but without success so far. I have read that pears do not have the same wild yeasts on them as apples. There is loads of information now on the internet, sometimes conflicting.

I have also tried freeze-distilling cider but have been disappointed with the results so far…And who knows, perhaps I'll even register with Customs and Excise and start selling some – one day.

Cider in London

If you like craft cider and you live in London, you're going to need our survival guide...

What should you do if you love cider and live in London?

a *Move to Bristol, sharpish*
b *Make your own*
c *Read our Survival Guide...*

Considering that Bristol is only two hours' drive away it seems amazing that London has so little to offer the cider drinker. Try making a resolution to drink only cider for an evening and, unless you choose your pub very wisely, you're unlikely to enjoy it much.

The dearth of decent cider put into context some of the more outrageously ignorant things written by national journalists during the cider tax revolt of March/April 2010. Wine writer Malcolm Gluck looked a bit foolish when he took the government's side in the fiasco, dismissing all British cider as factory-made rubbish and claiming that you can only find real artisan cider in Normandy and Brittany.

Perhaps Malcolm hadn't been west of Oxford in a while. Certainly, anyone exposed only to London cider could be left a poor opinion of the industry. There are two reasons for this. First, most pubs are either part of a chain or tied to a brewery, so they can't just get in a cider to try if they fancy it. Second, the people trying to sell cider and perry in London find it's too expensive to buy from smaller producers. If there's a wholesaler in the capital with a stock of fine West Country fare, they're keeping quiet about it.

Barry Topp presses through straw at New Forest Cider. They like that sort of thing in London.

But it isn't all bad news! Alongside one or two long-standing bastions of cider excellence, an increasing number of pubs now have beer festivals with a cider on the side, or even cider festivals, and if you know where to look you can find good cider any day of the week. You could almost imagine you're in Bristol.

Barry Topp: Ciderland's London Ambassador

Long before the clink of ice cubes attracted Londoners' attention to cider (It's Irish, you know, like Guinness), Barry Topp was Ciderland's Man in the Capital. He started selling his New Forest Cider from a thatched trailer in Borough Market in October 1998, when the Two Fat Ladies were on hand to open a one-off sixty-stall revival of the moribund market, and when the renaissance became permanent he stayed. In those days the thatched trailer spent the summer months travelling from steam rally to agricultural show, and in the winter it would appear in that Dickensian region beside London Bridge, wreathed in steam from the mulled cider warming Barry's clientele. But the 2003 licensing act, with its insistence on premises being fixed and permanent,

Barry Topp's New Forest Cider stall has been a fixture at Borough Market since 1998.

put an end to the trailer's rovings, and the Hampshire cidermaker got himself a stall – a 'cage' to use the correct term. Another move came just in time to avoid losing his pitch to a new railway development, and now he's sitting pretty, right in the middle of a flourishing market.

It's worth visiting even on the days when New Forest Cider isn't on sale, but better, obviously, when it is. The stall is licensed for On and Off Sales, so you can have a drink there and then to wash down your ostrich burger or chorizo roll, or order a bag-in-a-box and pick it up later. Or both. As well as draught cider from the New Forest – which is made the West Country way, with vintage fruit – and, if you're lucky, Barry's Normandy-style keeved cider, you'll find bottle-fermented Burrow Hill (Stoke Red or Kingston Black) and other high-end bottled ciders.

Alternatively you could visit New Forest Cider, staying the night if you felt like it at the B&B run by Barry's wife. Not far from Ringwood, this is the far eastern outpost of Ciderland proper. Cross the forest and you eventually reach Selborne, where Mr (Angus) Whitehead makes his popular ciders using the Eastern Counties approach of blending eaters and cookers with the odd cider apple thrown in.

As befits a market trader, Barry is a man of independent opinions, and he's fairly forthright about the NACM and what he perceives as its less-than-helpful attitude to craft cider makers. But we're not getting involved in politics here. We're talking London cider. So what are the options?

The Harp on Chandos Street has a great selection for the thirsty cider drinker.

The Harp Tavern

This pub, on Chandos Street about two minutes from Charing Cross, looks, as its name suggests, like a good Irish hole in the wall, and the interior seems to bear this out. Even at 5pm on an indifferent Wednesday the narrow bar is packed with gents of all ages and in varying stages of inebriation. This gem of a pub sells more real ales than you could throw a stick at, including some beauties from Harveys of Lewes, and better still, behind the bar in fridges are chilled flagons of real farmhouse cider and perry, imported all the way from Somerset and Herefordshire.

So there you are. Cider heaven, almost in the shadow of Nelson's Column. The only problem being that the place gets busier than the CoriTap on student night, but if you like a crowd you won't mind that…

Chimes

Philip Marron's Pimlico restaurant is an unusual sort of place, the only London eatery that advertises itself as a cider specialist (for now, at any rate). Producers at the cider-as-wine end of the spectrum like to talk about cider and perry as accompaniments to food, yet it's rare to see restaurants actively trying to coax diners away from wine. Chimes has been doing this for a quarter of a century, and in the process Phil has learnt a fair amount about life at the sharp end of the cider business.

When he set the place up in the early 1980s food was going global, in terms both of production and dining. In a move that anticipated today's local and organic movement, Phil decided to specialise in traditional English food, with cider as an obvious corollary. At the time cider was enjoying a boom in the capital, so it made good business sense too, and over the decades that followed Chimes developed an international reputation as London's only restaurant-ciderhouse. These days you'll find an interesting mix of tourists from North America and Europe, along with a long-serving cadre of regulars enjoying their Old Rosie or Merrydown.

The selection is, by Phil's own admission, fairly conservative, partly because his regulars know what they like but mostly because the logistics of getting cider from smaller producers to London for a decent price (and with a long enough shelf-life) are offputting, to put it mildly. He does get a delivery from Biddendens every couple of weeks, though, and is always on the look-out for new possibilities.

Food-wise, where else could you enjoy a starter of Whitby Pudding followed by Fidget Pie for a main course? Visit www.chimes-of-pimlico.co.uk to find out more.

Since the 1980s Chimes has been serving high quality English food, along with cider and perry.

Other pubs for cider drinkers

Barry and Phil both reckon that a gentle tsunami of half-decent cider is slowly washing over the capital, with Aspall, Westons and the odd surprise guest now available in a number of London boozers.
Check out the Listings for details, but you could make a start at:

The Southampton Arms (NW5)
The Green Man (Fitzrovia, W1)
The Bree Louise (Euston, NW1)
The Cider Tap (Euston, NW1)
The Pembury Tavern (Hackney, E8)
The Harp Tavern (WC2)

How To Make Cider

The best cider you'll ever taste is the one you make yourself. Go on, have a go...

Making cider is easy. Get a quantity of apples (preferably cider apples), crush them into a pulp, press the juice from the pulp, put the juice into a fermentation bucket, attach an airlock, wait until the juice has fermented then drink it. Making cider really is as simple as that. As long as you keep everything spotlessly clean and airtight you will end up with a very pleasant drink.

Making very good cider is slightly more complicated, and making fantastic cider takes years of experience. Making cider is an entirely natural process, which combines the wild yeast on the skin of the apples with the sugars inside the fruit to create a fermentation resulting in the production of alcohol. What is described below is a 100 per cent natural fermentation, here's how you do it.

A groundsheet or tarp is very useful for apple collecting.

1 **First pick your apples.** If you live in a cider apple area such as Somerset, Devon, Herefordshire or parts of Wales you should be able to source cider apples either for free or for a nominal amount. The price of apples varies every year, but in 2009 the going rate in Somerset was about £30 a ton if you picked your own and up to £100 a ton if the apples are supplied. A quarter of a ton of apples will make approximately 40 gallons of juice.

If you don't have a ready supply of cider apples, use ordinary apples. Use a blend of desserts, cookers and crab apples and keep a detailed note of the blend.

2 **Be prepared.** Wash all equipment thoroughly, sterilise buckets and presses and wash down after sterilising so that none of the sterilising fluid is left. Wash the apples and cut out any rotten bits.

3 **Crush the fruit.** Before you can press the juice from the apples you need to reduce them to a pulp. This can be done in a variety of ways from pounding them with a home-made device, to using a hand-operated fruit mill (scratter) or an electric mill (see equipment).

4 **Pressing time.** Transfer the pulp into a fruit press. Most small scale producers use a 'basket' press. These come in various sizes of up to about 60 litres capacity. The pulp is placed in a muslin bag inside the press and as the press is screwed down, the juice gushes out through the slats in the basket.

5 **Fermentation.** Transfer the juice into a fermentation bucket or demijohn, which has been thoroughly cleaned and washed out with sterilising powder. Fill the vessel as close to the top as possible. If you don't have quite enough juice to fill it, you can add some boiled but cooled water although this will reduce the alcohol content and will change the flavour. Place an airlock in the lid of the vessel and store. The warmer the place you store the bucket, the quicker the fermentation. A slow fermentation is general regarded as producing a superior end product, so don't worry too much if you need to store the buckets in an unheated garage or outhouse although if it is really cold, especially at the start, the fermentation can stick. Take a hydrometer reading. A typical blend of sweet, bittersweet and sharp cider apples should have a reading of between 1050 and 1055 which will result in a drink of between 6% and 7% alcohol by volume if the cider is allowed to ferment completely until the hydrometer reading is 1000.

6 **How long?** Assuming that you make your juice at the beginning of November, the cider should have fermented by mid January. Allow about 8 weeks for the fermentation. To check when fermentation is complete,

Picking up apples by hand is time-consuming, but it gives you a chance to chuck out the bad ones

The Totterdown Press team after a hard day's harvesting.

take a hydrometer reading of the pressed juice. Take further readings as fermentation progresses. When the hydrometer reads 1000 all the sugar has been converted to alcohol.

7 **Racking.** This is the process of siphoning the cider from the fermentation bucket into another vessel to leave behind the sediment or lees. The racking should take place when the fermentation is complete – when the flow of bubbles through the air lock has almost stopped or when the hydrometer reading is 1000. Some craft cider makers rack slightly earlier, but many leave the cider 'on the lees' for a few days after fermentation to allow a small amount of autolysis of the yeast. Carefully siphon the juice from the fermentation bucket into another clean bucket taking care not to disturb the lees at the bottom of the bucket. Siphon the cider though a funnel with gauze. Take great care not to introduce air into the cider. Direct the funnel onto the side of the receiving bucket in order to gently fill it. Do not squirt the cider into the bucket or create a frothy 'head'. Fill the new bucket to the brim and add an air lock (where practically possible you should brim fill to reduce head space).

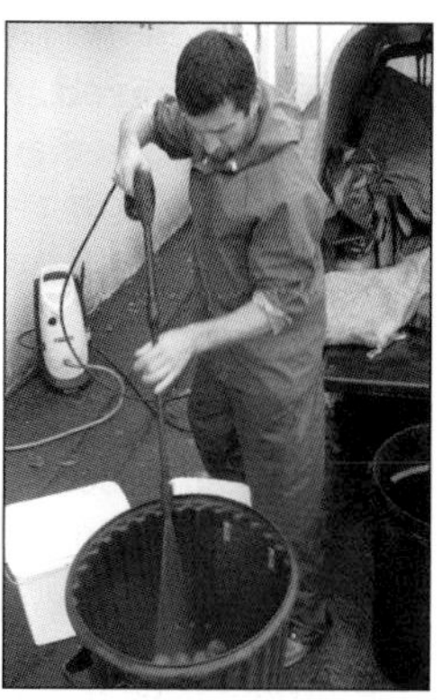

If you want to make great cider, keep everything squeaky clean.

8 **Secondary fermentation.** Assuming that fermentation is complete by mid January, you should now leave the cider until the air temperature rises. Early in March, as the temperature warms, the cider should undergo secondary malolactic fermentation. During this process the malic acid is converted into lactic acid and carbon dioxide. The result is a smoother drink. If you have sulphited the cider it is unlikely the malolactic fermentation will take place, though malolactic bacteria cultures can be added to promote the secondary fermentation.

9 **Bottles or barrels?** Depending how much cider you have made you may want to bottle it or transfer it into a barrel or demijohn. Bottling can be a laborious process. The most practical storage method for many small producers is to carefully siphon the finished cider into a five-gallon plastic barrel and to fit a CO2 cap. You can bottle small quantities of the cider from the barrel and give the barrel a squirt of CO2 to keep everything airtight.

10 **How long will it last?** Home made cider is best drunk within a year, but it will last longer if you keep the container airtight. Many producers add sulphite or camden tablets to prevent the cider going off.

Pressing apples is hard work, and you can expect to be covered head to foot in apple juice by the end of the day...

IS IT REALLY THAT EASY?

The short answer is yes. Making cider really is as easy as described above. However, there are several factors you should consider to refine the basic method into a production schedule that fits the amount of time and money you have available.

Time

Traditional cider-making is a time-consuming process. Allow at least a day to pick a quarter of a ton of apples and transport them to wherever you are going to store them. Some makers think it is best to store the apples for a couple of weeks before pressing to allow the sugars, acids and tannin to develop. However, many others feel that storing the apples can cause problems and that the best

Pressing apples through straw is incredibly hard work, but you end up with a delicious cider, slightly softened by the straw. Photo by Bill Bradshaw (www.billbradshaw.co.uk)

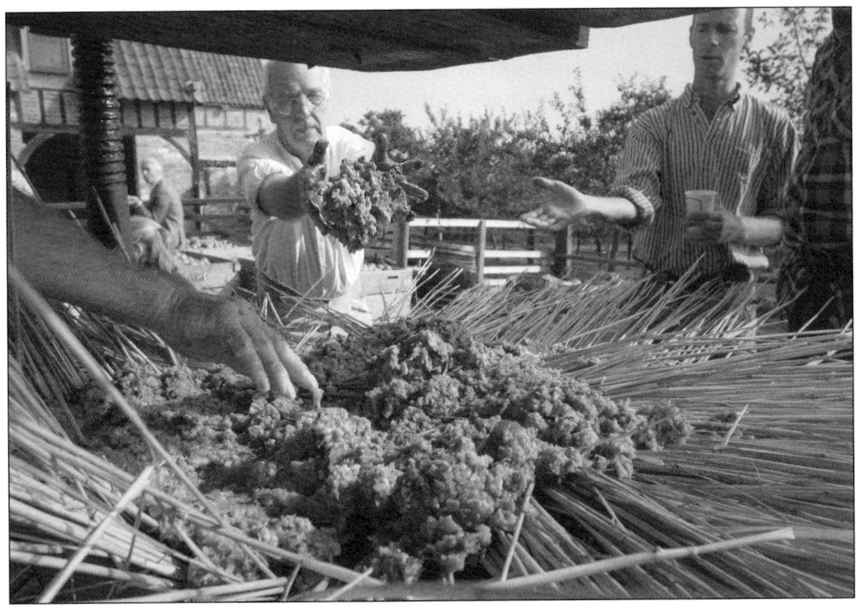

cider comes from apples picked and pressed as soon as they are ripe.

Scratting and pressing is also a time-consuming process. If you are using a basket press, allow at least a day and more likely a weekend to press quarter of a ton of apples and get all the juice into fermentation buckets. If you do take more than a day, everything will have to be thoroughly cleaned before the second day's pressing.

One of the unlikely time-consuming aspects of the pressing process is getting rid of the cake of dried apple (the pomace) that is left at the bottom of the press once all the juice has been extracted. It needs to be disposed of quickly because it smells and attracts fruit flies. It's easy enough to say, 'put it on rose beds' or 'feed it to pigs' but how many of us have a ready supply of hungry porkers? The easiest way to get rid of the pomace is to take it to the local tip as green waste. But you'll have to factor this into your pressing routine and allow enough time to get to the tip before it closes. Last year at the Totterdown Press in Bristol, the cidermakers offered the pomace on Freecycle. A local farmer picked it up within hours.

It's a time-consuming business, maturing your cider. But not that arduous.

Adding yeast

Whether or not to add yeast to the pressed juice is one of the most frequently asked questions by novice cider makers. The answer is emphatically that you don't need to add yeast. Wild yeast occurs naturally on the skin of the apple. However, many cider makers prefer to leave nothing to chance and therefore add their own yeast (available from home brew shops). If you add yeast, you must first get rid of the wild yeast. To do this sulphite the apple juice following the maker's instructions and add a cider yeast.

Adding sulphites

If you add sulphite to the juice you will kill off any impurities. Although some cider makers regard adding sulphites as a corruption of the natural process, it is understandable that they don't want risk the cider going rotten. Adding sulphite is advocated by those who view it as an insurance policy to prevent various faults from developing due to unwanted microbial activity, or to ensure that a specific cultivated yeast takes over from any wild yeasts. Cider barrels were traditionally sterilised by burning sulphur candles inside them. This left a residue of sulphite inside the cask. Nowadays the use of controlled amounts of sulphite can be done much more accurately than the haphazard use of sulphur candles. The other time that sulphites are commonly added is at the end of the process. If you are producing on a small scale there is really no need to add sulphite to the finished cider, but if you are producing thousands of litres, it's an understandable precaution. Total permitted is 200ppm.

Henry Weston got started with this great old press, but these days you don't have to do your own pressing.

TO PRESS OR NOT TO PRESS

Buying a fruit mill and press is likely to cost upwards of £500. Of course, they should last for years and produce thousands of gallons of cider, but there are alternatives…

1. **Use a commercial press.** Neil Worley is an expert cidermaker who lives near Shepton Mallet in Somerset and who won the gold medal at the Royal Bath and West Show in only his second year of production. He started making cider in 2006 and has never pressed an apple. Neil wanted to make cider in fairly large quantities (thousands of litres) so the outlay in time and money for a large press and scratter would have been considerable. Instead, Neil carefully selects his apples from local orchards having identified the specific varieties, pays the farmer to deliver to a local cidermaker, pays for the apples to be pressed and for the juice to be transported back to him. It's an unusual way of working, but it leaves Neil free to spend more time refining his cider-making skills rather than gathering and pressing apples.
2. **Rent a scratter and press.** Several companies rent equipment. Expect to pay up to £50 for a weekend depending on the time of year.
3. **Share a scratter and press.** Traditionally cider making was a community event with people working together to turn the apple harvest into cider. Given that

How many apples?

Cider apples are small and hard so it takes a surprising number to create a gallon of cider. A good rule of thumb is that 20lb of apples makes about a gallon. There are about 5 cider apples to the lb, so approximately 100 apples makes a gallon, so you will need about 500 apples to create enough juice to fill a 5-gallon fermentation bucket.

craft cider making is low-tech and labour intensive, the old way is most certainly the best. Make an event of the pressing, gather a group of friends and neighbours, eat, drink and press. Have fun!

Milling fruit at Severn Cider. A strenuous job but with one or two perks...

ADVANCED TECHNIQUES

Once you've made your first batch of cider and realised just how good it tastes, you'll probably want to experiment and refine your techniques.

Blending

Although some single apple varieties make a great cider it is generally accepted that blending a variety of different apples produces a superior drink. You can blend at various stages of the process.

1. Mix the apples when you press.
2. Blend the juice after pressing when it goes into the fermentation bucket.
3. Blend the finished cider.

Some producers blend cider which hasn't had a secondary fermentation with cider that has. You can also blend a small amount of acetic cider into a large volume of fresh stuff.

Keep detailed notes of the blend so you can reproduce and refine it every year. If you are producing large quantities of cider, it is worth keeping a sample in a demijohn so you can taste it as the fermentation progresses without disturbing the main batch. However, one of the peculiar things about cidermaking on a small scale is that juice produced on the same day from the same apple varieties and placed in fermentation buckets standing next to one another can ferment at a different rate and produce a markedly different cider, so there's no guarantee that a sample demi-john will taste exactly like the main batch, it's more an indicator.

Cold Racking

If you leave the cider to its own devices, all the sugar will turn to alcohol resulting in a very dry drink. If you prefer a sweeter cider you can stop the fermentation while some of the natural sugars remain in the drink. Use a hydrometer to measure the amount of sugar in the cider and taste the juice to gauge the desired level of sweetness. If using a hydrometer reading, the specific gravity for a medium sweet cider is about 1012 and for a sweet cider it's about 1018-1020. Place the cider in as cold a place as possible and rack into new vessels. Do this several times. The result is that you will gradually leave the yeast in the lees at the bottom of the fermentation vessel with each successive racking but the sugar will remain in the cider. Top up the cider with water to replace the juice that you leave at the bottom of the fermentation vessel with each racking. The resulting drink will be low in alcohol and it won't keep as well.

Cold Racking is a time-consuming process and there's always a danger that the fermentation will continue despite your best efforts. This is bad news if you have transferred the cider into bottles because they could explode. If you want a sweet cider the alternative method is to add saccharine (which won't restart the fermentation process) or you can add lemonade or a sugar solution to create the desired level of sweetness. If adding sugar or lemonade only add it to a batch of cider that is going to be drunk immediately.

The Fruit Shark ready for action. Many small producers find the Shark is perfect for all their scratting requirements.

Keeving

This is quite a complicated process but the results can be stunning. If successful the keeving process will result in a brilliantly clear, sparkling drink low in tannin. One of the key factors in keeving is to produce a juice that is high in sugar content so it is advisable to add dessert apples to the blend. For best results keeving should be done in cold weather when fermentation is slow (see The Joys and Perils of Sweet Cider).

Using a Hydrometer

A hydrometer measures the specific gravity (SG) of a liquid by measuring the amount of sugar. As the sugar is turned to alcohol, the hydrometer reading drops, so by making a note of the first reading of the freshly pressed juice (the original gravity or OG) you can estimate the strength of your cider when fermentation is complete, all the sugar has turned to alcohol and the hydrometer reading is 1000.

Original Gravity	Alcohol by Volume
1035	**3.7%**
1040	**4.3%**
1045	**5.2%**
1050	**6.1%**
1055	**7.0%**
1060	**7.8%**
1065	**8.5%**
1070	**9.3%**

Tom Bull of Severn Cider testing his pick-up to see just how many apples it will take.

GOING COMMERCIAL

Anyone can make cider, but who goes on to achieve long-term success, either in commercial terms or as an artisan prize winner? Do you have to live in a particular place, or come from a particular background?

Well who's out there right now? Andrew Quinlan of The Orchard Pig used to be in the Marines. Rose Grant is a retired electrical engineer. Ivor Dunkerton directed a TV drama back in the day. John Harris of Janet's Jungle Juice was a photographer. Tom Bull of Severn Cider works in a neighbouring quarry when he's not making cider. Dave Kaspar of Days Cottage was a teacher in a previous life. Keith Orchard worked in the furniture trade. Tom Oliver still has an alternative career in the music biz. Neil Worley works in magazine production and marketing. Alex Hill has the best of both worlds, supplying Ciderland with mills and presses through Vigo, and also making bottle-fermented cider on a small scale.

Everyone you ask seems to have a different story, a different way they fell into cidermaking. It was always that way though, wasn't it? Farmers planted apple trees in their pasture so they had the cider to fall back on when the bottom fell out of agriculture – as it has done so often in this country. When cider or perry enjoyed a boom, everyone downed tools and manned the presses. When the rest of the world went back to their imported wine, it was back to the fields. This didn't just apply to farmers, but to Somerset clergymen and doctors, cottagers and craftsmen from the Forest of Dean… you name it.

All of the people listed above have one thing in common. To varying degrees, and in very different ways, they are successful cidermakers. So what's the secret?

Perhaps the first thing to consider is what you're aiming to achieve. For example, James Marsden of Greggs Pit makes award-winning cider and perry but chooses to keeps his production small scale – check the website for the exact numbers. You might say that his winning ways and small scale of operation go hand in hand. Then you have Andrew Quinlan of The Orchard Pig, who set out on a clearly defined mission to produce cider on a much larger scale, to standards and using methods that suit him. There are excellent producers whose cider never leaves the village, and others who supply festivals and events around the country. So you need to ask yourself what it is you want to achieve, then go for it. These tips may help.

KNOW WHAT YOU'RE ABOUT

You'll notice that successful producers tend to have a particular focus or area or expertise. Frank Naish enjoys the respect of the cider world and his approach is fairly straightforward:

1. Press apples.
2. Transfer juice to barrel.
3. Leave in barrel until ready to drink.
4. Drink.

He's been doing this since before most of us were born and he's good at it.

But then there are makers who prefer to emulate the producers of Normandy and keeve every drop of juice they can, and others who have made the champagne method their own. If there's a method that suits you, then why not stick with it?

Inside the Burrow Hill still house where Julian Temperley makes his cider brandy.

MAKE A CONSISTENT CIDER OR PERRY

Each vat of fresh apple juice is a new world, full of competing organisms and with a unique chemical composition. It doesn't matter whether the container holds a gallon or 1000 gallons, each batch of juice has the

Equipment

If you intend to make more than about 20 gallons of cider it is worth investing in a fruit press and fruit mill (scratter). There are many presses and scratters on the market from companies such as Vigo (see Listings) and as a general rule of thumb buy the biggest press and scratter you can afford. A fairly recent arrival on the scratting scene is the electric mill the Czech-made Fruit Shark. It's a simple piece of kit, but a real workhorse and excellent value for money.

Here's what you need to get started if you are making more than 10 gallons. If you are just making a few demi-johns you can use kitchen equipment such as a mincer or food processor to juice the apples.

- One scratter
- One fruit press
- Ten five-litre fermentation buckets (enough to hold 25 gallons of cider and then rack into clean buckets(10x5 litres = 50 litres or a little over 10 gallons)
- A means of washing apples.
- A funnel
- A siphon
- Airlocks for fermentation buckets
- Sterilising powder
- Demi-johns, bottles or barrels in which to store the finished cider

potential to become a unique cider with its own flavour, body and strength. In some ways this is A Good Thing – you might end up with a prize-winner – but it goes against the whole idea of brand identity. We're used to a food or drink with a particular label having particular characteristics. A million cans of Coke all taste the same, and even drinkers of farmhouse cider demand consistency these days.

A consistent supply of fruit from the same orchards is helpful if you want to make consistent cider.

So how do you create a consistent cider?

1. Know and control your fruit supply. If you use fruit from the same trees every year you have a much greater chance of creating a similar cider. Each year's harvest is different, with attributes like sugar content influenced by summer weather and other factors, but you'll notice that successful cidermakers often have either their own orchards or ingrained, long-term relationships with local orchard owners.
2. Use a blend of vintage varieties. The wider the range of varieties, the more opportunity you have to blend different batches after fermentation and so create a cider that is recognisably yours.
3. Know your yeast. Some producers insist that you can only make a consistent cider by killing off wild yeasts with sulphite and introducing cultivated yeast. Others do fine with wild yeast, but this is a tricky area. If you press fruit from the same orchards, using the same equipment, in the same place, year after year, you will have a reliable wild yeast that will add individual character to your cider. But if you have to source fruit from different orchards each year, or if you move to new equipment or premises, cultivated yeast may be a better bet. Keith Orchard reckons wild yeasts work OK in a small batch of cider (say 50 gallons) but don't do so well in large batches.
4. Stick to scrupulous standards of hygiene. This goes without saying, but let's say it anyway.
5. Reject anything that isn't up to scratch. How stringent is your quality control? Would you sell cider from an iffy batch? Arguments rage about what you should do with acetic cider (to take one example), with some saying you can mix it into fresh cider in low ratios and others saying you should discard it (or turn it into vinegar).

Your answer is part of what defines you as a maker.

6. Use 'industrial' methods. You can create your own brand of cider using all the tools available to the modern producer: filtering, sugar or sweeteners, malic acid, pasteurization, sulphites, carbonation... That's what they do with Coke, and it seems to work OK for them.

Green Valley Cyder is made at the back of the Darts Farm shop near Exeter. Which isn't bad for business.

KNOW YOUR MARKET

Every successful cider producer has a market, whether it's a popular local pub, a caravan park or a national supermarket. The cider has to be tailored to the market, so either you find people who like what you're doing, or you adapt. You may think cider should be bone dry but if you're selling it to holidaymakers the chances are you're going to have to sweeten it.

The absence of a market is the single biggest deterrent to growth. You can win prizes galore, but without customers you're stuffed. So will people buy direct from you? Are there enough pubs in a ten-mile radius that will take your cider? Can you command a high enough price to pay for bottling – or pasteurisation, carbonation, etc? These examples may help:

- Green Valley Cyder has an excellent farm shop right next door – in fact the two businesses grew up side by side.
- Days Cottage cider and perry is sold alongside the producer's apple juice at the Bristol and Stroud farmer's

Making Perry – Top Tips

Perry is made in the same way as cider, by pressing the fruit and fermenting the juice. It is more difficult to make but perhaps not as difficult as some would have you believe. Perry pears can vary hugely in character and quality, from tree to tree and year-to-year, which is why the best producers know their fruit intimately.

1. Use vintage varieties. Most good perry pears have sufficient tannin and depth of flavour to make a great single variety perry. Don't bother trying to make perry out of dessert pears, unless you want a weak, flavourless brew.
2. Gather pears at the right stage of ripeness - not easy, unless you happen to live beside the trees. One or two varieties will keep a while, but most deteriorate extremely rapidly.
3. Know your pears. Perry pears aren't like cider apples. For one thing, they don't float, so if you stick them in a big tub of water they will disappear to the bottom. They may even dissolve. Some varieties need to macerate before pressing. Others don't.
4. Take the utmost care with hygiene, keeping the juice airtight, etc.
5. Be very wary of blending perries. Often they don't mix.
6. Be prepared to fail dismally – or to enjoy a fantastic, perry-soaked summer!

markets, where Dave and Helen have built up a loyal following over the past decade or so by being friendly and helpful, and offering consistent good value.

- New Forest Cider has London sewn up (see Barry Topp's story in the London section of the Areas section).
- Tom Oliver's good reputation, willingness to act as a spokesman for perry and constant travels have won him markets in Europe and the USA.
- Keith Orchard has teamed up with Tom to sell at the Slow Food market in Bristol – a good match for perry awarded a Slow Food Presidio.
- West Croft Farm (Janet's Jungle Juice) and Rich's are within staggering distance of the biggest concentration of caravan pitches in Europe. Their products are tailored to their customers' tastes.
- Like these two, Sheppy's is handy for the motorway. Perry's too picks up a lot of holiday traffic, though they're a little more out of the way – for them, the publicity that comes from winning big prizes is particularly useful.
- Aspall makes the most of its history and connection to the Golden Age of Cyder by selling cider in old-fashioned bottles that look a bit posh.

West Croft Farm is no distance at all from the caravan parks of Burnham and Brean.

Sometimes, unexpected changes can affect your market. The makers around Glastonbury were cut off from their markets when the Beeching axe fell in the 1960s. Previously the railway had provided affordable transport, but now companies had to invest in lorries, pay hauliers, or quit. Clapps of Baltonsborough went into cheese. On the other hand, the rise of the motor car and building of the motorways has created new markets.

Technological advances may be helpful or they may not. Websites and on-line ordering have proven more successful for makers of high-end bottled products than for farmhouse cider; it costs too much to ship a gallon of scrumpy.

Buying on eBay

The popularity of cider making is such that it's difficult to find bargains for scratters and presses on eBay. In fact, eBay can be more expensive than ordering direct from a manufacturer or from your local homebrew shop. However, eBay can be a good source of demi-johns, barrels and other brewing equipment.

Buy trees: If you've got room, why not plant your own cider apple trees? There are several eBay traders offering a wide variety of cider apple trees at reasonable prices.

PUB TROUBLE

Even prize-winning craft cidermakers like Rose Grant can find themselves struggling to persuade local pubs to sell their wares. The main issue seems to be the perennial problem of tied houses, with landlords often unable to sell anything except the factory cider dictated by the brewery (or management further up the pub chain). In one instance Rose convinced a publican to pursue the matter with the brewery, only to be told that the brewery itself was governed by its contract with the main cider supplier. Since this brewery owns 500 pubs, this is obviously not good news for the small producer. The pub's numerous guest beers, incidentally, were all made by companies owned by the uber-brewery.

But it's not all bad news. On another occasion Rose entered into an email discussion with the landlord of a Free House she hoped to supply.

"Initially he took the attitude of, why should he buy my cider when the Stowford Press on his bar came in considerably cheaper. My reply was that success is not just about the perceived profit from one cider versus another, rather it is more to do with the number of customers attracted to the pub. I suggested that if he were to put on a craft cider, 'word would get round' and the level of business would increase. After a few days he decided to buy a box and give it a try. I'm glad to say that my words came true. The pub did really well with its craft cider all through the summer and now regularly has a selection of five or more West Country craft ciders available."

While pubs everywhere are struggling to compete with cheap supermarket booze, some new developments can work to the craft cidermaker's advantage. CAMRA is actively promoting its vision of Real Cider and Perry to pubs across the country, and producers can now insure against punters buying a bad pint by using Bag-in-Box packaging. Most importantly, both landlords and pub-goers love a party – summer cider festivals are good business. Here are a couple of tips:

- Check out your local CAMRA – enter competitions, ask about festivals, get to know the movers and shakers, ask for advice on pricing, etc.
- Find Free Houses in your area. Offer landlords samples

Once upon a time cidermakers could sell their wares easily to local pubs. Nowadays it isn't so easy, but don't despair - it can be done.

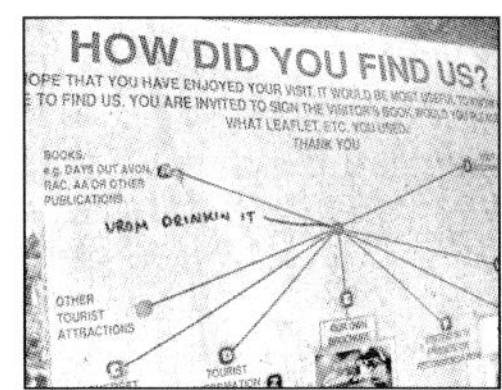

An early example of interactive marketing from Perrys of Dowlish Wake...

of your cider. Ask their opinion. Make friends with them. Suggest a cider festival or themed event and offer to help.

- Look out for pubs in your area that specialise in cider – Bristol has several and others are springing up around the country. Visit. Say hello.

Brands come and go. Some stick around longer than others...

BRANDING FOR BEGINNERS

A good brand is like a pair of boots that fits just right. You hear the name, see the label, taste the cider and everything seems to belong. Many of the best-known cider companies have been around for years, and their names have the ring of success about them. In the old days people mostly named cider after themselves: Mr Bulmer, Mr Weston and Mr Thatcher each left us their legacy. Taunton Cider chose to associate itself with the county town of Somerset, building on the heritage and traditions of the area.

Individual cider brands always had imaginative names, but the companies bore their owner's name like country shops. Today cider brands reflect wider trends. They're designed to get noticed or to appeal to a particular niche market.

The Orchard Pig is a cider success story - good cider and excellent marketing.

The Orchard Pig went from nothing to national in five years, building on the marketing expertise of one partner and orcharding skills of another. The cider is good, but the name and labelling are perfect – pitched at image-conscious drinkers who are into the River Cottage local food scene.

Burrow Hill did a similar thing back in the 1970s, attracting the new festival crowd with arty labels celebrating the lifestyle of posh hippies in the country. The hill itself, with its distinctive single tree, made a brilliant brand image, worked and reworked in diverse ways over the subsequent years. You can go there. Stand on the top. It's all part of the fun.

At a simpler level you've got companies like Wilkins, which rely for brand recognition on a humble sticker plastered onto countless plastic containers. The label is distinctive. It works.

So how do you create a brand? You need:

- An identified market.
- Catchy name based on a place or theme related to cider.

- A distinctive logo: could incorporate a tree, a bend in the river, an old press, even a rodent…
- The right packaging: screw top, crown cap, plastic container – each describes the cider inside.
- Your schtick, or USP: what is it about you and your product that makes you different from the rest? You could be using ancient, forgotten local varieties (Cornish Orchards) or barrels rescued from a shipwreck (Somerset Cider Brandy). Maybe cidermaking has been in your family for generations (Aspall, Sheppy). Perhaps you're using an unusual single variety (Thatcher's Katy) or unusual methods (Brimblecombe's antique press). You could be the only cidermaker in the country (Thistly Cross in Scotland). Maybe your cider is designed to be served over ice…

Coming up with an image and a slogan is a good thing. If it's the right image and slogan.

The next stage is to spread the word about your brand. You'll notice that whenever cider is in the news there's invariably a quote from Julian Temperley, accompanied by

How to get ahead in advertising

Modern creatives must sigh when they look back at the good old days, when you could say what you liked about cider, irrespective of whether it was true or not. A century ago the imagination ruled, and consumers were expected to work out for themselves whether the more outrageous claims were true. This anarchic state of affairs continued post-war, but as advertising standards were gradually imposed the ad executives had to find new ways to capture the attention.

- Whiteway (1917) give a lesson in aspiration-led marketing with the fabulously pretentious 'Whimple Spécialité'. Meanwhile their "Still Cyders: 'Dartmoor' and 'Exe Valley' Brands" are "veritable substitutes for Hocks and other Still Wines."
- Symons cider 1954: "This is Symons cider, Devon cider. When a large number of men tasted it recently against other well-known ciders, 2 out of 3 said at once, 'That's the one for me!'" How's' that for scientific marketing?
- Black is Back – the rebranding of Blackthorn in 2009 didn't go according to plan; in Bristol, billboards were altered to read 'Black is Crap' after regular drinkers found their favourite brew wasn't quite what it used to be.

Top jingle (sung by Adge and the Wurzels):

Coates comes up from Somerset,
Where the cider apples grow,
There's nothing like sweet cider
To make a party go.

Not a bad jingle:

Woodpecker Cider,
Hereford lightning,
Clean and bright.
What a refreshing change!

Not a very good jingle:

Diamond rings and pearls
Might suit other girls,
I think they may be a sham.
Don't we all discover
Stars above may shimmer
But nothing sparkles like a Babycham

at least one reference to Somerset Cider Brandy. It doesn't matter whether the news is good or bad, the important thing is that the name is there in black and white. So what can you do?

- Enter local and national competitions. If you win, make sure the world knows about it.
- Stage an event (Apple Day, Wassail), take some good pictures or invite a photographer friend along, then spread the news.
- Set up a blog or website – it's the first place anyone looks for information these days.
- Use social media – search for 'cider' on Facebook and Twitter and see how people do it. Bristol-based food magazine *Fork* has 2000 followers on Twitter, which means 2000 potential buyers for each issue. A good logo is a must.
- Get involved with a music/arts festival. It worked for Burrow Hill and Brothers Cider at Glastonbury.

Julian Temperley was onto a good thing when he first drove the Somerset Cider Bus to Glastonbury.

THE BORING STUFF

If you're going to sell cider you have to jump through a hoop or two. In some parts of the country you may have to do little more than fill in a form; in others you can expect lengthy inspections by health-ocrats who don't know the first thing about cider and assume that you're out to poison the local populace.

So what are the rules?

Tax And Duty

You can make and sell up to 7000 litres of cider or perry in a 12-month period without paying duty; if you go over that volume you have to pay tax on everything. These rules may change, though, so keep an eye on the cider websites. Also, you're supposed to register with HMRC, even if you're selling much less than 7000l.

According to The Cider and Perry (Exemption from Registration) Order 1976 (SI 1976/1206), all duty-exempt cider makers to apply to HM Revenue and Customs to actively claim exemption from registration. This is usually a formality but it is an offence not to claim exemption. So fill in HMRC Form CP33 and send it off.

If you're selling cider there's also the question of tax,

which is much too complicated for our tiny brains. Have a look at the HMRC website for information.

It's probably wise to keep off the subject of rats when the health inspector comes to visit.

Environmental Health

This is the part that can be tricky, especially if you live in a part of the country where cider hasn't been seen since 1532. Hygiene people don't warm to the sight of apples lying on the ground, nor are they fond of cobwebs, as Roger Wilkins once discovered.

But if you're selling cider you have to register with your local authority's Environmental Health department. This might just mean writing a letter, or it might involve a lengthy inspection of the whole process from harvest to bottling. Inspectors will be looking out for places where insects, rodents or bugs can get in and meddle with the cider. They'll want to see that your operation is clean – sterile where necessary. Actually this is no bad thing, as hygiene and good cider go hand in hand.

The main thing is, don't make jokes about rats adding body to the cider.

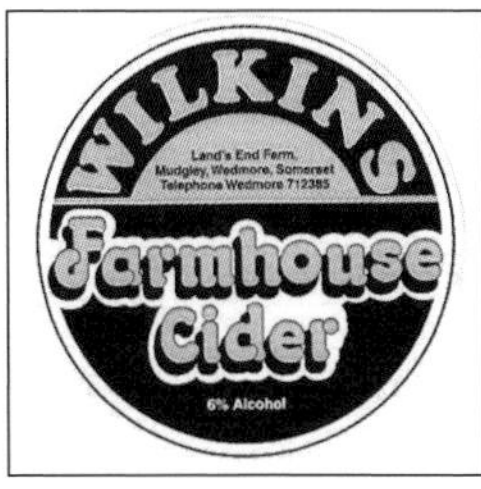

A fine example of a cider label. Simple, distinctive, and it says 'Wilkins'. Thirsty, anyone?

Licensing

Anyone who sells alcohol to the public needs a licence. You don't need one if you're supplying cider for someone else to sell, but you should make sure that they do have a licence.

This is too complicated an area for us to explore in detail, so we recommend looking up the Licensing Act 2003 at the Department for Culture, Media and Sport.

Essentially you need a Premises Licence if you're selling from the farm gate or out of your garage, and this will involve having plans in place for cleaning, hazards, etc. And if you're selling at events you need a Personal Licence. In both cases you'll also need insurance; ask around at cider events or check online groups for information on the best options.

Labelling

By law your label must show the alcohol content of your cider, to the nearest 0.5%, and the volume of cider in the container. Labels don't have to list ingredients – other than sulphites, if used – or give a best before date. Cider and perry in the Three Counties are governed by a PGI, so you can't call your cider Herefordshire Cider unless it has some connection with the county.

Record Keeping

You should keep good records of cidermaking and sales, for tax purposes, quality control and in case of inspection. Have a look at the Gregg's Pit website for a fine example of record keeping in the production of cider and perry.

It's a tough business - Taunton Cider's factory at Norton Fitzwarren is demolished...

Help And Advice

Cider may have a cheery image but it's a tough business. From corporate takeovers in Hereford to the struggle for supremacy in Bristol pubs, this is a business in which companies are constantly rising and falling. There's a legendary story that a certain Somerset cidermaker in the 1960s went round farms where cider production had recently lapsed and broke up the equipment to make sure no other bugger started up. You might be in it for the love of cider, but you'll be competing with people who are in it for the money. So don't expect another cidermaker to reveal their secret blend or give details of their financial dealings.

This being said, cider people do like to talk shop, and you can always ask advice on orcharding, technical problems, useful varieties and so on. In these respects the industry works together, and various bodies and support groups exist to share help and advice.

The National Association of Cider Makers, founded in the 1920s, is the biggest and most important, representing companies like Bulmers and C&C and working closely with the government on health issues, duty, etc. Of more interest to smaller producers are the NACM's affiliated members. Well worth checking these out:

- 3CCPA (Three Counties Cider and Perry Association). Contact: Helen Woodman, Gregg's Pit, Much Marcle, Ledbury, Herefordshire, HR8 2NL. www.thethreecountiesciderandperryassociation.co.uk
- SWECMA (South West of England Cider Makers Association). Contact: Bob Chaplin, Kilver Street, Shepton Mallet, Somerset, BA4 5ND. Tel: 01749 334000 E-mail: bob.chaplin@gaymercider.eu.com
- Welsh Cider Society. Contact: Paul Barrett, 0292 9226680 www.welshcider.co.uk

SWEET CIDER

PROPER DRY FARMHOUSE CIDER IS AN ACQUIRED TASTE AND SOME PEOPLE NEED IT SWEET

Dry cider may win prizes, but many drinkers are looking for something sweeter.

One of the most frequent questions asked of producers at craft cider festivals like The Big Apple is 'Do you have anything sweeter?' At a certain Somerset cider farm, meanwhile, a woman working behind the counter told us that her customers were in no doubt what they liked. "It has to be sweet," she told us. "Give them a taste of dry and they'll think you're trying poison them."

We've noticed the phenomenon elsewhere too, at cider bars and events where even the dry cider seems sweeter than it ought to. Nick Poole, pioneer of the Powerstock Festival, agrees that dry cider is a hard sell these days. He reckons people used to put up with the harsher flavour of old-fashioned farmhouse cider because it was either all there was or was much cheaper than other drinks. Nowadays people are paying as much for a pint of cider as they are for a pint of beer – more in the case of some bottled ciders – and they want the flavour they like. Sweet, appley, gentle on the throat…

So what do you do? Rod Marsh of the National Collection of Cider and Perry believes that drinkers who start out on Magners or somesuch can develop a palate. They might venture into more interesting ciders with a medium-sweet crowd pleaser, then gradually work towards the authentic dry Somerset cider – he's a Naish fan. He's seen this happen and reckons that you have to keep challenging people and encouraging them to move away from sweetness.

But other experts see sweetness as a good quality and point to the widely popular and often delicious ciders of Brittany and Normandy. Nick Poole, who has beaten the French at their own game, reckons that sweeter ciders have more flavour, with more of the apple coming through. But he's not suggesting that people sweeten a finished cider, he's talking about keeving the juice so that some natural sugars are left unfermented.

Cidermakers who want other people to enjoy their cider – whether commercially or for fun – have to consider this problem, so here are the basic choices:

Make Dry Cider. If People Don't Like It You Can Drink It Yourself.

This is what you'd call the combative approach. Make the cider you like and the rest of the world be damned. Not necessarily good for business, though it's amazing what people will drink if you tell them it's the most fantastic thing in the world…

Make Cider With A Sweeter Blend Of Apples

Perhaps this sounds a bit obvious but if you get the blend of apples right you can make a fully-fermented, unsweetened cider that tastes – not sweet exactly – but smooth and appley. We've tasted ciders made around West Pennard recently that have no harsh tannins and just the right balance of sweetness and acidity – none of that mouth-puckering quality that puts off novice drinkers.

Blend Cider Of Different Ages

The Gregg's Pit medium cider that won Gold in its category at The Big Apple in 2010 was a blend of ciders from 2008 and 2009, with the younger, fresher cider adding both a touch of sweetness and a bit of zip and zing to the earlier vintage. Being Gregg's Pit, the blend of apples was spot on to begin with, but the mixing of the ciders brought out the best in them. However, some makers claim you should never mix ciders from different years.

Keeve Your Cider

If you want a naturally soft, sweet cider, there's only one way to go. People often wonder why the cider drunk with crepes in Brittany is so different from most of the cider available in the UK, and the answer is that artisan cidermakers in that part of the world keeve their cider as a matter of course. They have to, because under the strict regulations that govern their endeavours, no other kinds of sweetening are allowed.

Keeving is an art, but it isn't as complicated as the terminology suggests. What keeving does is remove a proportion of the yeast from a vat of apple juice shortly after fermentation begins. This means that there's not enough yeast to ferment all the sugars in the juice, so you end up with a cider which is low in alcohol and sweet. To make the classic cidré bouche, the cidermaker bottles the cider just before fermentation ends, so that the yeast keeps working inside the bottle, generating the CO2 that makes the cork pop. This has to be timed just right, as an excess of gas can have explosive consequences.

Keeving is essentially straightforward, but might take a while to master. The process uses a pectin esterase enzyme and calcium chloride, which you can buy together as 'Kler Cidre', available from Standa Industrie, Caen, France. Vigo may stock it too. 1000 litre plastic containers are ideal for this.

1. Choose the right apples, which should be pectin-rich. Bittersweets work better than bittersharps.
2. Ensure apples are ripe before pressing, but remove any rotten fruit. The weather should be cool, so that fermentation doesn't start too quickly.
3. Crush the fruit. Leaving it to macerate for 12-24 hours before pressing will boost the pectin levels and give you a greater chance of success. Press.
4. Add the enzyme as soon as posible after pressing, using 100ml of enzyme to 1000 litres of juice. Stir. Leave for 24 hours.
5. To test whether the enzyme is working, add 1ml calcium chloride to 1l juice. You should see clots forming in the juice. If nothing happens after a few minutes,

You wouldn't catch these old boys glugging the sweet stuff...

leave it a few hours and try again.

6. Once the test is positive, add a litre of calcium chloride to 5l of juice, stir, then add to the 1000l juice. This is what happens next, according to Dr Andrew Lea:
   "Pectin methyl esterase removes methanol from the pectin chains. Calcium cross-links the chains to form a gel. Various molecules are attracted to and trapped within the gel, and therefore removed with it: asparagine (amino acid/ yeast nutrient), vitamin B1 (yeast nutrient) and yeast cells."
7. Fortunately all you need to do is wait patiently for the 'Chapeau brun' or brown hat to form. It's a thick, not very pleasant-looking brownish jelly. Can take a week to ten days to appear.
8. Scoop off with a stainless steel sieve. Wait for it to reform. Scoop again.
9. Rack the juice into another vessel and leave to ferment as usual.
10. Deciding when to bottle is a real art and will require some experimentation. Essentially, you need to rack the mostly-fermented cider about 10 degrees above your desired level, then wait until the fermentation has slowed almost to a standstill – but we thoroughly recommend consulting an expert (see Listings). For safety reasons you should bottle in champagne bottles with a wired-on mushroom cork.

An important premise of this book is that anyone can make cider, but not that many cidermakers can consistently produce a top quality keeved cider. It's a labour-intensive business that requires skill, attention to detail and the willingness to admit that a particular batch just isn't good enough. Tom Oliver is prepared for a failure rate of a third or more, although the cider is never wasted. But people expect a consistently good product, and anything that isn't up to scratch has to go.

The next step in the UK cider renaissance has to be a wholesale adoption of keeving, accompanied by a willingness among retailers to promote high-quality sparkling cider – we were in M&S in Bristol recently where they were selling a French cidre bouché, but no UK equivalent. This has to change. Unfortunately, however, any increase in duty will make it uneconomic for small producers to supply retailers, and we have already seen how the government responds to calls for help from small groups of artisan producers.

Sweeten With Sugar Or Apple Juice

Two straightforward approaches. If someone wants to buy a barrel of cider for an event you can ask them beforehand how sweet they want it and add sugar (dissolved in water) to taste. Leave the barrel too long and the cider may start to ferment again, depending on whether there's any yeast left, but if it's going to be drunk in the next couple of days it should be fine. Sugar is expensive, but many producers prefer to use it for bottled ciders, pasteurising the cider to prevent further fermentation and to stabilise the flavour.

Apple juice is a great natural sweetener for cider, bearing in mind that it will make the cider taste more appley and reduce the alcohol content. Cider sweetened with apple juice also has to be drunk quickly, as fermentation is likely to restart.

Sweeten With Artificial Sweeteners

You don't normally associate saccharin with 'real' food products – viewers of River Cottage would be appalled if Hugh F-W started sprinkling it on his organic porridge. But saccharin has been added to cider for a century and among producers of farmhouse cider it's perfectly acceptable – CAMRA have even enshrined its use in their definition of Real Cider. It's cheap, very easy to administer and of no interest to yeast, so you can see why people like it. Some of the more fastidious producers tend to frown on the practice, though not all ciders and perries from the region are saccharin-free. Since you don't have to tell anyone what goes in your cider or perry it's quite possible to say one thing and do another.

On the other hand some producers won't touch artificial sweeteners, and since they include some of the best makers of cider and perry in the country we assume that one can get along OK without them. To find out which sweeteners to use, and in what quantities, consult the literature or ask around. The sweetener of the moment is Sucralose, also known as E955. Sucralose is about 600 times sweeter than sugar, and twice as sweet as saccharin. So you don't need much.

The Cider Apple

If you want to make a strong, flavoursome cider that will keep for ages, get some proper apples.

You can make cider out of eaters, cookers and crabs, but the great cidermaking cultures of Northern Spain, Brittany, Normandy and the West Country owe their richness and longevity to a different kind of fruit. We think that the cider apple was first developed in Moorish Spain and brought north along the Atlantic seaboard by Basque traders, and from these distant beginnings thousands of apple varieties have emerged, flourished and, in many cases, vanished again.

Research at Long Ashton in the early 20th century confirmed what good cidermakers had known for centuries: the best cider is made with the best apples. The juice of cider apples ferments to give a cider that is strong, flavoursome and which keeps well. So what are we looking for in a cider apple?

First find yourself a cider apple orchard.

SUGARS: High sugar content means a strong cider, which isn't just good news from the drinker's point of view; ciders which are high in alcohol keep longer and better. You can measure the amount of sugar in apple juice with a hydrometer, which tells you the density of the juice – the specific gravity – and therefore the sugar level (see Making Cider section). Measure again after fermentation.

Most cider apples contain 10-15% sugar. Apples which are high in sugars but low in acids and tannins are 'sweets'.

ACIDITY: No, we're not talking psilocybin here (although some cider lovers swear that the trippy high you get from drinking lots of proper Somerset cider is caused by the magic mushrooms that get scooped up with the fruit). All apples contain malic acid, and the proportion in a cider apple contributes both to the flavour and its health and longevity.

Apples in which acids dominate the flavour are known as 'sharps', and they produce fresh, light ciders such as those traditionally popular in Devon. Cooking apples are also highly acid, and have often been added to farmhouse cider blends, but they don't have the same flavour and character as genuine cider sharps.

Collect lots of these.

TANNINS: We owe the rounded flavour, mouth-feel and amber colour of proper West Country cider to the high level of tannins contained in the best cider varieties. Tannins are naturally occurring phenolic compounds that protect apples from disease and injury. When the skin of an apple is broken, these complex molecules oxidise and turn brown, covering the exposed flesh in a layer of thick, brown juice that protects from attack by fungus or insect. If you cut a slice of an old apple variety the flesh quickly turns brown, do the same to a supermarket eater and nothing happens. The complex flavours of traditional apples owe a lot to the fruit's defence mechanisms; sweet modern apples would struggle to survive without pesticide protection.

Press them with one of these.

Cider apples that are high in tannins are known as bittersharps (tannin and acid predominate) or bittersweets (tannin and sugar). Bite into one and the taste sensation is quite horrifying. Crush a sackful, however, and the juice is sweet, with a rich brown colour from the oxidised tannins, particularly a group called procyanidins. These not only add flavour and body to the cider, but also afford antiseptic protection from Zymomonas mobilis, the organism that causes cider sickness and, to an extent, acetobacter, which turns cider into vinegar.

Tannins lend cider a flavour that is harsh and astringent or bitter and soft, depending on the fruit. Tremlett's Bitter is astringent, which makes it ideal for blending but quite intense for a single variety. Dabinett, on the other hand, is a top choice for single variety ciders because its tannins impart a rounded, bitter flavour that isn't harsh.

HOW TO GET CIDER APPLES

There is plenty of unused cider fruit lying around West Country orchards in the autumn – though not as much as there was a decade ago. But how do you go about buying some?

- Look on an OS map for areas where there are lots of orchards (marked with small green crosses), then pick a spot and go there in the summer. You could combine a cider tour with some apple research.
- You can also check the Common Ground website and the various orchard groups, national and local, for tips on where to go. You may find there's a cider orchard closer to home than you think.
- Talk to people in village pubs and farm shops, at markets and local garages, and you'll soon find out if an orchard owner has apples to spare.
- Make contact. Have a look at the trees. Negotiate a price, bearing in mind that the going rate is around £30-£40 a tonne if you pick your own.
- Ask the best time to collect fruit then come back in a van or large car. Two people can fill the back of a van in a few hours.

When harvesting apples be careful not to fall out of the tree. The broom is for shaking the fruit, not the climber.

HELP AND ADVICE

Orchard Link supports the owners of small, traditional orchards in Devon, by helping them find markets for fruit; they may be able to hook you up with an orchard owner. Take a look at www.orchardlink.org.uk.

- Yorkshire Orchards sell Dabinett in season along with a host of other apple varieties www.yorkshireorchards.co.uk

Essential Equipment

- Friendly disposition towards orchard owners, farmers and curious passers-by.
- Stepladder, preferably manned by someone who isn't likely to fall off.
- Sturdy broom for tree-shaking – the poor man's panking pole.
- Large groundsheet for catching apples.
- A couple of trugs.
- Twenty or so large hessian sacks (pet food shops and coffee companies are both good sources). Check for holes made by rodents before departure.
- Wellington boots, to prevent trench foot.
- Bread, cheese and cider.

- Somerset Orchards - www.somersetorchards.co.uk – make apple juice from cider fruit, but might be able to advise
- Try orchard groups for advice: see Listings for details.

HOW TO IDENTIFY A CIDER APPLE

Even with the help of a guide book identifying apples of any kind is tricky, to say the least. Some are distinctive, but often you find yourself with a range of apples that all seem to be misshapen, striped and/or russetted to a baffling degree. So you end up calling them 'the little stripy jobs near the hedge' just as people have for millennia.

The essential tool for the apple detective is a strong set of teeth and the courage to bite into something that will probably taste vile. What you're looking for is:

- A woolly, chewy texture, absolutely the opposite of the supermarket eater's juicy crunch.
- Sweetness – fairly easy to identify, but don't expect it to taste good.
- Acidity – makes you wince.
- Bitterness – the hardest taste to identify, because the least commonly encountered in non-cidermaking life. It's the mouth-puckering flavour that makes you want to remove your tongue and scrub it thoroughly.

Dave Kaspar of Days Cottage hard at work identifying apples.

If the apples come from the right place, they're probably the right apples. Photo by Bill Bradshaw (www.billbradshaw.co.uk)

If you blend varieties that have the desired texture and a combination of the taste sensations outlined above you will probably have a pretty decent cider; you can always make up the names.

TOP VARIETIES

There are hundreds of named cider apple varieties and hundreds of others that are known only to the men and women who collect them to make cider. Frank Naish, the veteran West Pennard cidermaker, uses at least two anonymous apples in his blend. In her *Somerset Pomona*, Liz Copas tells the story of the Red Jersey apple, which was sent many times from a farm in West Pennard called Laurel Grange; for years the same apple turned up under different names: Loyal Drain, Loyal Drang, Loral Drain, etc.

These are some of the best-loved and widely available cider apples:

Kingston Black (aka Black Taunton)

The most famous Somerset cider apple, believed to have originated in Kingston St Mary, just outside Taunton, is a bittersharp with an excellent balance of acidity and tannins that gives a characterful single variety cider. Some find the flavour too distinctive, however, and prefer to use Kingston Black in a blend with other fruit. If you're planning on planting it, be warned: it's a shy cropper and prone to canker and scab. At least it's easy to identify, though, with dark red fruit that can turn a rather sinister purple.

Kingston Black: A bittersharp with well-balanced tannin. Often used to produce a single variety cider.

Yarlington Mill

Another Somerset bittersweet found in both traditional and bush orchards, Yarlington Mill was supposedly discovered growing out of a wall beside a mill wheel in the village of Yarlington in the last years of the 19th century. Taunton Cider brought it to prominence in the 1970s, making the variety a mainstay of its new bush orchards.

Dabinett: Regarded by many craft producers as an essential ingredient in a good blend. Also an outstanding single variety.

Brown Snout

The secret to a Herefordshire apple's success is to be picked up and propagated by Bulmers, and so it is with Brown Snout, a mild-mannered bittersweet that came to prominence in the early bush orchard trials of the 1950s.

Brown's Apple

Another early-cropping variety originating in the mild climate of south Devon and capable of producing a huge crop in a good year, this is one of the finest sharp varieties. A staple of the Devon cider renaissance, the bright red fruit is easy to spot either in standard or bush orchards.

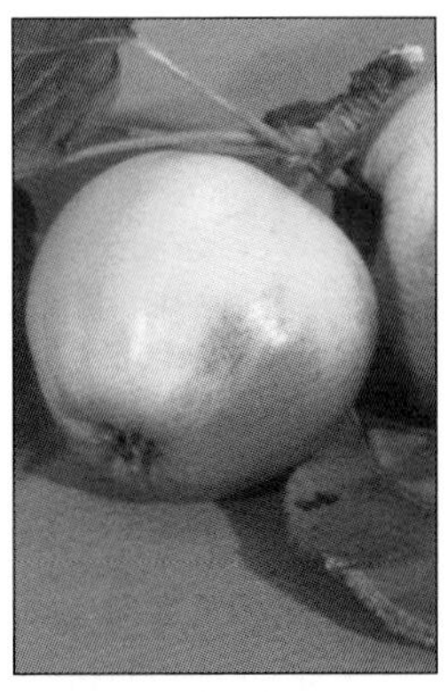

Yarlington Mill: Another firm favourite with many craft producers.

Dabinett

This late season bittersweet was found as a gribble in a hedge in Middle Lambrook, Somerset, by Mr William Dabinett, and propagated by a local nurseryman. Thanks to its balanced flavour and consistent cropping this is one of the most popular varieties; the fact that it prospers both in standard and bush orchards makes it particularly useful.

Michelin

Named after a passionate promoter of cider, this French variety was introduced to Herefordshire in the 1880s, and is now one of the most widespread bittersweets. Though by no means a classic apple, this ordinary-seeming green fruit is a top cropper.

Porters Perfection

Found mainly in the Martock area of Somerset, this medium bittersharp produces excellent cider. It's a late variety and not ready for harvest until mid November.

Porters Perfection: This bittersharp can produce an excellent single variety.

Foxwhelp

One of the classic bittersharps of Gloucestershire and Herefordshire, Foxwhelp is used in blends or fermented alone to make a single variety cider of character. A variety called Foxwhelp was one of the finest apples of the Golden Age of Cyder, but seems to have disappeared but for a few old specimens by the 20th century. As with Somerset Redstreak and the variety propagated by Lord Scudamore, today's apple may or may not be related to its forebear.

Tremlett's Bitter

A full bittersweet that flowers and ripens early; in a good year it can produce a huge crop of small red apples which are ready by mid-October. Despite its astringent flavour, Sheppys and others use Tremlett's Bitter to make a characterful, slightly challenging single variety cider.

Fair Maid of Devon

Once planted extensively by legendary Devon cider company Whiteways, this sharp has been put back to use by a new generation of producers in the county. Low in tannins, this is definitely one to blend. Fair Maid of Taunton, incidentally, is a milder sharp which is also known as Moonshines for its large, luminous yellow fruit.

Harry Masters Jersey

This late mid-season bitterweet is said to have been named after the Mr Masters who raised both it and Yarlington Mill in the Somerset village of the same name. There is often a lot of discussion of what makes a good blend on the cider workshop forum at www.ciderworkshop.com and HMJ is almost always recommended by experienced producers.

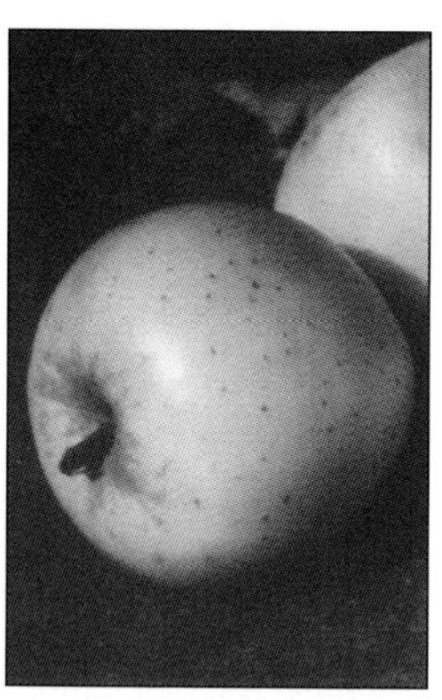

Morgan Sweet: One of the earliest cider apples, it also ferments quickly so is a good bet if you want cider for Christmas.

Morgan Sweet

Once this was a well-known Somerset dessert apple, and within living memory it was a Bristol favourite. But the rise of sweet, crunchy imports drove it out of the fruit bowl and onto the cider press, where it has a vital role to play as a cider apple that ripens early enough to produce cider before Christmas. Look out for this sweet, light festive cider.

Vilberie

Introduced from France by Bulmers during the company's early 20th century growth spurt, Vilberie is enjoying a comeback as new producers seek reliable bittersweet varieties. A late but heavy cropper.

Harry Masters: Many craft producers recommend a blend of Harry Masters, Yarlington Mill and Dabinett for a great cider.

Dunkerton's Late

A Somerset sweet which is green until ready to harvest in November, at which point in turns a glorious yellow. Low in tannins, it gives a light, sweet cider but is best blended.

Bulmer's Norman

A staple of orchards across the West Country, Bulmer's Norman was introduced in the early 20th century by the fast-growing Bulmers company, and achieved popularity for its vigorous growth and solid cropping; it is often used as a stembuilder. A bittersweet with a hard tannin that makes it best suited to blending.

THE FORGOTTEN VARIETIES

ACROSS THE COUNTRY ORCHARDS ARE BEING RESTORED AND RARE VARIETIES PROTECTED

A SOMERSET POMONA
The Cider Apples of Somerset
LIZ COPAS

A Somerset Pomona by Liz Copas is an essential reference book for craft cider producers.

Across the UK cider and apple enthusiasts have been seeking out lost or forgotten varieties, part of a wider hunt for fruit varieties of all kinds. In part this nationwide quest has been fuelled by the urgent need to halt the disappearance. Here are some of the great projects underway around the country.

Gloucestershire

Charles Martell has been hunting lost varieties of apple, pear and plum for decades, and has saved large numbers from extinction. On many occasions he has located the last remaining tree and taken graftwood from it. A classic example is Arlingham Schoolboys; the last tree in the village of Arlingham died in the 1990s but not before Charles had taken cuttings from it and grafted them successfully. The variety can now be found in his Gloucestershire Apple Collection and the Mother Orchard maintained by Dave Kaspar and Helen Brent-Smith at Days Cottage. Visit the Gloucestershire Orchard Group (www.gloucestershireorchardgroup.org.uk) for Charles' Pomona-in-progress.

Cornwall

In the late 70s Mary Martin returned to her native Tamar Valley to find the orchards she remembered in a terrible state. With her partner James Evans she set out to rescue the Tamar apples and their stories, combing the Cornish countryside for forgotten orchards and seeking out those old enough to remember apples shared by their parents and grandparents. In one case they snatched unburned twigs from a bonfire after new homeowners chopped down a particularly rare tree. In 1980 they began making cider and also began an apple collection, which is now preserved in the Mother Orchard at Cotehele. In a wild-looking orchard in Landuph, they tracked down the Colloggett Pippin, the shiny Onion Redstreak and the Tamar cider apple Tan Harvey.

Rare Cornish varieties are now being put to good use by Andy Atkinson of Cornish Orchards, whose cider offers a commercial future for the county's cider apples.

Dorset

Over the past few years Liz Copas has been working with Dorset cidermaker Nick Poole to find and document the county's lost cider varieties (see the Dorset section in Areas). The result of this hard work is that 400 trees are about to be planted, with 25 rare local varieties, including King's Favourite and Golden Ball. Visit Dorset Cider (www.dorsetcider.com) for details.

Welsh Marches

Since 1993 the Marcher Apple Network has been rescuing and promoting apple varieties along the Herefordshire/Powys border. This work led, in 2010, to the publication of the *Welsh Marches Pomona*, which describes 31 apples, many of them old varieties which have been re-discovered in local orchards. Visit the Marcher Apple Network (www.marcherapple.net) for details.

SINGLE VARIETY VS BLEND

Cidermakers tend to have strong opinions on this subject. Traditional producers like Burrow Hill or Wilkins work with a blend of top cider apples (Burrow Hill famously uses forty varieties) but in today's brand-crazed age the single variety cider is holding its own.

Blending is undoubtedly the best way to produce a rounded, reliable cider, since you're mixing sugars, tannins and acids according to an approximate formula that has proved successful for years. You're also likely to produce a cider that will keep, particularly if you can achieve the ideal mix of bittersweets and bittersharps.

Few cider apples have the character to produce a good single variety cider, although Kingston Black and Dabinett are renowned for doing just that. A quick survey of ciders available from commercial makers gives us Tremlett's Bitter and Dunkerton's Late as contenders, while Thatchers famously make Katy as well as Cox and Prince William. The only UK ice cider, made by Once Upon a Tree, uses Blenheim Orange.

For the small-scale cidermaker it may be worth making batches of single variety cider just to see what they're like, then blend them to taste. It's a good way of finding out what the reported qualities of fruit actually mean.

Thatchers Prince William is a fine single variety cider.

GRIBBLES

Many of today's great cider apples had humble beginnings, starting life as little more than weeds growing out of walls or wasteland – like the Granny Smith, found growing in an Australian compost heap. In Somerset it was once common for farmers to take the dry pomace left over after pressing and chuck it in a corner of a particular field for the cows to munch on. The seeds would be left to sprout, creating a rough and ready nursery of seedlings, or 'gribbles'. This may be a disastrous way of propagating apple trees – and could explain the often poor standard of cider in the Victorian countryside – but now and again the lottery of apple reproduction would produce a fantastic new variety. Dabinett and Yarlington Mill were both found by chance in Somerset villages, and subsequently put to excellent use.

CAN'T GET CIDER APPLES?

If you live in a flat in some city miles from cider country you may be wondering how on earth you can make proper cider. Ciderheads in the Eastern Counties would no doubt answer that you don't need special apples, since they've been making cider for centuries in that part of the world using blends of eaters and cookers.

Aspall uses a blend of Bramley and Cox, with the addition of bittersweet cider apples to give depth and body, and the Suffolk company must be doing something right as you can now drink its cider aboard Cunard liners.

And down near Canterbury in Kent, Rough Old Wife cider is also made using Bramleys, with Worcester and Crispin for sweetness. Not far away, Biddendens makes a fiendishly strong cider using cookers and eaters only.

So if you live in that part of the world, the best advice may be to visit your local cidermakers, find out what you can about their craft, and make the best of the fruit available. You can add tannins, though, by blending crab apples into the mix.

As well as being highly acidic, crab apples are rich in tannins; you can crush them just as you do other apples and add the juice to your blend. Crabs are a bugger to pick and it might take a few goes to get the proportions right, but on the other hand you can find them in parks and gardens all over the country, and you won't have much competition for the fruit. Now and again you come across a cider made of pure crab apples. It may not be to everyone's taste, but it is the oldest kind of cider – the original, if not perhaps the best.

With thanks to Liz Copas, author of *A Somerset Pomona*.

A lasting tribute to the cider apple: The Herefordshire Pomona.

The Cider Orchard

There is no place quite like a cider orchard. If there isn't one nearby, why not plant your own...

Orchards have been a feature of our landscape since the Romans arrived with their pruning knives and their disdain for the humble crab apple. It is quite possible that the Celts already cultivated the native fruit but they left no evidence of their pomological activities; the sacred texts that venerate the life-giving apple bough (which could be a reference to grafting) were written after the Romans had been and gone.

An orchard in the heart of Ciderland – the pub at Burtle sells its own cider.

Still, a two thousand year history is nothing to be sniffed at. Did orchards vanish when the Romans left? It hardly seems likely, after four centuries of influence over the population, and anyway the early Christian monasteries preserved the skills and tools of civilisation through the Dark Ages.

With the Normans came the first specialised cider fruit, and cider orchards have been with us ever since, the acreage ebbing and flowing as changes in taste, fashion and international security affect the demand for cider. Look at an 1870 Ordnance Survey map (www.old-maps.co.uk) and you'll see western Gloucestershire and Herefordshire blanketed in orchards; today remnants of this man-made forest survive, the boundaries unchanged, beside the river Severn at Minsterworth and elsewhere.

TRADITIONAL ORCHARDS

Until the 1950s cider apples were grown on standard trees. Eating apples and cookers may have been grown espaliered against walls or on bush-style trees, but cider orchards typically contained widely spaced trees with plenty of room between and beneath them for grazing livestock. They weren't planted this way because it looked scenic but because it was a system that worked: sheep or cattle kept the grass down, which kept the bugs down, and fertilised the soil; in return the animals ate windfalls and enjoyed both shade from the sun and shelter from the rain. Pigs and orchards went well together, as pigs snuffle up apples and bugs with equal relish.

At Wick Court Farm, near Arlingham in Gloucestershire, Jonathan Crump presides over a set-up that might have looked just the same five centuries ago. In an orchard covering no more than a couple of acres lives a small herd of chocolate-brown Old Gloucester cattle, whose milk is made into Single Gloucester cheese. The leftover whey is fed to the Gloucester Old Spot pigs that share the orchard with the cattle and spend their days happily turning windfalls into bacon and fertilizer.

Though in many ways a perfect system this isn't going to feed a city cheaply. Across Britain both orchards and fields have disappeared as farmers attempt to coax ever-greater volumes of milk, meat or corn out of the land. In Somerset particularly you can still find the typical small (less than five acre) farm orchards, but most date from before World War II. They're wonderful places, full of birds and insects and beautiful at blossomtime and in the autumn, but with a limited life span. Few apple trees live longer than eighty years or so,

World War II had a dramatic impact on farming. If the countryside of 1939 was still ruled by the horse and – to look at – hadn't changed much in a hundred years, the countryside of 1945 was in the throes of a revolution. Factories that had been rushing out tanks and planes turned to tractors and combines, and the few workers left on each farm learnt to drive and stopped drinking on the job. Sometime in the mid-1960s traditional farm cidermaking ceased to exist and in Somerset – so the story goes – a certain cidermaker went round the farms

Traditional orchards are descended from the wooded pasture of the middle ages. Widely spaced trees leave plenty of room for sheep – or cattle.

A caravan at Days Cottage.

smashing equipment to make sure it didn't fall into the hands of rivals.

At the same time orchards began disappearing from the landscape, despite a healthy market for cider apples. Why, you might wonder, would farmers go to the trouble and expense of grubbing up trees that could make them money? The answer is, they were paid to. Farmers from the 1950s to the 1970s grubbed up orchards, tore down hedges, filled in ponds and destroyed ancient woodland because successive governments paid them to do it in a misguided – disastrous, even – attempt to turn the countryside into a food factory. Then the EEC got in on the act, paying farmers to over-produce staples like grain and milk.

By the 1990s it was clear that traditional orchards were being lost at an alarming rate…

95% lost in Wiltshire since 1945
90% lost in Devon since 1960
75% lost in Gloucestershire since 1945
63% lost in Worcestershire since the 1970s
60% lost in Somerset since the 1960s.

Outside the Somerset Museum of Rural Life a sheep and a crow survey the apple crop.

COMMON GROUND AND APPLE DAY

The loss of local character across Britain prompted Sue Clifford and Angela King to launch Common Ground. The antithesis of Thatcherism, the new campaign group was set up in the mid-80s to celebrate the local and distinctive, and its most enduring and successful campaign has been to save traditional orchards and apple varieties.

Common Ground launched Apple Day on October 21, 1990, at Covent Garden, bringing fruit back to the old market after an absence of more than a decade. The next year saw 60 events across the country, and by the end of the 1990s that number had increased by a factor of ten. Now there are thousands of annual events run by the National Trust, WI groups, fruit growers, museums, horticultural societies and Wildlife Trusts.

> *From the start it was intended to be both a celebration and a demonstration of the variety we are in danger of losing – not simply in apples, but richness and diversity of landscape, place and culture too.* Common Ground.

Common Ground's fascination for the local and distinctive found its most vital expression in the campaign to save traditional orchards. Here's what Sue and Angela have to say in the fabulous '*Common Ground Book of Orchards*':

In orchards we and nature together have created an exuberant and a secret landscape – a treasury of genetic diversity and a repository of culture. For if an orchard is grubbed out for intensive agriculture or development, the loss for local distinctiveness goes deep.

The greatest loss of orchards has tended to be in and around villages, where a former orchard makes an ideal plot for a modest housing development – just look at the number of Orchard Lanes and Apple Tree Closes dotted around Somerset villages. In Carhampton, a village famous for preserving the winter ritual of wassail, the last of many orchards was threatened with development until local people put up a fight. A 600 signature petition, media attention and plenty of help from Common Ground and others led, in 1996, to the establishment of the Carhampton Community Orchard.

Common Ground has done more to change public attitudes towards apples and orchards than anyone else.

Expect the unexpected when you visit Burrow Hill. This llama is an inquisitive creature...

Now there are Community Orchards all around the country, and a still-growing awareness of the value and significance of orchards generally. At the Bath and West Show in 2009 the first Common Ground Special Award, for an apple juice or cider made by and from a Community Orchard or not-for-profit orchard, was won by Gabriel's Community Orchard in Pilton, Somerset.

A traditional orchard in Somerset. The trees have been left to grow as they like…

GRANTS TO PLANT AND GRUB

In 1987 Somerset County Council took a remarkable step. Noting the disappearance of traditional orchards from the landscape, it launched a programme of grant aid for the planting of fruit trees, and over the next decade more than 20,000 new trees were established in the county – still not as many as were grubbed up over the same period for housing or in the name of agricultural progress, but a start.

And the local authority has continued to take an active interest in orchards and cidermaking, hiring James Crowden to put together a cider map of the county and keeping a database of orchard owners who are sent regular newsletters.

Not to be outdone, Gloucestershire County Council also paid out money for tree planting during the 1990s. But at the same time the national government was continuing its disastrous post-war policy of paying farmers to grub up fruit trees. Presumably you could, at one time, have applied for funding to plant trees, then got a grant to grub them out again.

This traditional orchard is all that remains of the great Devon cider company Whiteways.

JOHN THATCHER AND THE SPS

No, not a Somerset funk band, but another chapter in the story of Her Majesty's Government's war on cider… Having spent decades paying farmers to grub up apple trees, the UK government announced in 2004 its deadliest attack yet on the nation's orchards. Following a much-needed reform of the EU's Common Agricultural Policy, farmers were to be paid according to their farm's cultivable land area, not according to crop production. This Single Payment Scheme required farmers to declare the acreage of land under cultivation – and orchards were not included. A field with a single apple tree would be designated as orchard, and therefore as non-farmland, and with a future change of use all but impossible, it looked as though the

PLANT YOUR OWN ORCHARD

APPLE TREES GROW FAST AND CROP QUICKLY, SO IT'S WORTH CONSIDERING PLANTING YOUR OWN

If you went out today and planted a small orchard of a half-dozen trees on dwarf rootstocks you could be making cider from the harvest in three or four years' time. That's assuming you have somewhere to plant said orchard and the wherewithal to buy the trees. Here are a few orchard start-up FAQs…

How much space do I need?
This very much depends on the trees. Fruit trees are usually sold as saplings with a label giving the variety, the rootstock and other info like growing conditions, size and the amount of time it might take for the first crop. All of these may vary, depending on the climate and soil. See Box on rootstocks, and ask orchard groups/local growers for advice.

Where should I plant apple trees?
Most of us don't have the luxury of choosing. Sandy soil won't support a big tree and waterlogged ground does not generally suit fruit trees – although you see plenty of apple trees on the Somerset Moors and Levels. Check for frost pockets before choosing varieties.

What varieties should I plant?
You might want a selection of fine Somerset varieties, but will they grow where you live? Worth remembering too that a Kingston Black grown in Sheffield will give you a different juice to one cultivated in Taunton. The best bet is probably to join one of the online cider groups or contact the National Orchard Forum and see if anyone else is growing cider apples in your area. If you are lucky enough to live in the West Country then what you want is a balance of bittersharps and bittersweets – see 'Cider Apples' for some suggestions. When choosing trees, bear in mind that early blossoming varieties will struggle in a location that is prone to late frosts.

Where should I buy them?
In 2009 we lost one of the best nurseries for cider apple varieties, when Scotts of Marriot was forced to close after more than a century in business. Fortunately there are a growing number of new nurseries and online sellers dedicated to fruit tree propagation – see Listings.

Do I really have to prune my trees?
In good growing conditions standard trees will grow upwards too fast for their roots, so pruning in the early years is essential. Otherwise, pruning increases the tree's health and productivity, and can make the tree more manageable. Though there are plenty of Somerset orchards brimming with fruit that haven't seen a pair of pruning shears in decades.

Where can I learn about pruning and grafting?
Orchard groups, nurseries and horticultural societies offer workshops all over the place, often in the winter. See Listings for some options.

What pests affect apple trees, and how can I deal with them?
The most notorious is the larva of the codling moth – the 'maggot' found in apples. You'll notice in some orchards a dark band around the lower part of the trunk of each tree – this band of sticky ointment prevents female moths travelling up the trunk and is highly effective.

mass destruction of orchards was imminent. Enter John Thatcher, who argued long and hard for the inclusion of orchards in the SPS. With Julian Temperley's assistance he succeeded, and the furore surrounding their campaign highlighted both the immense value of orchards in the modern countryside, and their fragility. In 2009 the National Association of Cider Makers awarded John its annual Fred Beech award for this outstanding contribution to the industry.

Wildflowers and grasses thrive in unsprayed orchards.

ORCHARDS AND WILDLIFE

One of the problems encountered by Common Ground is that orchards have no legal protection. You can apply for a Tree Protection Order on a particular tree, but in legal terms an orchard is little different from a field of wheat.

In a way this makes sense. An orchard, after all, is man made, and you can't expect farmers to have land just sitting around because the trees look pretty in blossom season.

But it's becoming increasingly clear that orchards have a vital role to play in towns and, even more so, in the countryside, as oases of wild nature. If you look online you can find acres of material on Biodiversity Action Plans and whatnot, but the simple truth is that modern agriculture is too efficient and too intensive for nature to thrive within and around it. In a modern wheatfield you'll be lucky to find so much as a beetle, but in an old orchard you can find anything and everything.

The bullfinch is either an orchard pest or a beautiful bird that needs the unofficial nature reserve of the traditional orchard to survive. Depends how you look at it.

For one thing an old orchard is one of the few places where grass and wildflowers are allowed to grow unploughed and unsprayed. The richer the botanical mix, the more insects there are and the more effective the pesticide protection offered by ladybirds, earwigs, hoverflies and wasps. The richer the insect mix, the more birds there are, with bluetits playing a particularly beneficial role.

Birds love orchards, both for food and shelter in the form of holes and hollows. In a traditional Herefordshire orchard you might find tree sparrows, wood pigeon, great tits, jackdaws, long-tailed tits, mistle thrush, spotted flycatcher, little owl, tree creeper, great spotted woodpecker and collared dove. Bats of different kinds also thrive among the old trees, as do foxes, badgers and other mammals.

In 1992 the UK government signed up to the Rio Earth Summit pledge to restore biodiversity, but orchards received no official recognition for fifteen years. Finally, in 2007, Natural England noticed the fuss being made by Common Ground and the People's Trust for Endangered Species, and by local campaigners such as the Gloucestershire Orchard Group, and teamed up with PTES to launch a nationwide orchard survey. Then, in May 2009, Natural England announced a £500,000 collaboration with the National Trust to revive traditional orchards.

Not that this gives orchards any legal protection. Farmers can still grub fruit trees as and when they please. The only way to stop them is to make apples worth growing, by making cider a lucrative business. Which means the wildlife of Britain is in our hands. We must drink more cider.

The noble chafer beetle (Gnorimus nobilis) is one rare bug, found almost exclusively in traditional orchards.

NATIONAL TRUST ORCHARDS

With so many grand houses in its care it's not surprising that the National Trust owns some 100 traditional orchards. Some have been managed for decades and the fruit sold commercially, while others have been restored recently, thanks to the Trust's new-found enthusiasm for all things pomological. In April and May 2010 the first Full Bloom Festival took place, with events following the opening of flower buds at Trust properties and community orchards from Cornwall to Cumbria. Check out your local Trust properties for apple and cider-related events, such as wassail and Apple Day celebrations. Highlights include:

Cotehele, Cornwall – The Tamar Valley was once covered in orchards. Now a Mother Orchard has been planted on the estate of this Tudor mansion, with 120 varieties, mostly near-forgotten Cornish apples collected and propagated by Mary Martin and James Evans. There's a stone mill, which you can see in operation on Apple Day – powered by Exmoor ponies.

Brockhampton, Herefordshire – In the heart of orchard country old apple and damson trees are host to associated wood decay insects such as the rare noble chafer beetle Gnorimus nobilis – the orchard bug-hunter's holy grail - and the mistletoe weevil Ixapion varigatum.

Hedge plantings of damson trees extend the orchards into the wider landscape.

Lacock Abbey, Wiltshire: Harry Potter fans may have already visited the crazy old monastery where large chunks of the films were shot. They may not have noticed the orchards and wildflower meadow, which are home to yellow rattle, hawkweeds, ragged robin, ox-eye daisy, bugle, veronica and vetches as well as various grasses and cowslips.

Barrington Court, Somerset – The most genteel cider orchards you'll see, and the cider isn't bad either. Lend a hand on Apple Day and celebrate wassail.

There are about 70 varieties of cider apple at Barrington Court in Somerset.

Killerton, Devon - 58 acres of traditional apple orchards, with 600 trees featuring 98 different varieties of apple including Slack-ma-girdle and Star of Devon, as well as two unique to the estate - Killerton Sweet and Killerton Sharp. Each year four tons of apples are picked by staff and volunteers, then pressed in a Victorian press.

Barrington Court Cider

Cider has been made in the grounds of this Tudor mansion for years, but the most recent renaissance got under way just a few years ago. There are ten acres of orchards surrounding the exquisite formal gardens of Barrington Court, planted with cider fruit that found its way into the presses of local cidermakers - Burrow Hill is only a couple of miles away, so this is prime cider country. But in 2006 the market for fruit abruptly dried up as other local orchards came on line.

This turned out to be A Good Thing. Barrington Court had been the first house ever bought by the National Trust, back in 1907, and the Trust were looking for ways to celebrate the centenary. What could be better than making a few barrels of Somerset's finest? With seventy-odd varieties of top cider apples there was no shortage of fruit, but the cidermaking equipment that had been on the estate was long gone. Signs went up at Trust properties in the area and before long Roger Wheaton offered the services of his mill and press – not Vigo's latest but a fantastic antique mill and a press constructed from great slabs of elm. A proper old farm press and definitely not light. Fortunately, Roger owns a haulage company in Chard, so transport wasn't an issue.

So the apples were pressed and the juice fermented and bottled as 100BC. the cider went down a storm, so next year they made some more. And then some more the year after that…

Now the pressing has become an Apple Day event, with volunteers gathering fruit and operating the press – which is good news for chief cidermaker Rachel Brewer. They made 1,900 litres in 2009, which works out as, er, a few more 70cl bottles. You do the maths.

The cider certainly isn't the cheapest in the county, but it flies off the shelves of the Barrington Court shop. Maybe this is partly thanks to its rarity and its connection to the place, but the cider is good too – perhaps a bit young when we tried some in late April but full of flavour.

APPEAL TO THE NATIONAL TRUST!

We reckon you should be doing more. With such a large potential market for your products, surely you should be selling top craft ciders in your shops nationwide. This would provide a valuable market for the best small-scale cidermakers AND do far more to promote orchards in the long term than the Natural England project.

ORCHARD PIG GROUND FORCE

Charlie Dimmock in an orchard? Sadly not. Orchard Pig Ground Force is, nevertheless, a wonderful scheme – in fact you'd be tempted to call it groundbreaking were it not all about keeping the ground unbroken.

The relationship between apple growers and cider makers has always been tricky. To grow apples requires a commitment of time and capital on the part of the orchard owner, and there is no guarantee that there will be demand for fruit the year after planting, never mind five or ten years. The cider maker will tend to buy fruit as cheaply as possible, but if there's a lot of demand or a particularly poor harvest he will have no choice but to pay whatever the orchard owner asks.

Percy Bulmer learned this in the early days of the Hereford company, and after one disastrous year Bulmers made long-term deals with orchard owners across the Three Counties, telling them which varieties to plant and guaranteeing a market for the fruit.

Subsequently, the condition of orchards has reflected the state of the cider industry. In Somerset the traditional farm-scale orchards continued to be replanted, in some cases, until the 1970s, when companies like Taunton Cider started planting their own, high-yield, bush orchards. Today Thatchers grows a lot of its own fruit in modern orchards, but still takes in apples from elsewhere, while larger companies have been accused of importing apple pulp from Europe.

When Neil McDonald and Andrew Quinlan set up The Orchard Pig in 2005 they found themselves with a quandary. Based at the West Bradley Fruit Farm, they had only limited access to cider orchards, yet they were surrounded by orchards that had been allowed to deteriorate during the pre-Magners cider slump. Neil came from a farming background and had both experience of

Old orchards and old buildings go together. This is Muchelney Abbey in Somerset.

Bees and orchards also go together.

orchard management and a fascination for the subject, so he set up Orchard Pig Ground Force, the first company to specialise in orchard maintenance services including planting, pruning and harvesting. OPGF manages 800 acres of orchards that are owned by other people, often bartering the harvest for maintenance (mistletoe removal, etc) and planting.

In 2009 one local orchard owner was offered £40 a tonne if OPGF picked the fruit, or £100 a tonne if he did the harvesting. In a good year this can mean a fairly decent income; in a bad year, it doesn't. Either way, these sums are way better than those offered by other, larger cider makers in the area – who have access to the international apple market. With the housing market depressed and the cider market robust it makes sense for orchard owners to let OPGF keep their trees healthy.

The orchard of the future? Growing apples on vines at Thatchers.

THE MODERN CIDER ORCHARD

One of the achievements of the Long Ashton Research Station was the propagation of new cider apple varieties that grow on dwarfing and semi-dwarfing rootstocks. Experiments in the 1950s demonstrated that a bush orchard could produce far more apples than a standard orchard the same size, and much more quickly.

The downside was that these new varieties were more susceptible to pests than their standard predecessors, and needed spraying with chemicals including DDT and lethal organo-phosphates like parathion and schradan – the insecticides investigated by Rachel Carson in her 1962 eco-classic Silent Spring.

So it took a while for the bush orchards to catch on, but by the 1970s Taunton Cider and other companies were switching over to orchards that produced high yields and could be harvested by machine.

The most intensive modern orchard might contain 1300 trees per acre instead of the 48 traditionally grown in orchard pasture; the trees bear fruit within five years rather than twelve, and are grubbed out and replaced after twelve-fifteen years, rather than fifty.

The process of innovation and development continues, as larger cider companies try to make their production more efficient. Walk up the lane behind Thatchers in Sandford and you'll see the full spectrum of orchards, from traditional pasture dotted with venerable old trees, through orchards in which the trees stand in densely packed rows, like tall hedges, to the most recent addition – apple trees so carefully nurtured for maximum efficiency that they resemble vines.

Some still swear by the old varieties and the standard trees which – in their proper unsprayed habitat – display remarkable resistance to disease and require little or no chemical attention. For others innovation and discovery are part of what makes cider so exciting: new apples, new flavours, new possibilities…

A fine old perry pear in the orchard at Gregg's Pit, Much Marcle.

GRAFTING

The apple does not grow true from seed. If you plant the seed of, say, a Kingston Black, the resulting tree will not bear the sought-after dark fruit but some other apple – possibly a great cider apple, but more likely a crabby

Rootstocks Made Simple

If you go to buy an apple tree from a nursery the label will have on it a number preceded by M or MM. This refers to the type of rootstock. Apple trees are propagated by grafting or budding material from the desired variety onto the root and lower stem of a tree bred for that specific purpose. Since the rootstock determines the vigour with which the tree grows, and so its eventual size, you need to get the right one. M is an abbreviation of East Malling Research Station where rootstocks were scientifically categorised in the 1920s. Not that the numbering is very scientific; rootstocks aren't numbered in order of size but according to their position in the EMRS nursery… MM stands for Malling-Merton and refers to the next phase of research, in which East Malling collaborated with the John Innes Institute at Merton. Makes perfect sense now, doesn't it? You might also come across more recent additions to the rootstock family, prefaced by G or CG (Cornell-Geneva). People in northern climes should check out new work being done on Siberian crabapple rootstocks.

M27: Only 5ft high and needs full support throughout its life. Can be grown in a pot, but don't expect too many apples.

M9: Top dwarfing rootstock used by the National Fruit Collection at Brogdale, and in modern cider orchards. Will produce a tree 8-10 feet high and in full bearing within five years. Expect around 55lb/25kg per tree. Needs staking.

M26: A cross of M9 and M16. Reaches 8-10 feet unpruned, but does not like wet or clay soil. 70lb/30kg plus.

MM106: Semidwarf which can grow to 11 ft. Doesn't need staking and doesn't mind wet. Resistant to woolly aphid. 100lb/45kg.

M7: Semidwarf that needs staking for first 4-5 years. Very hardy and fruitful. Can tolerate wet.

MM111: Half-standard (10-12 feet). Resistant to woolly aphid. Up to 300lb/150kg.

M2: Very similar in size and vigour to MM111.

M25: Standard tree, typically 12-15 ft high and correspondingly wide. Only suitable for large gardens and pasture, but ideal if you want a traditional orchard. Up to 400lb/180kg.

specimen that isn't much use to anyone. This mutability is a good thing, in the sense that it constantly throws up new varieties, but the only way to ensure that you get the apples you want is to graft a twig – or scion – from the desired tree onto a rootstock. The cultivation of apples spread with this knowledge and the equipment that went with it, from Persia into Ancient Greece and slowly westward across Europe, until the Romans planted the first orchards in Britain. It's one of the defining features of civilisation.

If the scion determines the fruit, the root stock determines the shape and character of the tree; formerly hardy native crab apples were used, and today you can choose from a bewildering range of stocks that are numbered M5, M26 and so on, like motorways.

You can buy scions of sought-after varieties. Training in grafting (and pruning) is offered by the Gloucestershire Orchard Group and other organisations (see Listings).

Some cidermakers still insist on using fruit from traditional orchards – this is Burrow Hill.

Q&A LIZ COPAS

NATIONAL ASSOCIATION OF CIDER MAKERS' ORCHARDING ADVISOR AND AUTHOR

What got you interested in cider and perry?
Working in the Pomology department at Long Ashton Research Station. Well, as a cider pomologist, how could I not be interested in the end product?

Do you have a treasured memory of a particularly good cider or perry?
Yes. The Long Ashton cider and perry was legendary. People used to make any excuse to visit the Research Station, inevitably ending up at the cider house to fill their boots with bottles and demi-johns. The House of Commons bar stocked our cider and perry.

How do you account for the recent surge of interest in cider and cidermaking?
Getting the products on the supermarket shelves with quality presentation, showing lots of imagination with different tastes and bottling. Cider has become an alternative drink for all and moved away from the scrumpy image. Also Magners TV advertising did a lot of good.

Do you have a favourite apple variety?
Probably a well-balanced Dabinett. I am also very partial to a good drop of Stoke Red. For a naturally bittersharp variety I think it makes a much better cider than Kingston Black

If you could drink cider in any time or place, where would it be?
It would be good to taste the Hereford Redstreak cider as made in the mid 1660s. I wouldn't want to stay there too long though.

Any advice for the novice cidermaker?
Read the books on how to do it and hopefully avoid the pitfalls

What's your most precious bit of cider-related gear?
Records made at LARS in the early days.

Tree to Tree

We follow the cidermaking journey from an orchard near Glastonbury in Somerset to the Apple Tree pub in Bedminster, Bristol via a South Bristol press on the slopes of Totterdown. Pictures by Beezer, Sean Busby, Richard Jones and James Russell

Shaking apples from the tree: some people use a panking pole, while others prefer a more hands-on approach...

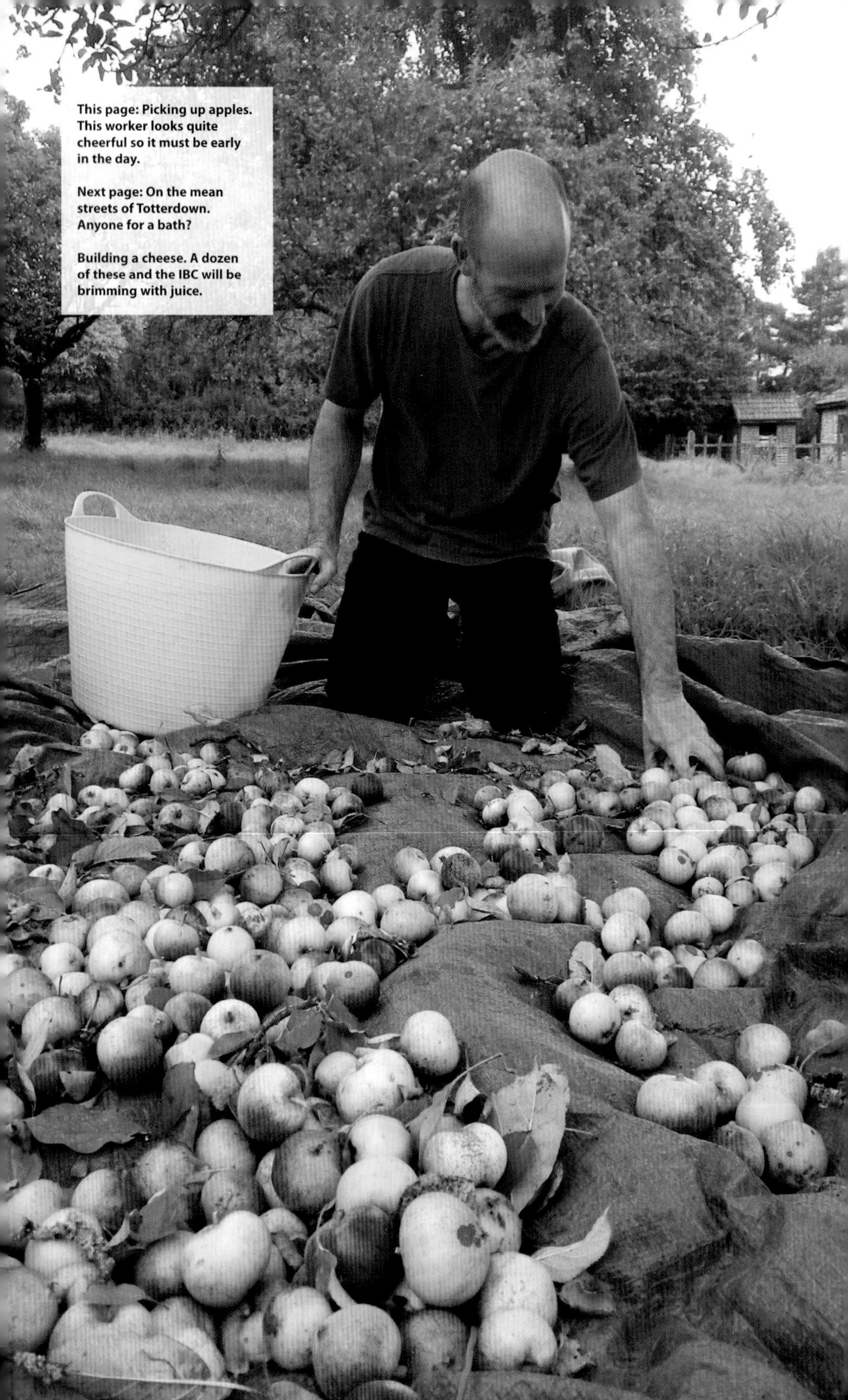

This page: Picking up apples. This worker looks quite cheerful so it must be early in the day.

Next page: On the mean streets of Totterdown. Anyone for a bath?

Building a cheese. A dozen of these and the IBC will be brimming with juice.

TOTTERDOWN PRESS
THE APPLE CHAPEL

The Leominster Morris strut their stuff at Gregg's Pit, Much Marcle, during the Big Apple festival. Orchards respond well to a bit of song & dance, especially at Wassail time...

DRY
BLACKTHORN

After 20 years living and working in Tokyo, music and fashion photographer Beezer returned to his old haunt The Apple Tree in Bedminster, Bristol and found that very little had changed…

The next generation... The youngest member of the Totterdown Press looks on as the juice flows.

Tasting Notes

Cider and Perry History

Our native drinks have a long and sometimes distinguished history

To the dedicated cider enthusiast it should come as no surprise that the origins of our favourite tipple are as cloudy as the finest farmhouse brew. People have always made the most of fruit, and it's safe to say that the unfortunate Cheddar Man and his murderous Stone Age chums ate and perhaps cooked crab apples. Did they also cut them up and ferment them in water to create an unpleasant but intoxicating beverage? Did a neolithic Roger Wilkins hold court in a Wedmore cider cave?

Alas, we will never know, as a cup of cider leaves very little for the archaeologist to dig up. In Britain the first records of orchard cultivation come from the Romans, one of whose varieties, Decio, is supposedly still grown in Somerset. But to the Romans an apple was strictly for eating – a digestive aid with erotic overtones – and they were fortunate to live in England during a prolonged warm spell that allowed vineyards to flourish across the south.

It's likely that people did make some kind of fermented apple juice and in the middle ages the juice was extracted from crab apples by age-old methods described thus:

Gather crabbes as soon as the kernels turn black, and lay them in a heap to sweat and take them into troughs and crush them with beetles. Make a bagge of coarse hair-clothe and fill with crabbes and press and run the liquor into hogsheads.

Leave in the barrel for a couple of months and you would have a cider of sorts – people still make cider

Pomona, the Roman goddess of orchards. The Romans loved apples but weren't too keen on cider.

from crab apples today, although this may not suit every taste. Was this the kind of drink that was served to St Colombanus when he visited the King of Burgundy in 600? It's difficult to say. What we do know is that, five hundred years later, a different kind of cider was being made, sold and enjoyed in monasteries and on estates from northern Spain to Devon. This cider was strong and flavourful – a match for ale and even wine.

So where did this new drink come from? The Romans had mills and presses capable of extracting apple juice with reasonable efficiency – an olive and an apple offer similar challenges – and with the decline of the Empire the technology and know-how passed into the hands of Christian and Islamic powers. Fruit growing was a valuable industry around the shores of the Mediterranean, where agriculture experts took advantage of the warm climate and long growing season to experiment with new varieties.

By the time William the Conqueror landed in Sussex, the Moors had taken over Spain, introducing new fruit varieties along the way. From central Spain the new tannin-rich apples found their way to the Basque country, and from there traders took grafts of the best varieties north along the Atlantic seaboard to Normandy, where climate, soil and populace proved highly receptive. Fuelled by cider, the Normans made short work of Harold's Anglo-Saxon ale swillers at Hastings; a hundred years later the presses at Battle Abbey were in full production…

King Arthur's resting place? Or a medieval tourist trap?

A delivery of apples, 1930s style.

GLASTONBURY AND ARTHUR

Glastonbury Abbey may not seem the most urgent port of call for the cider lover, but one highlight of the ruined monastery's grounds is a fine orchard of standard trees that was planted by Taunton Cider in the 1970s – the latest in a long succession that began in the early days of the abbey, when the apple tree was not just a source of fruit but an important mythic symbol.

Anyone who has spent more than ten minutes in the strange Somerset town will appreciate that the definitive story of King Arthur, Avalon and Glastonbury is unlikely to be written. The name Avalon made its first appearance in 1136, in Geoffrey of Monmouth's *Historia de Regum Britanniae,* as the magical island of apples (Insula Pomorum que Fortunata uocatur) where Arthur's sword Excalibur was forged, and where he was taken to recover from wounds sustained at the Battle of Camlann. The *Historia* and its sequel, *Vita Merlini*, dealt in myths and legends, so it must have come as a surprise to the 12th century literary world when Arthur's grave turned up in Glastonbury.

According to another less than reliable Medieval historian, Gerald of Wales, Henry de Sully ordered a search of the abbey grounds when he became Abbot in 1190. Some particularly zealous monks dug five metres into the ground to discover a massive treetrunk coffin and a leaden cross bearing an inscription: Hic jacet sepultus inclitus rex Arthurus in insula Avalonia. ("Here lies renowned King Arthur in the island of Avalon").

It didn't seem to worry anyone at the time that the Abbey had suffered a terrible fire less than ten years before, which had destroyed the Old Church – one of the oldest religious buildings in the country – and taken Glastonbury off the pilgrimage map. Rather, the discovery only served to fuel the nation's Arthur-mania, and in 1278 Edward I himself came to Glastonbury to preside over the reburial of the great man's bones before the Abbey's High Altar.

For almost three hundred years, Glastonbury Abbey was one of England's top tourist destinations, with visitors

Cider fruit and monastery ruins - Glastonbury Abbey as it is today.

On his death, King Arthur was taken off to the Isle of Apples – Glastonbury, if you believe the monks.

relying on the monks for their bread and cider. Fortunately for them, Glastonbury in the 12th century really was an Isle of Apples. Every monastery had an orchard, which often doubled as a cemetery, and a hundred years after the Norman invasion specialist cider apples – pearmains – were well established. There is no reason to doubt that Glastonbury was any less suited to apple cultivation a thousand years ago than it is today – and if you have a wander around the cider orchard you'll see that this is a very good place to grow apples.

A century ago, in fact, the surrounding country was one massive cider orchard, with local cidermakers, inspired by the good work done by Sir Neville Grenville at nearby Butleigh Court, using the now-vanished railway – the Strawberry Line as it was known, because it carried summer fruit from Cheddar – to ship their wares to London and the Midlands. Between the wars Clapps of Baltonsborough enjoyed national fame, and more recently Frank Naish, of West Pennard, has achieved renown as the country's oldest cider maker. Not far away, in West Bradley, The Orchard Pig now makes excellent use of the region's cider fruit.

Apples and cider were vital to life in medieval England, specially in the monasteries.

THE GOLDEN AGE OF CYDER

A cider-loving time traveller could only have one destination: the late 17th century, when a cider as strong and flavourful as Canary wine was made from an apple variety called Redstreak. This miraculous fruit was discovered in France by John, Viscount Scudamore, and planted on his extensive Herefordshire estate during the 1630s. From it was made a cider that was full-bodied, fruity, and of a sparkling yellow hue. This 'speedy, vanishing nittiness', as one writer called it, owed a lot to a timely invention: bottle glass.

Some years earlier, James I had ordered glassmakers to stop using valuable timber as a fuel, forcing them to burn coal instead of charcoal. The new fuel burned hotter and as a result it became possible to make glass that was strong enough for bottling.

Previously glass bottles had to be encased in leather or wicker, and were too weak to be transported, but the new verre anglais was strong enough to hold even pressurized liquids, such as cider undergoing a secondary fermentation. Nobody knows exactly who first made this dark green bottle glass, or when, but the location may well have been Newnham-on-Severn, which is close to the coalfields of the Forest of Dean and in the heart of 17th century cider country.

It's likely that Scudamore and his secretive cidermaking cronies were adding sugar to bottles of cider and wiring down the corks decades before the French invented champagne. This would explain why the drink became so popular during the Civil War and Commonwealth. By the time Charles II was restored to the throne – and he wasn't called the Merry Monarch for nothing – everyone was drinking, making or writing about cider, cyder, sydar or plain old sider. Samuel Pepys had a drop now and again, while John Evelyn – a founder of the Royal Society and expert on trees and forestry – devoted a book to the subject. *'Pomona'* (1664) is a book about fruit-growing, with nationalist tendencies. In the introduction Evelyn assures his readers:

That if at any time we are in danger of being hindred from Trade in Forreign Countries, our Englic Indignation may scorn to feed at their Tables, to drink of their Liquors, or otherwise to borrow or buy of Them, or of any their Confederates, so long as our Native soyle does supply us with such excellent Necessaries.

And he had a plan, to wit:

Our Design of relieving the want of Wine, by a succedaneum of Cider (as lately improv'd)…

Many 21st century governments would do well to take notice. Evelyn believed that a country still impoverished by civil war – and beset by enemies abroad – could be healed and strengthened by a drink that supported in its production farmers, coopers, glass bottle manufacturers, merchants, shipping companies and other related businesses. It also saved vital stocks of grain that might otherwise have been used for brewing beer and provided a healthier alternative (it was widely felt) than beer or wine. In a way that now seems highly improbable, cider was at the centre of national discourse and taxed the greatest minds of the age.

Of the numerous books published the most famous is

John Worlidge showed people how to make a living from cider. A man ahead of his time.

John Worlidge's *Vinetum Brittannicum* of 1676, a treatise on every aspect of orcharding and cidermaking. With advice on varieties and rootstocks, soil types, pests and irrigation, the respected agricultural reformer offered landowners great and small the chance to make their fortune in cider. According to his calculations a farmer could plant one acre with a hundred Redstreak trees and, after ten years, earn double his original investment in a single season. As far as Worlidge was concerned, cider was it.

> *Yet is there not any drink known to us generally palatable as cider: for you may make it sute almost with any humorous drinker: it may be made luscious by an addition of a quantity of sweet apples in the first operation, pleasant being made with Pippins or Gennet-Moyles only: racy, poignant, oily, spicy with the Redstreaks and other sorts of fruits, even as the Operator pleases. And it satisfies thirst, if not too stale, more than any other usual drink whatsoever.*

John Evelyn was one of the great figures of the 17th century. He thought that home-grown cider was A Good Thing.

The campaign worked. So successful did the cider industry become that cider overtook both wine and ale as the drink of choice among Londoners, and the landscape of the Three Counties changed as farmers claimed and enclosed common land. Most of west Gloucestershire was enclosed long before Parliamentary Enclosure began, with landowners planting apple trees in pasture land, on arable fields and in hedgerows – and forcing their tenants to do the same. In 1636 George Wyrral of English Bicknor, Gloucestershire, leased parcels of land for 21 years, and obliged tenants to plant and graft a set number of crab stocks. After two decades the trees would have been in their prime.

Some parishes, like Taynton and Kempley, had more than 10% of land under orchard by the end of the 18th century, and most of the county west of the Severn had a coverage of over 5%, with most orchards planted close to villages or clusters of cottages. For many cottagers the apple crop was their biggest source of income, so it was understandable that orchards should be planted close to home. Perry was also extremely popular and had the great advantage that one tree could bear as much fruit as several apple trees; you can still find perry pear trees from that period standing alone in fields or growing in hedgerows.

The Golden Age of Cyder gave us something else: poetry. John Philips, John Milton's nephew, carved an unusual niche as the nation's Cyder Poet and in his 1708 epic, Cyder, he outdid Worlidge by giving would-be cidermakers all the right advice – in verse. Here he is, talking about the art of grafting:

Let Art correct thy Breed: from Parent Bough
A Cyon meetly sever; after, force
A way into the Crabstock's close-wrought Grain
By Wedges, and within the living Wound
Enclose the Foster Twig.

Makes perfect sense, and it scans too. But Philips doesn't stop there. As far as he is concerned, cider is an integral part of the national character, and he contrasts the gentle, communal world of the English cider drinker – who shares a loving cup –with the intemperate, aggressive lands of the vine. The poem ends with a vision of the Royal Navy conquering the world, until cider Shall please all Tasts, and triumph o'er the Vine.

Unfortunately the gentry's fondness for cider didn't

John Philips, the Cyder Poet.

Villagers collect the autumn apple harvest in Minsterworth, Gloucestershire. (Picture courtesy of Minsterworth Community History Project).

last, so that by the end of the century even Gloucestershire landowners were serving imported wine to guests. It would be a while before the next Cyder Poet came along…

He wasn't called the Merry Monarch for nothing. Charles II's Restoration was fuelled by cider and perry.

THE CIDER MILL

Unlike a grape, which can be squished between thumb and forefinger, an apple gives up its juice with the greatest reluctance. Early cidermakers didn't bother trying to crush apples, but instead steeped pieces of fruit in water to make an insipid brew; their medieval descendants let nature do most of the work for them, leaving apples until they were black and half-rotten and then pounding them in a trough to release the juice.

Until the 20th century West Country cidermakers tended to leave fruit on the ground to soften. It was a common sight, in the low-lying Moors of central Somerset, to see the crop of a whole orchard bobbing about in late autumn floodwater. But even softened apples need to be crushed before pressing. In Ancient Greece a similar challenge was presented by the olive, and in response the engineers of Athens created the *trapetum*, a mill that crushed fruit under a stone wheel. The Romans went one better with the *mola olearia*, which featured two wheels on a shared axle, revolving around a central pivot. Forms of this mill still exist in southern Europe, while a different version was later used to crush apples.

In fact one or two cidermakers still use a stone edge-runner mill today, and you can have a go at using one yourself each October at Hellens in Much Marcle. The principle is straightforward: a wheel rolls around a deep groove cut in a circular piece of stone, usually with an elderly or particularly docile horse providing the motive power, crushing apples placed in its path. But it isn't the weight of the stone that crushes the fruit, but the grinding effect of the asymmetrically cut stone working against the rough sides and bottom of the trough.

These mills are heavy, cumbersome and must have been extremely expensive. Yet they are to be found in crumbling cider barns and farmyards in parts of Ciderland where there was a good supply of suitable stone, or easy access to river transport; there are plenty along the banks of the Severn, in an arc stretching from Awre to Taynton, but few in Dorset or Devon. Around the Forest of Dean, which abounds in small quarries, you may come across stone mills and press beds abandoned in sheds or built into the walls of buildings. Keith Orchard has a wonderful old stone mill complete with wooden and iron fittings, while James Marsden of Gregg's Pit uses a stone base for his press. Perhaps that's why he wins so many awards…

Life became a lot easier in the 1660s, when cider impresario John Worlidge patented a new kind of mill. Named 'Ingenio', this device employed a wooden cylinder studded with iron pegs to break up the fruit, and it had the undoubted advantages of being lightweight, comparatively cheap and hand-operated.

Few have survived – it's doubtful, even, that the wooden machine was durable enough to compete with the stone mill – but Ingenio served as a model for future generations of 'scratchers' or 'scratters'. In the 19th century mobile apple-pressing outfits roamed the countryside, dragging a wagon-mounted scratter and press from farm to farm; later, scratters were powered, via a belt drive, first by steam engine and then tractor. You can watch a steam-powered scratter in action at New Forest Cider.

Mills like this were used for centuries, especially in The Three Counties. You can still find them in use here and there.

TAXING TIMES

Excise duty was imposed on cider for the first time in 1643, making it a possible, if unlikely, cause of the English Civil War, but nobody collected it with much enthusiasm. This situation continued until 1763 when the prime minister, Lord Bute, announced a Bill that raised the tax to ten shillings per hogshead. He needed the cash to pay for the Seven Years' War, which had proved an expensive victory.

Cider was still enjoying its Golden Age and the tax was resisted by an army of noblemen, clerics and farmers, who published all manner of lampoons and broadsheets portraying Bute as a Scottish tyrant. Protesters objected particularly to the inspection regime threatened by the Bill and William Pitt the Elder joined in the fun, invoking the ancient legal principle that an Englishman's home is his castle saying: "The poorest man may in his cottage bid defiance to all the forces of the crown. It may be frail – its roof may shake – the wind may blow through it – the storm may enter – the rain may enter – but the King of England cannot enter." Bute resigned but the Bill was pushed through by his successor, only to be repealed in 1766.

"Rejoice! Here's welcome News, Come let us merry be,
King George, our gracious King, in his great Clemency,
So kindly has consented his Subjects' Wants to ease,
By taking off the Cider Tax, which does the Kingdom please"

There was even better news in 1830, when the government of Lord Wellington repealed all taxes on cider. During World War I the exchequer again turned to the nation's cider presses as a source of income, but taxation was stopped in 1923. For fifty glorious years cidermakers were untroubled by government, but in 1976 Chancellor Dennis Healey spotted a source of revenue – all too scarce in those cash-strapped times – and pounced. Since then the tax on cider and perry has remained in place, strongly influencing the development of the industry.

Known as the Cider Monument, the Burton Pynsent Monument commemorates a gift of land from a Somerset landowner to William Pitt the Elder, opponent of the 18th century cider tax.

Tax and the Cider Industry

A cidermaker is allowed to produce up to 70 hectolitres (1539 gallons) in any twelve-month period, tax-free, but go over the limit and the whole output is taxable.

Mr Healey's intervention had a disastrous effect on the industry, which flatlined for several years. It had just started to pick up when, in 1984, the Tories raised the rate of duty, sending cidermaking into decline for the rest of the decade. Further rises have followed, culminating in the spring of 2010 with a proposed hike of around 14% by the Labour government. The proposal led to a torrent of protest, as journalists and Tory politicians evoked the spirit of 1763. By the beginning of May, a Facebook group launched in response to the proposed tax had 57,000 members, and cider producers were enjoying a surge in popularity not unlike the famous Magners effect of 2005/6. The tax increase was temporarily shelved, but at the time of writing it seems likely that duty will increase over the coming years.

Promoters of artisan cider and perry find themselves with a problem. After all, the poor reputation of cider rests on its popularity among street ranters and cider punks, and this in turn is down to the low duty levels that make cider cheaper than lager of equivalent strength. Raise the duty rate and the big cider companies would stop selling huge plastic containers of cut-price death juice. But how to protect the small-scale or artisan producers? Could it be that our obsession with alcoholic strength is the root of the problem? Some propose to tax cider on the basis of its juice content but how do you test juice content? Any such test would be based on certain bio-chemical markers that the tester would look for, and any large-scale cidermaker would be able to alter the make-up of their cider to ensure the right result…

We don't want to see the removal of the 7000l exemption, or even its replacement by a 0% band. Once the principle of levying duty on all cider is in place, it will only be a matter of time before that 0% becomes 1% and so on. The flowering of craft cidermaking explored in this book would never have happened without the exemption, and only the most short-sighted or health-obsessed of governments would seek to remove it.

A SHORT HISTORY OF BULMERS

As a boy HP (Percy) Bulmer suffered from asthma and couldn't go to school. Unqualified for any profession, he decided to set up in business – something to do with eating or drinking, his mother suggested, 'because neither ever go out of fashion'. Well, it happened that his father, Rev CH Bulmer of Credenhill, Hereford was a great friend of Dr Hogg, editor of *The Herefordshire Pomona*, and had himself written substantial chunks of the magnificent book.

So, in 1887, Percy Bulmer hitched up a pony, Tommy, to his neighbour's stone mill and made around 4,000 gallons of cider, filtering the finished product through cloth bags and bottling it. His brother Fred – a Cambridge graduate – abandoned his ambition to become a teacher and joined him in the business, and, with a loan from their father, they bought a plot on Ryelands St, Hereford, and set about increasing production. In June 1889 the budding cidermakers won several prizes at the Royal Agricultural Show held in Windsor Great Park, but it was by no means obvious what they should do next.

The story of the next twenty years is instructive for any would-be cidermaker. At the time the cider industry was at a low ebb, with production and consumption a small-scale West Country affair. There was no specialised equipment to be had, nor, more importantly, was there much of a market for cider. Fred Bulmer embarked on a national sales tour that took him from 'the Isle of Wight to Dundee', and discovered a nation so ignorant of cider that many people didn't know what it was. With no budget for advertising, the brothers instead wrote booklets describing their business and products and sent these to potential customers in the drinks trade, slowly building up a list of

Percy Bulmer started making cider in 1887.

The Cider Monument

High above the village of Curry Rivel stands a tall column, dedicated to the memory of Sir William Pynsent. Pynsent was a highly successful businessman in the thriving Somerset cider trade. He was of course vigorously opposed to the 1763 Cider Bill, and was so grateful for the support of William Pitt the Elder that he changed his will, and left the Burton Pynsent estate to Pitt. When Pynsent died in 1765, his relatives were shocked to find they had been left with only a thousand guineas each. They contested the will, but failed in their challenge, and Pitt became the new owner of the Burton Pynsent estate. He commissioned Capability Brown to design the monument to remember Pynsent; local builder Philip Pear took care of the construction.

some 20,000 clients scattered around the country; not long afterwards they hired a professional salesman.

A similar DIY approach was needed in the cidermaking. With no equipment to be had locally, Bulmers went looking in France and in 1890 brought back a mill and press – in fact a wine press and not particularly suited to apples. In 1891 the brothers hired an ancient Clayton & Shuttleworth steam engine, which had been used to drive threshing machines; two more presses were added the following year, one a 17-ton monster from a candle factory.

Surrounded by expert pomologists as they were, it's no surprise that the brothers began experimenting early on with apple varieties, planting their own orchard with useful-looking trees then contracting local growers to plant the best varieties. By the 1920s Herefordshire orchards were dominated by Bulmers' favourites, apples like Brown Snout, Bulmer's Norman and Michelin.

The Bulmer brothers' capacity for learning was seemingly endless. After a failure in the Herefordshire apple crop in 1890 forced them to buy in overpriced Somerset fruit, they experimented with bulk storage of cider – a process that culminated in 1975 with the construction of the world's largest alcoholic drink container – their 1.6 million gallon Strongbow tank. And they would talk to the most unlikely people in the continual search for new ideas. On a visit to a German sugarbeet factory, for example, they saw how beets were floated to the mill along water-filled channels, being washed in the process. Couldn't the same be done with apples?

On the same trip they also learnt how pomace could be dried and processed for cattle feed. Later dried pomace was used to make pectin (the stuff that makes jam solid), and Bulmers became one of the world's biggest players in pectin production (try saying that after a few jars). This ability to adapt and evolve saw the company through more than a century of growth. In 1919 carbonation was introduced, and a few years later Woodpecker began rolling off the production line in new screw-topped flagons. Fred Bulmer had always been concerned for workers' rights and, as the business grew, the family kept ahead of national developments in staff welfare, implementing pension schemes and building houses and sports facilities. During World War II staff were fed

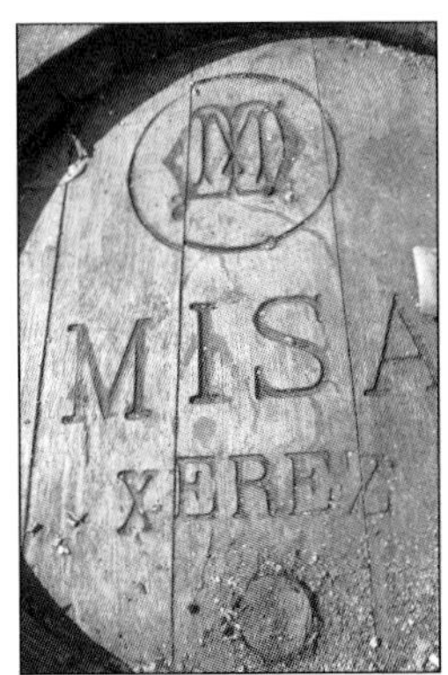

Sherry and whisky barrels have been recycled by cidermakers for centuries.

After World War II Bulmers bought out many of its competitors.

CHAMPAGNE CIDER

FOR MOST OF THE 20TH CENTURY CIDERMAKERS SOLD CHAMPAGNE CIDER. NOT ANY MORE...

When the Bulmer brothers were laying the foundations of their empire they looked to France for help and guidance. They had once bought a corking machine from a company called Taillard, in Epernay, and Percy Bulmer went there and introduced himself to the boss. He in turn introduced Percy to a champagne maker called Desmonet, who showed no hesitation in showing the Herefordshire lad how champagne was made. By 1906 the company was making its own champagne cider, which was relaunched in 1916 as Pomagne. Other makers followed suit, with Clapps of Baltonsborough marketing their wonderfully-named Avalagne – Champagne of Avalon – and several Devon-based companies selling similar products.

But Bulmers remained the biggest producer. For more than half a century Hereford supplied the world with champagne cider, until, in 1974, champagne maker Bollinger took the company to court over their use of the c-word. Bulmers won, but stopped making Pomagne, aware perhaps that it was only a matter of time before the EEC made Champagne a protected geographical designation.

Considering the history of cider's Golden Age, there was a certain irony in this legal battle and the decisions that followed. In his book *Ciderland* James Crowden lays out detailed evidence and arguments to support the claim that the method legally owned by a French winemaking region was in fact invented in the Three Counties. But we let it go somewhere along the line and, besides, Scudamore and co. didn't call their revolutionary sparkling beverage 'champagne', which is what the fuss is all about.

So from the late 1970s onwards, cidermakers started referring to their bottle-fermented products as 'Traditional Method', which is the permitted Euro-term for non-Champagne champagne-style drinks. And during the late 1980s and early 1990s several makers saw the growing popularity of sparkling wines and set about creating new ciders in this vein. Alex Hill of Vigo was one, and Julian Temperley another.

Julian had set himself the challenge of recreating the Golden Age of Cider in modern Somerset, and achieved a measure of success when critic Jilly Goolden took a sip of his Kingston Black bottle-fermented cider on the BBC's Food and Drink programme and cried, "This has got muscles, this has got brawn, I think it's gorgeous."

But the celebrations at Pass Vale Farm were short-lived. Back in 1996 the Tory government had been threatened with infraction proceedings by the European Commission, because the duty on domestic bottle-fermented cider was considerably less than that on imported sparkling wine of comparable strength – this, in the EC's opinion, constituted protectionism in breach of Article 95 of the Treaty of Rome. The Treasury leapt into action. Working alongside the NACM, it began realigning the duty rates, and the Blair administration carried on the good work. The result? In the 1999 Budget the duty on sparkling wine was reduced by 20 per cent, while on bottle-fermented cider it was increased by 20 per cent.

Protest in the House of Commons was brushed away by Lord McIntosh of Haringey:

"There are fewer than 30 producers of bottle fermented sparkling cider. Of those, 15 are exempt from the measure because their output per annum is too small; bottle fermented sparkling cider represents a small proportion of the total output of the remainder. I am sorry for the individuals concerned but this is hardly an industry of the kind that merits the massive attention which the DTI gives to industry throughout the country."

Well, it's good to know where you stand, isn't it? So now we're awash in cheap Cava and Prosecco, and bottle-fermented cider remains a treat.

at the works canteen. As a business, however, Bulmers was a ruthless competitor, and after the war the Hereford company set about swallowing its rivals. In 1948 it acquired Godwins Cider of Hereford, intending to market its Golden Godwin perry as a rival to Babycham, and also took over the Gloucestershire Cider Company. Other takeovers followed, among them WM Evans in 1960, Symonds Cider (makers of Scrumpy Jack) in 1988 and Inch's (of White Lightning fame) in 1996. Flotation on the stock exchange in 1970 preceded three decades of growth, until, by 2001, the company had a multiplicity of interests not only at home but also in Australia, China, South Africa, and elsewhere.

It was too much. The following September the company's share price collapsed. A quarter of the firm's Hereford employees were laid off, the Australian business was sold, and in 2003 HP Bulmer was finally taken over by a rival firm: Scottish and Newcastle. Which was in turn taken over by Carlsberg and Heineken.

Launched in 1960, Strongbow is named after the Norman knight Richard de Clare, Earl of Pembroke, who was nicknamed Strongbow after his feats with the longbow. With this kind of pedigree it isn't surprising that

The ladder has always been one of the essential items of equipment for the cidermaker. Picture courtesy of Minsterworth Community History Project).

Loading a wagon with apples. You can see wagons like this at Perry's Cider in Dowlish Wake.

Strongbow walloped rivals Dry Blackthorn and Merrydown, to become the world's best-selling cider – and the tramp's friend. Despite the recent success of Magners, Strongbow remains by far the most popular cider, accounting for three out of every five pints of cider consumed in UK pubs. Since 2002, apparently, the consumption of Strongbow from giant plastic bottles has declined, and people are buying cans instead. So what are the street ranters drinking for breakfast now?

A refined drink for ladies...

The nation's most popular cider is exported all over the world.

LONG ASHTON

Agricultural recession traditionally gives a fillip to cidermaking. In the late 19th century the British countryside was in the grip of a profound slump caused by the importation of cheap food from the Empire and America, and sure enough a cider revival began.

In Herefordshire Henry Weston began pressing apples commercially in 1880, and seven years later Percy Bulmer's works produced its first 4000 gallons of bottled cider. Between times the glorious *Herefordshire Pomona* was published – a massive two-volume affair that included not only illustrated descriptions of numerous fruit varieties but also essays celebrating the Golden Age of Cyder.

French cidermaking was also undergoing a renaissance, introducing new scientific principles and practices – in particular the analysis of different apple varieties. In Somerset, by contrast, cider was still being made with the bare minimum of science for local consumption, and with the passing of the Truck Acts and shrinking of the rural workforce, it seemed that Somerset was in danger of missing an opportunity to improve standards and tap the markets revealed by Bulmers.

This was certainly the opinion of Sir Robert Neville Grenville, Squire of Butleigh Court in the rich cider country south of Glastonbury. A man of his time, Grenville trundled around the lanes in a steam-powered car of his own invention, and in 1893 he turned his attention to cider. With the help of London-based analyst FJ Lloyd he collected examples of local cider apples, and began subjecting them to rigorous scientific study. For the first time the sugar content, acidity, tannin levels and other characteristics of farmhouse cider apples were assessed and tabulated, and the information used to improve cider quality.

After ten years the Board of Agriculture agreed that this valuable work needed a permanent home, and so the National Fruit and Cider Institute was established in Long Ashton near Bristol in 1903, on land leased from Lady Smyth, owner of the Ashton Court Estate. Cambridge man BTP Barker was put in charge (no first names in those days) and a cider house built. Working on the premise that you can't test cider apples without testing cider, an annual tasting day was inaugurated in 1907; by the 1930s it had become one of the major booze-ups of the Somerset calendar, attracting a thousand cider-lovers at a time, and in the meantime cidermaking had been transformed from a haphazard farmhouse affair into a major industry run on rigorous scientific principles. Working closely with the county's senior producers, and under the auspices of Bristol University, Barker analysed over 2000 apple varieties, promoting a number as vintage varieties and dividing them into the categories of sweet, sharp, bittersweet and bittersharp (see 'Apple Varieties' section). He also set out recommendations on everything from orchard management to cider house hygiene, and in doing so inspired a renaissance in Somerset cidermaking.

Redvers Coate worked for a year at Long Ashton before setting up his cider works in nearby Nailsea in the 1920s,

The *Herefordshire Pomona* celebrated the cider apple and helped launch a Victorian cider renaissance.

Cidermakers In The Dock

Everyone's heard of Bulmers, the Tesco of English cider, but fewer people knew the name Aston Manor until the summer of 2003 when Michael Hancocks, a 63-year old shareholder in the company, was tried for a dastardly cider-related crime.

Bulmers make Scrumpy Jack, a world-renowned brand. Aston Manor make Frosty Jack's. Enough said. But Hancocks bore a grudge against his successful competitor, so serious a grudge that he launched an extraordinary conspiracy against the Hereford-based company. With the assistance of chemist Richard Gay he endeavoured to introduce contaminated yeasts into Bulmers' production line, but the Bulmers employee recruited as inside man shopped the crooks to the local police. The plan was to contaminate cider over a period of months in the hope that drinkers would abandon Bulmers and switch to Aston Manor; instead Hancocks was convicted of conspiracy to defraud the maker of Woodpecker and Strongbow and sentenced to eighteen months.

Not that Bulmers has led an entirely blameless existence. In 2008 the cidermaker and its water treatment company were each fined £300,000 for breaches of the Health and Safety at Work Act after a deadly outbreak of Legionnaire's disease was traced back to two cooling towers at the Hereford plant. Two people died and twenty others were seriously ill during the 2003 outbreak; oversights and corner cutting had left the cleaning of water in the towers 'woefully inadequate', the judge said. Legionella bacteria had apparently been flourishing inside the towers.

In 2006 Bulmers sold around 68 million gallons of cider, around half the total UK output.

LONG ASHTON

NICK BRADSTOCK RECALLS WORKING AT LONG ASHTON RESEARCH STATION IN THE SIXTIES...

It was a very callow youth who would take the bus from Hotwells to the 'Cider Institute' in Long Ashton, just outside Bristol virtually every morning from the autumn of 1966 to late spring 1967. A shilling each way carried me into a world apart – from what I later recognised as the usual research station and from the world at Taunton Cider where, straight from school, I had been taken on as trainee cider maker in the summer of 1965 to do my six month 'cider student' course.

They say that if you remember the 60s then you couldn't have been there, true of the world of rock 'n roll perhaps but my memories become more vivid as time advances. This course was one that, if it existed now, some people would give their eye-teeth for – a blend of the academic, the scientific, the practical and the pragmatic, just like a well-made cider really. Of course, I didn't recognise it as such then....

The courses were tailored to the needs of each sponsoring employer and, as in my case, most cider makers wanted to apply research to improve their ciders and perries. At that time, much was understood about growing apples and pears but not so much about the final product. Little did I know it but I was in for a crash-course in all that was good and wholesome. Six months would never be enough and the learning never stops.

My fellow student, Geoff Aldridge from Teign Cider, and I were thrown in straightaway. There was very little of the now-deemed essential course syllabus, planning and programme and a couple of interviews and discussions with our tutor, Dr Fred Beech, were enough to start the process. A voyage of discovery was beginning.

Fruit was already coming into the Cider House and the pressing need was to get it pressed. Not willy-nilly but in careful order and according to precise instructions devised as part of the research programme. Under the careful eyes of John Llewellyn, the Cider House Manager, and Jeff Williams, the Cidermaker, Geoff and I toiled manfully at the small Beares pack-press, the Alfa-Laval centrifuge and, when we were deemed sufficiently responsible – that took some time – the juice evaporator and aroma concentrator.

Pressing is dull, dirty, cold and tiring work but it's essential to have experienced it in order to understand how hard it is. Operating the centrifuge and evaporator might have been warm and comfortable by comparison but noisy, dull and still demanding. Something would always need adjusting just as one's attention wandered – very little of automatic control systems in those days.

Then there was the complementary work in the lab. Mainly getting in the way of the expert and, as I now know, world-respected food and drink scientists doing fundamentally important work with balance, flasks, petri dishes and little in the way of electronics – such wizardry that now allows almost instant answers to what 45 years ago would take perhaps days to achieve.

Names and characters from that period are worth a book in themselves but having mentioned Fred Beech, there's only room to mention his boss, Alfred Pollard who went back in direct succession to the founding cider-chemist Lloyd who in turn had done the scientific work for the man who almost single-handedly resurrected cider in the 1890s, Squire Grenville of Butleigh to whom we owe so much and the foundation of the National Fruit & Cider Institute – at Long Ashton.

by which time Taunton Cider, Thatchers, Wilkins, Clapps of Baltonsborough and Showerings were all in business.

LARS continued its pioneering work through the middle years of the century, experimenting with new apple varieties and bush orchards (which took off in a big way in the 1970s), and testing pesticides; a former milkman in the village recalls driving in the early morning through a yellow fog of poisonous chemicals. In the 1950s Professor Barker wrote a comprehensive guide to perry pears, employing the practical, no-nonsense style for which he was well known in the world of cider – no one has yet written a better one. Earlier, wartime analysis of blackcurrants had led to the invention of Ribena.

By the 1980s the role of LARS was changing, and its work on fruit and cider was greatly reduced. Takeovers and changes in direction over the following decade led to the announcement, in 1999 that it would close.

"Long Ashton has done a huge amount for the cider industry," Martin Thatcher told reporters at the time. "They developed a lot of the techniques that are used today in cidermaking. They helped to work out what made the cider really good, batch after batch."

Today the orchards are gone, and one of the county's least sympathetic housing developments stands in their place, the odd pear tree and some nostalgic road names the only clue to the past. Actually that's not quite true. Liz Copas, who worked for many years as a pomologist at LARS before moving on to work for the National Association of Cider Makers, poured her great knowledge of cider varieties into a beautiful and informative 2001 book, *A Somerset Pomona*, which should be in the bookshelf of every cider lover.

French winemakers helped Bulmers when they first started making champagne cider – and thought nothing of them using the name.

Coates was a household name in the 1960s.

CIDER TRUCK

A FARM LABOURER IN THE 1850S MIGHT BE PAID 15 PER CENT OF THEIR WAGES IN CIDER...

It may sound like the delivery service we've been waiting for, but Cider Truck was once an integral part of working life in the countryside. With the Enclosures Acts of the eighteenth century the loss of common land meant that many agricultural workers had no way of growing their own food, and became reliant on the farms that employed them for sustenance.

This situation suited farmers nicely, since they could pay their workforce mostly in kind (bread, cheese, beer or cider) and give them only a pittance in cash. In 1796, William Marshall surveyed the state of agriculture in Gloucestershire and had this to say about the county's labourers:

Their wages are very low, in money; being only 1shilling a day. But, in drink, shamefully exorbitant. Six quarts a day, the common allowance: frequently two gallons: sometimes nine or ten quarts; or an unlimited quantity.

He noted that this worked in the farmers' interests if there was a good apple crop and plentiful cider, but not if the crop failed and employers were forced to shell out on malt and hops for beer. Unsurprisingly, no one took much notice, and fifty years on there was hardly a farm in England that didn't have a cider orchard attached. According to the Journal of the Royal Agricultural Society in 1843:

The advantage of an orchard upon a farm of sufficient size for the supply of cider for the labourers and for the use of the farmer's family is so generally appreciated in certain districts as to be thought almost an indispensable appendage... In the expressive language of the farmer it yields a harvest without a seed-time.

While this might conjure images of bucolic, cider-supping yokels, the reality of men, women and children all imbibing large volumes of cider as part of their wages did not please the reformers of the day, and after decades of campaigning, Cider Truck was outlawed in 1887. By this time the rural workforce was shrinking and machinery becoming more common, more complicated and, potentially, more dangerous, and gradually the farm orchards declined and died out.

Not that anyone in Somerset took much notice of the new law. Within living memory the cider house was a central feature of many farms; a frequent visitor like the postman would have his own mug, hanging from a nail beside the tapped barrel. Julian Temperley remembers a workforce that was still powered by cider. In his youth, if you wanted a hedge cutting you sent a man out with a billhook and a gallon of cider.

Once a vital part of the agricultural economy (a worker in 1850 consumed around 15% of his wages in cider), the farm cider orchard became redundant after World War Two. Around Somerset you can still see these orchards, usually covering less than five acres and dotted with old, mistletoe-covered and bramble-bounded trees, connected to the nearest farm buildings by a well-used track.

Ten years ago it looked as though these orchards would soon disappear through neglect – an apple tree only lives 80 years or so – but the revival of interest in cidermaking is having a knock-on effect as people replant old orchards with new trees. Once again villages are coming together around the cider press, particularly in west Dorset where the Powerstock Festival has inspired a host of community cider clubs, only people are now doing it for pleasure, not as part of a dubious pay deal.

CIDER & PERRY THROUGH HISTORY

THE EARLY YEARS As the first human settlers migrate across Europe they eat whatever they can lay their hands on, including crab apples. By the Iron Age crab apples are being cooked, dried and – who knows? – perhaps fermented.

55AD The Romans arrive in Britain, bringing the tools and skills to plant orchards and vineyards. They're not cider drinkers, however.

500AD St Guenole of Brittany chastises himself by living on a diet of water and perry. Really hard monks lived on perry alone.

600AD Thierry II, King of Burgundy and Orleans, serves Normandy cider to St Columbanus.

800AD Charlemagne orders that apples and pears be planted across his European empire. Each of his estates must retain skilled brewers to make not only ale but also perry and pomacium – a form of cider.

C11th

1014 First written record of cider making in the Basque country.

1066 The Normans come ashore in Sussex, which is bad news for King Harold but good news for cider lovers as they bring with them specialised cider apple varieties like Pearmain.

1080 Ibn Bassal, Moorish superintendent of Toledo in Spain, writes a Book of Agriculture, with sections on orchard skills like pruning and grafting.

1098 Foundation of the Cistercian Order, which values manual labour and cultivation. Fruit-growing and related activities like cidermaking become popular and widespread over the next two hundred years.

C12th

1100 The Basques of northern Spain and southwestern France have a well-established tradition of cider making.

1184 Glastonbury Abbey is ravaged by fire, which destroys the internationally famous Old Church and puts a big dent in the abbot's finances.

1190 Six years later, monks at Glastonbury Abbey 'find' the tomb of King Arthur, confirming the link between the Somerset town and the magical Avalon – or Isle of Apples. A boom in tourism sorts out the abbot's cash-flow problems. Today an orchard of top cider varieties grows near the site, as it has throughout most of the intervening centuries.

C13th

1212 Battle Abbey is making a profit from sales of cider, proving that the Norman Invasion is A Good Thing.

1230 A royal charter lists cider presses as a source of income for Bishop Jocelin of Bath. Records from across southern England suggest that the cider press is now a common feature of monastic life.

1260 Orchards and cider making mentioned in the parish records of Woolaston in west Gloucestershire.

1270 Large quantities of Normandy cider are being shipped to Winchelsea.

1299 The manor of Runham in Norfolk pays taxes to Edward I in the form of 'wine made of pearmains'.

C16th

1500 onwards Cider production in the South Hams region of Devon takes off, as trans-Atlantic sailors and travellers use cider as a remedy for scurvy.

History

1530s Henry VIII declares war on the monasteries. Centuries of expertise is lost, and the elderly Abbot Whyting of Glastonbury is brutally executed at the summit of the Tor. On the bright side, the gluttonous monarch uses some of his ill-gotten gains to send Royal fruiterer Richard Harris on a Continental spending spree. He comes home with a great store of graftes, especially pippins.

1553 Gilles de Gouberville distils cider and writes about it in his diary – the first mention of the Norman spirit now known as Calvados.

1588 Julian Le Paulmier, physician to French king Charles IX, writes a book praising the medicinal qualities of cider.

C17th **1615** Fear over the nation's timber supply – or greed, it depends who you ask – leads James I to ban the use of wood as a fuel for glass making. Experiments with coal lead to the invention of bottle glass.

1630s Viscount Scudamore returns from the French court with the Redstreak apple, which thrives on his estate at Kingston Lacy. Redstreak Cyder is born. Meanwhile, Louis XIII of France imposes crippling taxes on wine. In Normandy, vineyards are pulled up and replaced by orchards.

1643 A tax is imposed on English cider, but rarely collected

1650 Fruit experts appeal to Oliver Cromwell for state aid in a national scheme for the planting of fruit trees. The Golden Age of Cyder is in full swing, and the fermented juice of the apple is touted as a solution to problems as diverse as the shortage of bark for tanning and the unhealthy effects of drinking too much ale. The Puritans may have been cultural killjoys, but they did enjoy their cider.

1660 After the upheavals of the Civil War and the Commonwealth, the Restoration of Charles II brings an upsurge of interest in husbandry and gardening. When John Evelyn publishes the second edition of *'Silva'*, his jaw-dropping book on forestry, he adds a companion volume, *'Pomona'*, which promotes cider as an alternative to wine. John Worlidge patents the Ingenio, the world's first scratter.

1676 John Worlidge publishes *'Vinetum Britannicum'*, the first comprehensive guide for cider makers. It is now every gentleman's patriotic duty to drink English cider rather than imported wine. The 2nd edition of 1678 includes the first mention of distilled cider by an English writer.

1685 The Duke of Monmouth's Rebellion culminates in the disastrous Battle of Sedgemoor. 150 Somerset people are executed and hundreds of others are transported to the Americas.

1696 Cider is booming. Bristol, Gloucester and Newnham-on-Severn have eleven glass bottle manufactories between them; there are only nine in London.

1697 Celia Fiennes travels through Somerset, noting the fruitfulness of the orchards. She isn't too impressed with the cider, though, writing: 'In most parts of Somersetshire it is very fruitfull for Orchards, plenty of apples and peares, but they are not curious in the Planting the best sort of fruite which is a great pitty, being so soone produced and such quantetyes, they are likewise as careless when they make cider – they press all sorts of Apples together, else they might have as good sider as in any other parts, even as good as the Herrifordshire – they make great quantetyes of Cider, their presses are very large, so as I have seen a Cheese as they call them which yielded 2 hoddsheads – they pound their apples, then lay fresh straw on the press, and on that a good lay off Pulp of the apples, then turne in the ends of the straw over it all round and lay fresh straw, then more apples up to the top.'

C18th **1708** Following the example of his famous uncle, John Milton, John Philips writes Cyder, an epic poem that combines nationalist sabre-rattling with practical advice for the cider maker. Adge Cutler he is not.

1718 Earliest record of the Hagloe Crab, a fine Gloucestershire cider apple.

1725 Clement Chevalier inherits Aspall Hall Farm in Suffolk and begins making cider.

Aspalls remains an independent cider maker today.

1727 Symonds Cider founded. It will remain in family ownership until 1984, when it is bought by Bulmers. Their Scrumpy Jack cider is still sold today, though it isn't quite what it was.

1743 James Lind, ship's surgeon, demonstrates that cider is a remedy against scurvy. Not as effective as lemons, but a lot more fun.

1754 Ellis's *Compleat Cyderman* confirms that cider is the antidote to gout and scurvy, "our reigning British disease".

1750s Enclosures Acts make landless labourers increasingly reliant on farmers for employment and sustenance. It becomes the norm for farmers to pay workers in kind, and cider orchards spring up on farms across England and Wales.

1763 A new tax on cider provokes widespread demonstrations. Its Scottish promoter, Lord Bute, is burnt in effigy. Not for the first time, government policy has a less than happy effect on the cider industry, which goes into long-term decline. The tax is repealed in 1766.

C19th

1805 The Napoleonic Wars disrupt the wine trade and encourage a boom in perry. Many surviving perry pear trees date from this period.

1820s Parson Thomas Cornish starts making cider at Heathfield Rectory near Taunton, Somerset.

1830 Lord Wellington revokes all taxes on cider. He remains a national hero to this day.

1839 270,000 gallons of cider exported from Jersey to England. By the end of the century,

Devonshire Colic

The people of Devon suffered in the 17th and 18th centuries from a peculiar illness. This sickness, the symptoms of which included dreadful stomach pains, cold sweats, nausea, paralysis and sometimes death, struck at times when cider was drunk in the largest quantities – at harvest particularly – and it affected the heaviest drinkers the worst.

Known as Devonshire Colic, the sickness was thought by doctors to be caused by the rough, acid quality of the cider. Then George Baker, a physician from the famous cider making region of South Hams, noticed the above symptoms were similar to those of lead poisoning, and analysis of samples showed that the cider was in fact contaminated with lead. But where had it come from, and why was it only a problem in Devon?

At the time apples were usually crushed before pressing in a circular stone mill, powered by a horse. In other counties these mills were made from stone hard enough to withstand acidic apple juice but soft enough to carve whole from the quarry face, but in Devon the native granite was far harder to work; mills had to be assembled from blocks of stone and the gaps filled with lead. Acids in the apple juice reacted with the metal to form poisonous acetate of lead, which was imbibed with every hearty draught.

In 1767 Baker published his results, causing an uproar in his home county, where cider makers refused to accept that they had been poisoning drinkers for a century or more. At the time South Hams cidermakers had a lucrative business curing sailors and other travellers who arrived in Plymouth suffering from scurvy, so they were unlikely to admit their guilt. But once lead was removed from cidermaking equipment Devon Colic became so rare that an incident in January 1864 made The Times:

A fine young labouring man, named George Foxall, has just died at Powick, Worcestershire, from the effects of cider, which had been poisoned, as it is believed, by having been made in a mill which had been repaired with lead, and in which the liquor had been left standing.

The young man was employed by Mr Pullen, a farmer, and from him had a daily allowance of cider. He drank the poisoned cider on a Wednesday, took to his bed with stomach pains the next day, and died the following Tuesday, in great torment.

WALTER RAYMOND ON CIDER

'WHEN THERE IS TOO MUCH MIRTH IN THE BARREL, THE CIDER MUST BE RACKED...'

Not everyone agreed that Somerset cidermaking needed to be rescued by scientists to prevent it sliding into extinction. Countryside chronicler Walter Raymond expressed a view that was probably shared by many – only these weren't the people writing letters to *The Times*... In 1907 in '*The Book of Crafts and Character*' he describes the old and new ways of making cider, and it's fairly clear which he prefers from the following extract...

My friend Farmer John Buck prefers the good old way. Cider-making in the old way has little science, but abounds with picture-making subjects. Wagon-loads of fruit of all colours from pale yellow to deep purple are hauled into the farmyard and up to the 'pound-house' door. Within is the mill to grind the apples, and outside an old horse plods round and round unceasingly to turn the mill. The ground apples are called 'pummy'.

This pomace after standing a few hours is taken to the press – a quaint old machine, with a screw and sockets to take a bar, like a capstan. There it is put up between layers of straw, and as much as the press can take at one time is called a 'cheese'. the bar is turned until the press creaks. The sweet juice drips into the trough below, and the heavy, acid, yet sugary smell of it fills the air. As, under pressure, the cheese protrudes, the sides are sliced off and piled upon the top, until at last, when squeezed dry, it has diminished to one-quarter of the original 'pummy'.

The new cider is put in butts; and then follows always a doubtful time, for fermentation must not be too rapid. 'There's nothen like a vrost at the right moment' is a maxim with Farmer John Buck. And a lucky frost is certainly a wonderfully fine cider-maker. Without it a good cider-maker must be forever putting his ear against the stave to listen.

Is the ferment humming, or singing, or roaring?

When there is too much mirth in the barrel the cider must be racked – that is, drawn off at once. Thus fermentation is stopped and has to start again. Oceans of excellent cider have been made in this way.

'Zo a drop o' good cider won't do us no harm.'

But in the new way a great deal more care is taken. The apples are selected with care and scientifically blended, the juice of all the best varieties having been analysed. The fruit is never allowed to lie on the ground, is crushed by steam between bell-metal crushers, and horse-hair cloths have replaced the old layers of straw. The pomace never stands, but passes straight out of the mill into an hydraulic press which drains it at once to the last drop. The juice runs away into keeving barrels, in which fermentation can be scientifically regulated.

Then it is racked into pipes of large dimensions. Last of all it is filtered through sterilised cotton pulp, from which it runs out fine in colour and uniform in character. There are brands fruity or dry, according to the apples used, and the manufacture is so exact that their qualities scarcely vary at all. Some are used for bottling, and the sparkle is quite natural.

This filtered cider is said to be most useful to persons with a tendency to gout or rheumatism. Farmer John Buck declares that it has not the strength of the old-fashioned make. He says a bucketful would never go up into any man's head.

But what of that? Very soon, like the rest of us, the total abstainers will be hilariously singing:

'Zo a drop o' good cider won't do us no harm.'

exports from the Channel Islands slump in the face of home-grown competition.

1870-1900 As disease ravages French vineyards, cider production quadruples. In Paris, cider is drunk in preference to wine.

1880 Henry Weston starts making cider commercially at Bounds Farm, Much Marcle, Herefordshire. Westons continues to trade as an independent business.

1885 The Herefordshire Pomona, edited by Dr Robert Hogg, is published by the Woolhope Naturalists' Field Club. Only 600 copies are printed.

1887 The last of several Truck Acts outlaws the payment of wages in cider. In Somerset nobody takes much notice. In Hereford, meanwhile, Percy Bulmer follows his mother's advice to start a business relating to food or drink, as they 'don't go out of fashion'. The first 4000 gallons of Bulmers cider are made, filtered and bottled.

1891 The Whiteway family starts making cider at Whimple, near Exeter.

1893 Robert Neville Grenville of Butleigh Court, Somerset, enlists the help of chemist FP Lloyd and begins studying Somerset cider.

C20th **1903** Grenville's work leads to the foundation of the National Fruit and Cider Institute at Long Ashton, just outside Bristol. This will become the Long Ashton Research Station. Over the next few years the juice of over 2000 apples will be analysed, and defined as bittersharp, bittersweet and so on.

1904 Thatchers cider begins production. A century later the company makes the widest range of ciders you can imagine.

1906 Bulmers starts to produce champagne cider, marketed under the name of Cider De Luxe until 1916, when it is cunningly renamed Pomagne.

1911 Arthur Moore, the Spurways' cider maker, leaves Heathfield and joins forces with George Pallet in a new venture at Norton Fitzwarren, near Taunton. Three years later the Heathfield Cider House closes its doors.

1917 Roger Wilkins' grandfather moves up from the Moor to Lands End Farm, Mudgley, nr Wedmore, and begins making cider.

1920 The National Association of Cider Makers is founded.

1920s Breweries gradually take control of pubs via the 'tied house' system. Prevented from supplying their local pubs, many small-scale cidermakers go out of business.

1921 Perrys Cider founded by blacksmith Bill Churchill. Moore and Pallet's business in Norton Fitzwarren is launched as Taunton Cider.

1924 Redvers Coate works at the Long Ashton Research Station, then borrows money to open a cider works in Nailsea.

1930s In partnership with Bulmers, William Magner starts making cider in Clonmel, calling the brand Bulmers. Just to confuse us, it will later be sold in the UK as Magners.

1939-45 As in the Great War, wartime grain shortages limit beer production. People drink cider instead.

1950s Long Ashton Research Station experimenting with bush orchards. Fearing grain shortages, both the French and British governments pay farmers to grub up orchards and plant cereals.

1953 Showerings launches its new sparkling perry, Babycham onto the national market. It enjoys spectacular success.

1956 Showerings buys Coates and moves production to Nailsea. Babycham becomes the first alcoholic drink and only the second product to be advertised on TV in Britain.

1966 Adge Cutler and the Wurzels record their first album at the Royal Oak in Nailsea, within staggering distance of Coates. The single '*Drink up thy Zider*' makes the Top 50.

1960s An academic researcher finds many farmhouse cider makers have recently ceased production – the decline in the rural workforce and introduction of tractors and other machinery are to blame.

1970s After a series of high-profile legal battles, the EEC declares that 'Champagne' refers to a region not a process. Cidermakers are no longer allowed to use the name. Babycham is unaffected, since the 'cham' is short for 'chamois', ie the adorable fawn, and has nothing whatsoever to do with sparkly French wine.

1970s French makers adopt the familiar cidre bouche style of bottle-conditioned cider.

1971 Two years after the retirement of Redvers Coate, Showerings merges with Gaymers and Whiteways. Production moves to Shepton Mallet and the Nailsea factory closes.

1974 Adge Cutler is killed in a car accident. Somerset has lost its bard.

1974 The Butchers Arms, Carhampton, threatens to cancel its annual wassail because of lack of support but doesn't. Taunton Cider holds its first wassail, which is followed by a bumper crop.

1976 Labour Chancellor Dennis Healey imposes excise duty on cider. Producers who make more than 1500 gallons a year are liable to tax. The industry immediately goes into a decline.

1980s Bulmer's has 60% of the UK cider market and is the world's second biggest producer of pectin, derived from dried pomace.

1981 Sussex farmer John Pile buys cider from Perrys and Sheppys for resale at Middle Farm, Firle. Soon after he establishes the National Collection of Cider and Perry.

1982 Alex Hill buys his first fruit press in Budapest, Hungary. A year later he imports twenty-four. Vigo Ltd will go on to supply the mills and presses of the UK's 21st century cider renaissance.

1984 Tentative signs of growth in the UK cider industry are killed off by an increase in duty.

1986 Somerset Royal Cider Brandy is founded by Julian Temperley of Burrow Hill Cider. The following year the two French alembic stills, Josephine and Fifi, are put to work.

1987 Somerset County Council launches an ambitious programme of grant aid to revive orcharding in the county. Over the next ten years 20,000 trees are planted.

1989 The Big Apple Cider and Perry Trials are launched by a group of Herefordshire producers. In 2010 there were over 180 entries.

1989 Whiteways, the famous Devon cider company, closes down. A group of former employees rescues oak vats and other equipment and begins making cider down the road. Today Green Valley Cyder is going strong.

1990 Common Ground launches Apple Day. Over the next two decades it becomes England's unofficial autumn holiday, and a campaign to make it an official holiday is gaining momentum.

1990 In Canada the first Ice Cider is made. Twenty years on there are fifty-plus producers, and one in Herefordshire – Once Upon a Tree of Putley.

1993 The Marcher Apple Network is launched.

1994 120 acres of perry pears are grubbed out at Combe Florey, Somerset, as the popularity of Babycham reaches rock bottom.

1995 Taunton Cider is taken over by Matthew Clark, which will in turn be swallowed by Constellation Europe, a division of the world's biggest booze business. Its cider 'arm' is given limited independence as Gaymers of Shepton Mallet, producer of Blackthorn, Olde English and other brands. The Norton Fitzwarren plant is closed and demolished.

1995 Bulmers buys Inch's Cider, manufacturer of White Lightning. The nation's street drinkers rejoice.

1995 The Brothers' cider bar appears for the first time at Glastonbury Festival.

HEATHFIELD RECTORY

HOW THE DRY BLACKTHORN STORY STARTED WITH A CIDERMAKING VICAR

Heathfield Rectory near Taunton: humble beginnings for a multinational company.

In the early 19th century Parson Thomas Cornish started pressing apples at Heathfield Rectory, near Taunton in Somerset, and his son, also Parson Thomas Cornish, kept up the good work. By the 1840s customers included Queen Victoria (1 hogshead prime) the Bishop of Bath and Wells (1 hogshead), and the fashionable Carlton Club in London (2 casks).

According to a Somerset cider story, the elder Parson Thomas Cornish was preaching in his pulpit one Sunday morning when the door of the church opened and a man ran in. 'Maister, the Zider do Tuzilly!' cried the man, at which the Parson sprang down from the pulpit and dashed off to the Cider House.

With this level of care the cider business prospered (history doesn't record the state of the congregation). By the end of the century the Spurway family had taken over, but in 1914 Reverend Edward Popham Spurway, the last of Heathfield's cider-making vicars, retired. The famous old casks were acquired by a local shopkeeper for rhubarb wine.

The Heathfield tradition continued, however. Three years earlier the Rectory had lost its chief cidermaker, Arthur Moore, who had set up a rival business with George Pallet in Norton Fitzwarren. After World War One this company was launched as Taunton Cider, and after World War Two it was still going strong. Keeping up with industry developments (kegs and carbonation, lorries and forklifts), Taunton bought out local rivals such as Quantock Vale and Ashford Vale, Bruttons and Horrells.

Taunton Cider ad from 1978

Arthur Moore, master cider maker, came to Taunton in 1911. I suppose you could say he's responsible for the ciders we sell today, because though old Arthur's long gone now, his art, and it is an art, remains.

Autumn Gold and Blackthorn – from The Taunton Cider Company – where I'm happy to say the cidermaker's art is still recognised.

Eventually Taunton became a victim of its own success, when its Dry Blackthorn brand achieved mass market popularity. A takeover by Matthew Clark plc, a drinks wholesaler, was followed by a move to the company's giant Shepton Mallet plant. In 1995 the Norton Fitzwarren factory closed and has since been demolished. You can still buy Taunton Traditional in some Bristol pubs, but Blackthorn is the only significant survivor.

And not even Blackthorn is sacred. In 2009 the Gaymer Cider Company (as Matthew Clark's cider division is known) canvassed drinkers and then relaunched the cider with what Gaymer called a 'slightly mellower' flavour. In the ensuing protests advertising billboards bearing the message Black is Back were altered to give a less enthusiastic message, and drinkers in Bristol switched to Other Leading Brands (we're neutral here at the Naked Guides) or even, God forbid, beer. In a final twist, Gaymer was bought by C&C, the Irish parent of Magners, who then brought the old Blackthorn back again.

What would Parson Thomas Cornish Senior make of it all?

History

1996 Under EU pressure, UK government begins the process of raising duty on Champagne-style ciders and perries to a prohibitive £2 per litre. The increase becomes law in the 1999 Budget.

1997 The Gloucestershire Orchard Group is founded.

1999 The closure of the Long Ashton Research Station is announced.

C21st **2000** The Campaign for Real Ale presents its first awards for Real Cider (Gold - Westons Old Rosie) and Perry (Gold – Dunkertons Perry)

2000 The first Chinese-made Woodpecker cider goes on sale in Shanghai and Beijing. Bulmers also has operations in the US, Australia, South Africa, New Zealand and Belgium.

2001 The first Powerstock Festival is held as a village hall fundraiser in west Dorset. It will catalyse a revival of cidermaking in the county.

2001 Michael Hancocks, a shareholder in Birmingham cider company Aston Manor, conspires with others to tamper with cider made by its rival, Bulmers.

2003 Bulmers loses its independence in a takeover by Scottish and Newcastle. It is now part of Heineken.

2003 The Long Ashton Research Station closes its doors. Its land is sold for housing.

2004/5 As the government prepares to introduce the Single Payment System for UK Farms it becomes known that orchards are not to be considered agricultural land. A campaign led by John Thatcher forces a U-turn and saves countless orchards.

2005 Three Counties Perry is added to the Slow Food Ark of Taste, one of only four UK products.

2005/6 Britain goes mad for Magners, after the Irish cider maker hits on the brilliant idea of serving cider over ice. A massive advertising campaign celebrates orchard country. Suddenly Everybody Loves Cider.

2007 The UK government recognises the value of traditional orchards as wildlife habitat. Orchards continue to be grubbed up for housing.

2008 Bulmers fined for Health and Safety lapse that caused an outbreak of Legionnaire's disease. Proving that there's something to be said for making cider on a small scale.

2009 Magners (C&C) buys Gaymers.

2009 At the Bath & West Show, Common Ground presents the first award for a cider produced by a Community Orchard.

2009 The National Trust and Natural England team up for a two-year £500,000 orchards campaign.

2010 Government plans for a hefty rise in cider duty are met by vigorous opposition, led by a Facebook protest group with over 50,000 members. The tax is shelved, but an increase remains likely.

2011 Launch of Stella Artois Cidre, accompanied by a massive and not very comprehensible advertising campaign. What's next, Le Snakebite?

2011 Reports suggest US cider sales went up 25% in 2011 – brands include Woodchuck, Strongbow, Magners, Crispin and Ace... Even better news: you can now buy The Naked Guide to Cider stateside!

2012 Westons revamp Old Rosie brand, amid concerns that 'the personality of a cider named after a steam engine was not coming through'. Surely the 7.3% alcohol helps?!

2012 A nice plug for Julian Temperley when a model of Burrow Hill, evidently built by the Teletubbies' set designer, took centre-stage at the Opening Ceremony of the London Olympics.

Q&A BILL BRADSHAW

PHOTOGRAPHER FOR THE ONGOING *IAMCIDER* PROJECT. BILL IS BASED IN LANGPORT, SOMERSET

What got you interested in cider and perry?
Apple Villages 2004, a heritage project I was involved with. I was asked to document their work and it was fantastic. That's where my journey started!

Do you have a memory of a particularly good cider or perry?
I tend to remember a different place for each cider or perry I try, depending on where exactly I was and what I was doing when I tasted it for the first time. One of my earliest cider memories was sneaking a mouthful of farmhouse out of my parents' larder when I was about 14 or 15. It was breakfast time and it tasted amazing!

What's your favourite apple variety?
I love Tremletts Bitter, I think it's a really under-rated apple for single variety ciders. Sheppys do a bottled one and I love it, it's really crisp and tasty. There's always time for a Tremletts.

If you could drink cider in any time or place, where would it be?
I would love to have a few pints with Pop Larkin on a sunny summers evening "Perfick!" (*The Darling Buds of May* by HE Bates)

What can we do to ensure that orchards are still flourishing in 50 years' time?
Educate. I think if people truly understood the magic of an orchard, the orchard year and the beauty of nature's bounty first hand, the orchards will flourish. Full Bloom/Blossom festivals, Apple Days, Wassailling etc really help. I think more people should use orchards for celebrations, they're fantastic places to celebrate whether it's a picnic or a wedding. It would be great to get people using them for pleasure more.

How do you account for the recent surge of interest in cider and cidermaking?
It's interesting, I'm very aware of cider's renaissance at the moment because I have been photographing it for a while and I've followed its rise. I suppose its a combination of things: the popularity of doing-it-yourself food and cookery, the value of provenance, crap mass produced alternatives...

Do you have any advice for the novice cidermaker?
Sterilse effectively. A lot of effort is involved in sourcing, collecting, pressing, fermenting and bottling, even for a small batch of cider. If you trip up at any stage it all becomes futile.

Can you tell us about your best and/or worst moment as a cidermaker?
The first batch I made became infected and started growing on the surface of the cider at the final stage – maturation in the bottle. I was gutted, six months wasted. It was a good lesson though, you can't be clean enough.

What,is your most precious bit of cider-related gear?
I have a decent collection of cider books that I love.

Any suggestions for ways of sorting out the duty problem?
When the Government introduced a cider tax in the 1763 there were riots in Somerset, maybe we should try that again. That'd make it topical.

Anything you would like to add?
Yes, why doesn't someone write an Enciderclopedia?

For more information on IAMCIDER, visit www.billbradshaw.co.uk

Cider Culture

Cider and perry have their own culture and traditions, drinking places, festivals and fans...

TRADITIONS AND FOLKLORE

There are as many traditions associated with cider and orchards as there are villages and towns where cider is made and drunk. Of these the best-known is wassail, the annual blessing of the apple trees which takes place, in Somerset at least, on Old Twelfth Night (January 17). We recommend Jon Dathen's book '*Somerset Cider: Folklore and Customs*' to anyone who wants to delve deeper into the subject.

A cider mug is a precious thing – and quite right too.

Spilling A Drop For Luck

Following a completely unscientific study we reckon that it's much harder to carry a full pint of cider from bar to table than it is to carry a pint of beer. In the old days cider drinkers would pour a cup onto the ground before they got started drinking, as an offering to the Earth that provided the cider, and to prevent spills.

Lazy Lawrence

In Somerset the oldest tree of the orchard is venerated as the home of the Apple Tree Man, otherwise known as Lazy Lawrence or the Colt-Pixy. It is to this tree spirit that wassailers offer their cider and toast, waking him for the new season with their pots and pans, horns and shotguns. On Sedgemoor people would place a primitive rag doll, or mommet, in an apple tree to ward off evil spirits.

In *The Golden Bough*, Sir James Frazer describes a similar French practice:

'In Beauce, in the district of Orleans, on the twenty-fourth or twenty-fifth of April they make a straw man called "the great mondard." For they say that the old mondard is now dead and it is necessary to make a new one. The straw man is carried in solemn procession up and down the village and at last is placed upon the oldest apple-tree. There he remains till the apples are gathered, when he is taken down and thrown into the water, or he is burned and his ashes cast into water. But the person who plucks the first fruit from the tree succeeds to the title of "the great mondard." Here the straw figure, called "the great mondard" and placed on the oldest apple-tree in spring, represents the spirit of the tree, who, dead in winter, revives when the apple-blossoms appear on the boughs.'

Do you know how this song goes? If you do, let us know.

Lazy Lawrence defends orchards from apple thieves in the form of a wild-eyed colt, who will chase persistent scrumpers, kicking and biting. He and his fellow pixies – orchards have more than their fair share of faerie folk – need to be looked after. In particular you should always leave a few small apples on each tree at the end of harvest. These will help orchard birds survive the winter too.

Black Rat And Cider Toad

Moles 'Black Rat' cider is named after an abiding legend, that farmers would help along a slow fermentation by adding a rat to the barrel. Some would say that you can't make proper farmhouse cider without a rodent to give the cider some body.

This may sound a bit bonkers but the tradition has some good science behind it. Wheat and barley have more often been added to give body than rat flesh, but a slow fermentation will respond to a dose of raw meat as yeast feeds on the proteins. Being highly acidic, a vat of cider will dissolve a leg of mutton or even a horse's hoof, leaving no evidence of adulteration. In a recent conversation on the Cider Workshop pages, microbiologist-cum-cidermaker Andrew Lea expressed an opinion that raw meat would indeed provide thiamin and free amino acids for the yeast to work on, and made a rough calculation of how much steak you'd need to feed a 40 gallon barrel of cider: about 6oz or, in layman's terms, a fairly measly helping.

Well, we all know that a cider barrel can hide a multitude of sins…

Another legend, which really is quite odd, involves the addition of a live toad to the vat. Supposedly the toad would swim around in the cider, which was cleansed as it passed through the creature's body, but we're left with a couple of questions. Why didn't the toad dissolve in the acid cider? Besides, would you clean something by passing it through a toad?

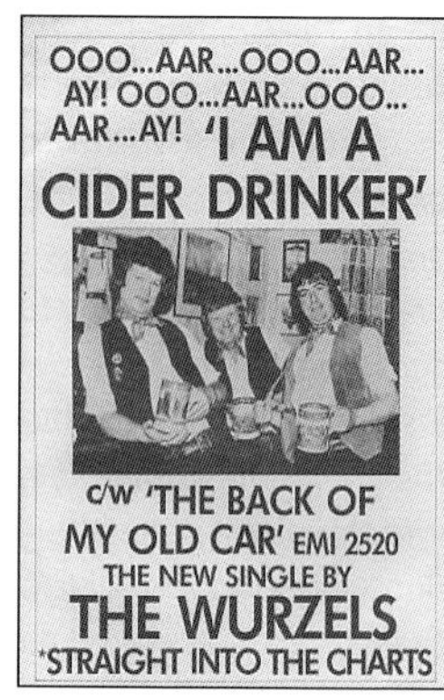

OOO...AAR...OOO...AAR...
AY! OOO...AAR...OOO...
AAR...AY! 'I AM A
CIDER DRINKER'
C/W 'THE BACK OF
MY OLD CAR' EMI 2520
THE NEW SINGLE BY
THE WURZELS
*STRAIGHT INTO THE CHARTS

Adge and the boys took on the Beatles with their first hit single.

WASSAIL

Wassail Song

Old Apple Tree we wassail thee,
And hoping thou would bear;
For the Lord doth know
Where we shall be
Till apples come again another year;
For to bear well and bloom well
So merry let us be.
Let every man take off his hat
And shout out to the old apple tree!

A Short History…

There was a time in the last century when the tradition of wassailing the apple trees came close to dying out. Nowadays wassail is an extension of the Christmas party season, and you can throw toast at apple trees at events all around Somerset and beyond. But through much of the 20th century celebrations were much more muted, with the Butchers Arms in Carhampton keeping the tradition going pretty much single-handed. And in 1974 the pub announced that it was giving up too.

The age of this peculiar winter rite varies depending on who you ask, but 'waes hael' is a Saxon expression meaning 'good health' and the habit of sharing a cup with friends and neighbours was imported by the German invaders in the 7th and 8th centuries. Before the Norman Conquest wassail was a village affair; on Christmas Eve revelers would go from house to house, entering by the front door, having a glug or two of mulled ale from a shared cup, singing, then leaving by the back. This is probably how the tradition of door-to-door carol singing got started.

When folksong collector Cecil Sharp went gathering wassail songs from around Somerset a century ago he found two dozen variations and one or two references that implied a long and unbroken history. The Curry Rivel wassail song goes like this:

Wassail! and wassail! all over the town;
The cup it is white and the ale it is brown;
The cup it is made of the good old ashen tree,
And so is the malt of the best barley.
For it's your wassail! and it's our wassail!
And it's joy be to you, and a jolly wassail!

There follow several verses imploring "Master and Missus" for bread, cheese and cider – which, in spite of the traditional reference to beer, was almost certainly the beverage on offer. Then the last verse:

The girt dog of Langport he burnt his long tail,
And this is the night we go singing wassail!
O Master and Missus, now we must be gone;
God bless all in this house till we do come again.
For it's your wassail! and it's our wassail!
And it's joy be to you, and a jolly wassail!

The two-handled cup is an important part of cider culture. Often shared between friends, it reflects the communal nature of cidermaking.

The growing popularity of wassail is a bit baffling, until you remember that it's celebrated in mid-January, when people will happily sing at trees for cider. Photo by Bill Bradshaw (billbradshaw.co.uk)

'The girt dog of Langport' refers to the Danes, who would often come up the River Parrett to attack Langport, the ancient inland port a few miles from Curry Rivel. Alfred's defeat of the Danish leader Guthrun in 878 came as a relief to the local population, who were still celebrating it a thousand years later.

Visiting wassail still takes place in Curry Rivel and in one or two other villages, but sometime during those long centuries the main focus of the ceremony shifted from village to orchard, and people began singing versions of the familiar song. When John Aubrey went traveling around England after the Civil War he described how people in the West Country 'Goe with their Wassell-bowle into the orchard and goe about the trees to bless them, and putt a piece of tost upon the roots'. It was also usual to bash pots and kettles or fire off guns, to awaken the spirits of the orchard.

They carried on doing this every year, unnoticed and unrecorded, until the 19th century, when working people moved in great numbers from country to town and all the old rural traditions began to die away. Before World War I there were a few farms around Minehead where wassail was still considered an essential part of country life; by 1920 the custom had all but disappeared and in the 1960s a researcher who traveled around Somerset interviewing farm cidermakers failed to find a single person who knew anything about wassail.

Legend has it that the Butcher's Arms kept the tradition alive through the century until, in 1974, it announced that lack of interest was forcing it to stop. Carhampton's 20 orchards had fallen into neglect and were rapidly being grubbed up, so it didn't look as though there would be anything to wassail for much longer anyway. In the end the Butcher's Arms kept on holding its annual wassail on the evening of January 17, as it still does.

A year earlier Taunton Cider had held its first wassail – which was followed by a bumper crop – starting a revival which has accelerated in the last few years. Taunton was responsible for a new addition to the wassail tradition, the choosing of a young Wassail Queen to do the toast-proffering business.

Meanwhile, there's a tradition in Bristol of banging pots and pans to celebrate the New Year. Is this a legacy

Cider culture has given us some notable artworks, such as this fine woodpecker. Must be worth at least a quid.

Back in the Golden Age of Cyder the gentry bought themselves fine cider glasses. Photo from NACM.

of wassail? Or just something that seems like a good idea after too many pints of cider?

January 17: Old Twelfth Night

As a ceremony marking the end of Christmas and looking forward to the new year, wassail was held for centuries on Twelfth Night. Then, in 1752, Britain adopted the Gregorian Calendar and the year shifted slightly so that Christmas fell eleven days earlier. Around the country most people grumbled and adapted but in Somerset there was consternation. Suppose they wassailed the apple trees on the new date and it didn't work?

There was only one way to find out, and that Christmas people travelled en masse to Glastonbury to see whether the Thorn planted by Joseph of Arimathea flowered on the new Christmas Day or the old. Not surprisingly it bloomed on the old date, and so Somerset wassail continued to be held on Old Twelfth Night.

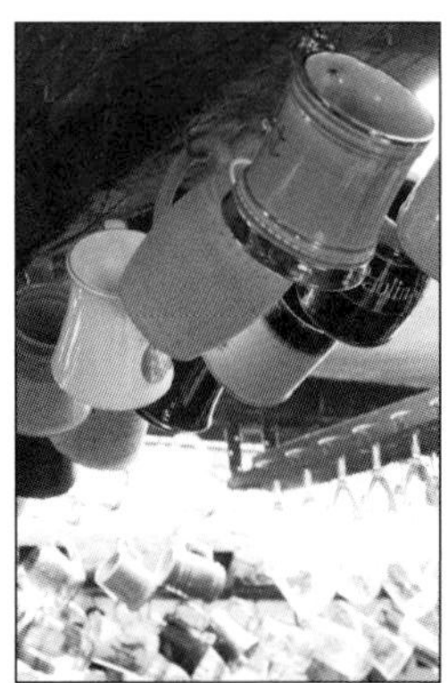

At Ye Olde Cider Bar in Newton Abbot cider mugs belonging to regulars hang above the bar...

Instant Wassail: Just Add Cider

Anyone can do it. All you need is an apple tree, a loaf of bread and a couple of friends. And some cider.

1. Make mulled cider and put in a bowl. In cases of extreme urgency, chuck cider in a pan, add gin as required and spice up with ginger.
2. Make toast.
3. Gather pots and pans, trumpets, drums – anything that makes a noise.
4. Transport the items above to the orchard.
5. Dip toast in bowl and place among branches of tree. You could send a child up the tree with the toast if you like. Or throw the toast. You're not supposed to eat it though – it's for the birds.
6. Raise bowl to senior tree and sing or chant the Wassail Song. You could walk round the tree if you like, or dance about. Whatever you like – it's your wassail!
7. Bash, blow or bang your instruments. Shout and scream. Make a real old racket.
8. Drink, pass bowl, drink some more.

Why Wassail is good science

It may sound like a lot of folkie nonsense, but there's some sound science behind wassail. OK, there's some fairly bad science as well, like the stuff about waking the spirits of the orchard, but offering cidery toast to robins and blue tits is a pretty shrewd move. In the spring these birds play a vital role in eating pests, and you want as many of them living and nesting in your orchard as possible. For the same reason it's a good idea to keep old, even dead, trees for birds to nest in.

In the old days wassail involved firing shotguns into the branches of the tree, and the great Edwardian nurseryman George Bunyard thought this slightly hazardous activity made sound sense, since gunshot wounds would encourage cankers to form in the bark of the tree, and cankers prevented the downward flow of sap from branch to trunk. More sap in the branches meant a more fruitful tree. More great cider science.

Celebrating Wassail on Old Twelfth Night. Photo by Bill Bradshaw (billbradshaw.co.uk)

TOP WASSAIL DESTINATIONS

These will vary year on year. Most take place on Old Twelfth Night (Jan 17) and support local charities. Some have limited space, so call ahead for info.

Butcher's Arms

The undisputed wassail capital of the world, this pub in Carhampton, not far from Minehead, kept the tradition alive through a long period of disinterest among the general public. They almost gave up once but kept going, and today the January festivities have acquired cult status. Unfortunately the survival of wassail has not prevented all

Wassailers At Heathfield

At the turn of the year came the wassailers. They assembled quietly outside the drawing room of the Rectory – we were never expecting them – and then their rustic songs began:

Wharton ol varmer he had an old cow
Why he didn't know 'an
So he built some barns to keep him warm
A little more zider won't do us no 'arm
Arm me boys, 'arm, 'arm me boys 'arm,
A little more zider won't do us no 'arm
The men had blackened faces: they mustn't be recognised by the spirits as they'd come to drive off the apple trees…

And so to the backyard where the cider flowed and they danced with the maids. There the songs were not quite so polite because the rector's lady wasn't present.

(Rev. Francis Edward Spurway, interviewed by the Bishop of Bath and Wells).

but one of the village's 20 orchards being grubbed up. Look out for the mulled cider made to a secret recipe that has been passed from landlord to landlord.

West Croft Farm

If you're looking for the Glastonbury, sorry, Pilton Festival of wassail then this is it. The maker of Janet's Jungle Juice has put the dark side of Brent Knoll on the winter party map with an exuberant fiesta of music, mild tree worship and cider. Expect a candlelit procession, roast hog and more.

Wilkins

Not to be outdone, Roger Wilkins has been wassailing for a decade now, with hundreds of people making their way down to Land's End Farm to bless his trusty apple trees – handy that they're just across the lane from the cider barn. Look out for Chris Jagger, brother of Mick, who often performs at Rog's shindigs.

Rich's

Has the great advantage of being the easiest to get to. Tickets are a bit pricey but you get a mug of stew to soak up the cider and proceeds go to the charity picked by the Burnham Rotary Club. The Mangledwurzels have played there in the past.

Somerset Rural Life Museum

A more genteel affair, perhaps, than some of the above, but numbers are limited and tickets tend to go quickly. In the past they've had cider and apple juice from Hecks, apple cake and a ceilidh band. A Wassail King or Queen is chosen to lead the procession by the unusual method of hiding a dry bean in a cake. Whoever gets the bean (without choking on it) does the honours.

Barrington Court

Well-known these days for its cidermaking, Barrington Court hosts a major wassail event, complete with Mummers and Morris men. Look out for curiosities like a giant wicker apple on top of the bonfire.

Thatchers holds its own wassail every year.

If there's cider to be had, the Mangledwurzels will probably be playing...

THE CIDER HOUSE

In the past the way cider was drunk reflected the way it was made. Fashionable London folk of the 1660s may have drunk their Redstreak like wine, from elegant, engraved glasses, but villagers across the West Country gathered around the barrel to share the cider they had helped to make.

The barn or shed in which the cider was stored and shared was known as the cider house, a casual, non-commercial institution that was an integral part of village life – and unknown to anyone outside the village. As industrial cidermaking took off in the last decades of Victoria's reign, draught and bottled cider was sold alongside beer in pubs around the country, and gradually the village pub replaced the cider house, even in Somerset.

For a glimpse of the old country cider house, the top destination has to be Rog Wilkins' Lounge Bar, which is a bare, draughty room adjoining the main cider barn at his farm overlooking the Somerset Levels. The place is a bit fancier these days than it used to be, with a mural of Rog decorating one wall, but the window still has no glass in it and the chairs are a mismatched assortment of office and kitchen rejects. If this is a bit disconcerting to the uninitiated, the strangest thing is the manner in which business is conducted.

When you walk in, Rog or one of his staff asks if you want Dry, Sweet or Medium, and pours you a half pint from one of three hogsheads that stand side by side in a corner of the barn.

If it's pressing time, the man himself will probably stop building a cheese, come over to pour you a drink, then go back to work, leaving you to enjoy your cider. You might be wondering how much it is, how you pay for it, how strong it is, and what happens next. By drinking your half are you signing up to some wholesale deal? This is a different world from the uniform, regulated world of the pub. Outside, across the road, you can see the trees on which the apples grew to make this cider. The barn is filled with the smell of apple juice and the racket of the mill. And the cider is being made right there, in front of you; you can see the physical effort that goes into the making.

The cider house: a place often full of boxes and cans of paint where people meet to make and to drink cider.

November is the best month to visit Rog Wilkins at Land's End Farm. The pressing is in full swing by then, although Rog starts pressing early-cropping Morgan Sweets in September. If you visit in the summer months, the experience is more of a tourist trip, with hen parties out from Bristol and families doing the Somerset tour. Go when the old boys are sat round, gossiping about village life, on a nasty afternoon in autumn or winter.

A classy example of ciderhouse interior decor. This is from West Croft Farm.

One Handle Good, Two Handles Better

The tradition of drinking from a communal bowl goes back at least to the Saxon age, when secular ceremonies of friendship and goodwill became ingrained in our culture. Perhaps the practice grew out of the need, in Medieval society, to create bonds of friendship outside the family, and it remained deeply ingrained in village life for centuries. In the 17th century it became fashionable to drink from a bowl flavoured with spices and toast – which also has a part to play in the ritual of wassail – from which derives the phrase 'making a toast'.

Shakespeare lived and worked before the Golden Age of Cyder – how differently might a cider-fuelled bard have seen the world? – but he did mention communal drinking

Owls and other vessels

There are as many kinds of cider container as there are varieties of cider, from the champagne bottle through to the no-nonsense plastic container. Today's artisan producers tend to prefer a beer bottle with a crown top, or variations on the wine bottle, but there's nothing quite like walking away from a Somerset cider barn with a gallon of nectar banging against your leg.

Once cider was sold in earthenware jars or jugs – you can buy them at junk shops and use them to clutter up the house – which have been replaced today by the brown plastic flagon.

Stone jars were popular among country workers as they kept the cider coolish, but there were numerous other vessels to be had. The most common was a small wooden barrel known as a firkin, but in the days of Cider Truck many working men swore by the hedgehog or owl. Walter Raymond, a sharp-eyed if nostalgic author of country sketches, described this in 1907:

'An 'owl' was an earthenware vessel of primitive shape, having two little ridges like epaulets upon its shoulders, with holes through which to thread a leathern thong – a good stout bootlace might sometimes serve the turn – whereby it might be hung up or carried.

"It may be this was the origin of the saying 'as drunk as an owl'... But alas! the owl is now a thing of the past.

'The last owl I ever had,' lamented an old carter as, one day at noon, he sat on the hedgerow bank and sliced a large onion with his pocket-knife, whilst the plough rested at the end of the furrow, 'got broke up twenty year agone. And he were a odd-sized owl, for he did hold vive quart."

when Puck, the wicked spirit of *A Midsummer Night's Dream*, says:

And sometime lurk I in a gossip's bowl,
In very likeness of a roasted crab,

A century later, John Philips drew a rather cosy picture of cider drinking in his epic poem, which begins with a weary farmer, exhausted after his labours, heading into the cider house...

His honest friends, at thirsty hour of Dusk,
Come uninvited; he with bounteous Hand
Imparts his smoaking Vintage, sweet Reward
Of his own Industry; the well fraught Bowl
Circles incessant, whilst the humble Cell
With quavering Laugh, and rural Jests resounds.
Ease, and Content, and undissembled Love
Shine in each Face...

It's a bit wordy, but you can picture the weary men chewing the fat while the bowl passes from hand to hand. Presumably this kind of drinking had its rules, with the cider equivalent of bogarting a joint being frowned upon.

The primitive bowl evolved over the years into the cider mug, a large two- or three-handled vessel, often decorated with cider-related images, which is shared. You can buy these cups at some of the cider company shops, and they're easy enough to find online, on eBay and elsewhere. Get one, and try sharing a cup of cider with the people you made it with.

The best ciderhouse interiors are created using those two magical ingredients, time and neglect.

Make Your Own Cider House

You'll probably have gathered by now that people hold very different views about cider and perry, but we think it's all about doing your own thing. Cider has rarely been as commercially important as beer or wine, but that's mostly because it's a drink people tend to make themselves for their own pleasure. Who knows how many groups of friends and neighbours are gathered right now in sheds and garages around the country, enjoying a cup of their own cider?

Anyone can make cider, and anyone can create a cider

house – it's just the place where your cider lives. But if you really want to get into the spirit of the thing and design something a bit more stylish (imagine one of those home improvement programmes where they have to turn a 30s semi into a mock-tudor mansion while the owner's out buying some fags) here are some tips:

- Start with a shed, garage or other form of shelter, where you store the cider while it ferments and matures.
- Display your cider with pride – up on a shelf, not hidden on the floor behind an old bike.
- Get in some chairs, not a patio set but a motley collection of discarded office chairs and hospital rejects.
- Arrange dusty old bottles, ancient garden tools, pilfered pub ashtrays, old brooms, beer crates, out-of-date trade calendars, dead bikes and suchlike to create atmosphere.
- Provide a good pile of old newspapers and magazines, the more dog-eared and mildewed the better (Wilkins has this down to a T).
- Fill your quart mug, switch off your phone, settle down and enjoy…

Cider houses often have a timeless quality. This is Brimblecombe in Devon.

Thoughts On Cider

From Christopher Middleton, A Writer in New England (C1910)

Falstaff once said that he had forgotten what the inside of a church looked like. There will come a time when many of us will perhaps have forgotten what the inside of a saloon looked like, but there will still be the consolation of the cider jug. Like the smell of roasting chestnuts and the comfortable equatorial warmth of an oyster stew, it is a consolation hard to put into words. It calls irresistibly for tobacco; in fact the true cider toper always pulls a long puff at his pipe before each drink, and blows some of the smoke into the glass so that he gulps down some of the blue reek with his draught. Just why this should be, we know not.

Also some enthusiasts insist on having small sugared cookies with their cider; others cry loudly for Reading pretzels. Some have ingenious theories about letting the jug stand, either tightly stoppered or else unstoppered, until it becomes "hard." In our experience hard cider is distressingly like drinking vinegar. We prefer it soft, with all its sweetness and the transfusing savour of the fruit animating it. At the peak of its deliciousness it has a small, airy sparkle against the roof of the mouth, a delicate tactile sensation like the feet of dancing flies. This, we presume, is the 4.5 to 7 per cent of sin with which fermented cider is credited by works of reference. There are pedants and bigots who insist that the jug must be stoppered with a corncob. For our own part, the stopper does not stay in the neck long enough after the demijohn reaches us to make it worth while worrying about this matter. Yet a nice attention to detail may prove that the cob has some secret affinity with cider, for a Missouri meerschaum never tastes so well as after three glasses of this rustic elixir.

That ingenious student of social niceties, John Mistletoe, in his famous *Dictionary of Deplorable Facts* – a book which we heartily commend to the curious, for he includes a long and most informing article on cider, tracing its etymology from the old Hebrew word 'shaker' meaning "to quaff deeply"-- maintains that cider should only be drunk beside an open fire of applewood logs…

FINDING A CIDER HOUSE

The old village parliament may be a thing of the past, but there are a handful of pubs outside Bristol which specialise in cider – and one or two that sell no beer at all. Most of the information on the internet about cider houses is woefully out of date – it's one of those instances of people reproducing stuff from other sites without bothering to check for themselves – so check recent reviews before making a special journey. And don't panic if you see no Bristol boozers below – they're on the Bristol Cider page.

Round the back of the Bull Hotel in Bridport, The Stable is the most impressive new cider house around.

The Stable, Bridport

The new kid on the block, the Stable has emerged as part of the Great Dorset Cider Revival. Twenty years ago few people would have put their money on a new cider house opening in Bridport, but subsequent developments have made this western corner of Dorset one of the most vibrant regions of Ciderland.

Tucked away behind the Bull Hotel, the former stables were acquired by the hotel's owners in 2008 and transformed into a Dorset-style pizza joint; the idea of making this a cider house as well grew out of the vibrant cider culture in the area coupled with the owners' determination to do something different. So far it seems to be working, with families enjoying the pizza and drinkers raving about the cider. Interestingly, the toughest job at first wasn't convincing people to drink cider but getting hold of the stuff to sell them. Now they're up to forty-odd, a mixture of the usual suspects and some local favourites like Cider By Rosie. The food is crucial though. They told us that trying to focus on cider alone would have been a financial disaster… Future cider house owners, take note.

Monkey House, Defford

Since the death of her husband Graham, Gill Collins has found it hard to keep this rare cider house going, and by the time you read this the Monkey House may be no more.

With its thatched roof, hanging baskets, wooden barrels, and air of unspoilt charm this is one of those timeless places people love to revisit every few years – to find everything as they knew it before. The world, however, keeps moving, with increasing duty and regulation and with expensive maintenance to keep that quaint roof waterproof. The Monkey House has been in Gill's family for generations, formerly as a bakery and shop and for many years as a genuine cider house (no beer, wine or spirits, just barrels of Woodmancote Cider), and she is reluctant to let it go. But she's in a Catch-22 situation; to make the place pay for itself she needs to attract more custom, but it's the quiet charm that attracts people.

There's a theory about how the cider house got its name, which was expounded neatly by Graham, "It's said that many years ago a cattle-driver left the cider house a little the worse for wear, and fell in some brambles, scratching his face. When asked how his face had been scratched, he replied 'A monkey scratched me!'"

The question is, did he really 'fall in some brambles'?

Originally the Monkey House made its own cider from an adjacent orchard, but the orchard was grubbed up around 1960 and cider production stopped. Nevertheless, one of the Bulmer family took a sample back to Hereford and produced Bulmer`s Woodmancote, a dry hazy gold farmhouse cider. This arrives in large barrels, and the difficulty of manoeuvring these barrels is one of the factors that may force Gill to close up shop.

There ought to be a way to save a unique institution like this, but it seems to be beyond us. At the time of writing the Monkey House is open at different times every day except Tuesday. Check before you travel.

The Crown Inn: an excellent local pub in the heart of the Three Counties.

Ye Olde Cider Bar, Newton Abbot

Tom Oliver and Andy Atkinson (of Cornish Orchards) are both graduates of Ye Olde Cider Bar, and both have put their training to the best possible use (see the Devon chapter). Yes, maybe they were supposed to be studying at Seale-Hayne agricultural college down the road, but when it comes to cider you can't beat good hands-on experience…

The Crown Inn, Woolhope

Cider history buffs might recognise the name of this Herefordshire village. Founded in 1851 to study the natural history of the county, the Woolhope Naturalists' Field Club was and still is based in Hereford, but took its name from the Woolhope Dome, an outcrop of Silurian rocks around the village. Of its many achievements, perhaps the greatest is *The Herefordshire Pomona*, which the club issued in parts between 1878 and 1884, with over 400 paintings reproduced as hand-coloured lithographs.

Today the village is the home of The Crown Inn, whose owners Matt and Analisa previously spent eight years running the Scrumpy House restaurant at The Bounds, Much Marcle. So you'll find plenty of Westons, as well as cider and perry from the best local makers.

Owner Charlie Newman makes his own cider, which isn't half bad. And has also put together a Fossil Museum. Yes, the Square and Compass is the pub with everything...

The Square And Compass, Worth Matravers

What a fantastic pub – genuinely one of the nation's finest. We spent a happy summer afternoon there not so long ago sampling cider in the sunshine – Cider by Rosie on draught and also the pub's own cider, pressed round the back by landlord Charlie Newman.

He is the latest in a long line of Newmans, who have been running the place and entertaining visitors for more than a century – Charlie's dad Ray was around when we were there, resplendent in long white beard. Father and son are avid fossil collectors, and you can take your pint and have a gander at the clay pipes, ancient coins and dinosaur skeletons in their fossil museum.

The place doesn't seem to have changed much in a century. Drinks are still served from a hatch in a narrow stone hallway, and food still means 'pasty'. You can sit outside and look out over the valley that runs down to the sea; footpaths lead right to the water's edge, though you'll find a rocky little cove rather than a beach. Probably best to do the walking part first and the cider second.

Music also plays an important role at the Square and Compass, which was a magnet for bohemian types between the wars and continues to attract a marvellous variety of people. Check the website to see who's playing.

The Railway Inn, Newnham-on-Severn

We came across an internet forum where someone had suggested taking the train to the nearest mainline station at Stonehouse in Gloucestershire and then walking to the Railway Inn. Fortunately, someone else pointed out that this would also mean swimming across the river, which is probably not a good plan. There used to be a station in Newnham, but now the nearest is Lydney. We had a lift to the pub with Tom Bull, of Severn Cider, who gallantly recommended a bottle of Harechurch Cider. And very nice it was too.

The Railway seems on first impression to be a no-frills small-town pub, but take a look behind the bar and you'll see why cider fans are prepared to swim the Severn to get there. There are – how many? – forty or so different bottled ciders and perries, with plenty of local stuff you'll be hard pressed to find anywhere else. Three centuries ago Newnham was a national centre for the manufacture of bottles (which may have been used for the world's first 'champagne-style' drink), so it's good to see so much glass cooling in Dave's fridge.

The Railway Inn has a fantastic range of bottled ciders – just don't try to swim there...

Eli's, Aka The Rose And Crown, Huish Episcopi, Somerset

Well it sells beer too, but Eli's has achieved the status of Legendary British Pub through the simple policy of staying more or less the same while everything else has changed around it. The first pint was served at the Rose and Crown in about 1800, and the place later became known as Eli's after a Victorian landlord whose family still runs the place. Stephen Pittard and his sisters are the fourth generation, and they're quite fortunate to still be in business after a flash flood in December 2008 forced the thatched pub to close for six months.

Reviews suggest that you still walk in to a tap room and serve yourself from barrels lined up against the wall. This isn't the case any more, and when we visited everything seemed to be out of a keg. The Burrow Hill was certainly fizzy. But it's still an unusual set up, with a till perched on a tiny stump of a bar in a small room at the heart of the pub. Stone-flagged rooms spread out in all directions from this centre, and there's a skittle alley if you fancy trying your arm. Definitely Tardis-like in there, and just to confuse you further there's an Ordnance Survey map on the wall of one room that has Eli's at the centre.

Nice shady garden, and apparently you can camp in a neighbouring field... Check before you go, though.

The Bristol And Exeter Inn, Bridgwater

If the cast of *Shameless* go on summer holidays they probably stop here on the way, to be greeted by a barking dog and a chorus of voices crying 'Shut it, Scrumpy!'. Cider may have gone upmarket in some parts of the world but on St John Street, Bridgwater, it is the drink of people who like to drink plenty and don't want to pay too much for the privilege. Rich's (ask for 'rough') at £2 a pint? What is this – the 1990s?

Landlord John Wootten was chairman of the North Star working men's club in Calne, Wiltshire, at the age of 17. Fifty years on, he made headlines in the local press by refusing to pass on the infamous 2010 cider tax rise to his cash-strapped customers. John wants to keep his customers and he wants to keep his pub going at a time when hundreds are closing every year. Good for him.

But is this a cider house? An in-depth internet survey suggested that the B&E was one of the country's great cider destinations, a bastion of old time cider culture. It isn't. It's an intimate, down-to-earth working man's local – go to Bedminster, Bristol and you'll find five like it on one street. Not that it is any less valuable for all that. It serves its regulars well, but it isn't necessarily the place to go and sample the best of West Country fare.

A proper working man's local – the Bristol and Exeter, Bridgwater.

Cold Nights: Hot Ciders

Though we tend to think of cider as a summer drink it used to be enjoyed year-round in country pubs. On cold nights it was served with ginger or gin, heated by the simple method of plunging a red-hot poker into a cup, or in a metal 'boot' placed in the fire. Today inventive bar staff make mulled cider with the milk-steaming gadget on a coffee machine. You can also make mulled cider at home. This recipe is from the National Cider and Perry Collection in Sussex.

Mulled Cider

4 pints of still, dry farmhouse cider
3 apples – washed, cored and sliced
2 oranges, washed and sliced
Juice and zest of 1 unwaxed lemon
2 tsp ground mixed spice
8 whole cloves
2 cinnamon quills snapped in half
6 tbsp light soft brown sugar

Heat without boiling for 10-15 minutes

CIDER IS GOOD FOR YOU

'Generally all strong and pleasant cider excites and cleanses the Stomach, strengthens Digestion, and infallibly frees the Kidneys and Bladder from breeding the Gravel Stone.'
John Evelyn, 1664

"Cider bad for you? Don't make I laugh,"
Roger Wilkins, 2010

It isn't unusual for promoters of a product to bang on about its health benefits. Guinness was marketed as a health-giving drink for decades; today red wine is touted as a source of antioxidants. Drink stout, meanwhile, and you'll live as long as the Queen Mother. So what about cider?

In 1609, so the story goes, twelve men, good cider drinkers all, performed a Morris dance at Hereford races; their combined age was a remarkable 1200 years. The equation of cider with long life goes back much further, though, to the Celtic veneration of the apple as the fruit of youth and immortality. When King Arthur was fatally wounded, he was, according to the old tales, ferried off to the Celtic otherworld of Avalon – Isle of Apples – to recuperate. Perhaps early Britons picked up on the fact that a severed apple twig will come miraculously to life if planted in fertile ground, or grafted onto a tree (see History section for more on Arthur).

Thanks to their acid content, apples have always been valued as an aid to the digestion, and the same applies to cider. Perry, meanwhile, retains its early reputation for 'dissolving the belly', as 16th century medicine described its purging effect. At a time when the significance of roughage in the diet was not understood a regular dose of perry was probably essential.

As John Evelyn noted in 1664, cider is also strongly reputed to prevent the build up of calcareous material that creates kidney stones, although it doesn't seem that anyone has ever put this long-held belief to any scientific test. The claim in a 1913 Bulmers advert that "...cider is strongly recommended by medical men as a cure for gout and rheumatism" would struggle to avoid censure from modern advertising watchdogs.

Not only is cider good for you, but making cider keeps you fit as a fiddle.

Also known as the Rose and Crown, Eli's is a great little pub.

How else is cider good for you? A couple of centuries ago you would have been wiser drinking cider (or, in an emergency, beer) rather than water. Typhus and other waterborne bugs don't survive long in the acid-rich, alcohol-infused environment of the cider barrel, so if your drinking water is polluted cider is a better bet.

Although 21st century tapwater may not taste great, it's unlikely to kill anyone, so we can't rely on the excellent excuse available to our alcoholic forebears. Looking on the bright side, though, cider does less damage to your waistline than beer, and if made in the traditional manner it shouldn't contain any of the additives that can find their way into a bottle of supermarket plonk. In fact, it shouldn't contain anything except apples, hence the widespread belief (held in spite of plentiful empirical evidence to the contrary) that farmhouse cider won't give you a hangover. Becuz it's pure, see?

Then there's the red wine guzzler's best friend, the antioxidant. To the general public, an antioxidant is Batman to the Joker's free radical, that cancer-causing ne'er do well. Beyond that, none of us has a clue, but every now and then the papers announce that Drinking Red Wine is Good for You because of its antioxidant content. Cider too:

"A diet rich in antioxidants may help to protect against disease, and our research confirms cider has the same levels of antioxidants as red wine," said Dr Caroline Walker, a scientist at Brewing Research International. A second set of studies at the Institute of Food Research, Norwich in the UK found that antioxidants are rapidly absorbed by cider drinkers enhancing the health benefit. And another recent report, on the health benefits of apples, found that they contained high levels of the anti-oxidant Quercetin, which has been found to kill the herpes virus.

You can take things too far, however, as a retired Somerset farm labourer explained to Jon Dathen:

"There's always some that take it too far. Some of they boys lost everything, jobs, wives, and cared for nothing but the cider, drinkin' perhaps ten to twelve pints a day, an' that was the old strong farmhouse brew. Go mad in the end they would. We'd say of anyone who weren't quite right, that they'd 'gone to Wells', 'cos that was where the sanitarium was, where the worst cases ended up."

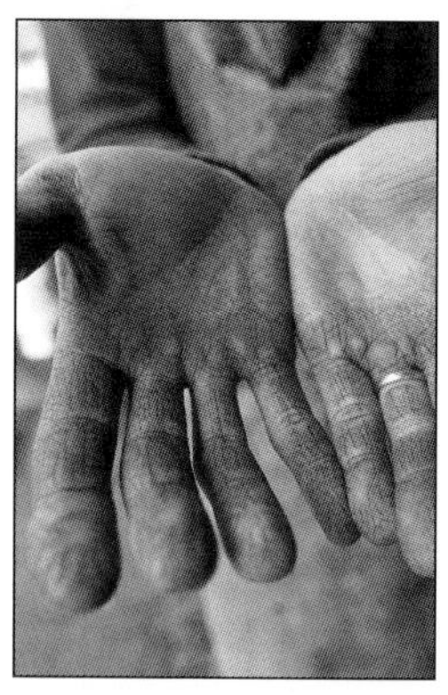

Cidermaking isn't too good for the hands, though... Photo by Bill Bradshaw (billbradshaw.co.uk)

Scurvy

When Europeans started exploring the world's oceans at the end of the 15th century sailors began falling prey to a ghastly disease. Victims displayed horrible symptoms: their gums bled, old wounds opened up and their legs became covered in dark purplish ulcers; increasing weakness followed, then came violent haemorrhages and death. This was distressing, not only for the victims but also for their employers, and as early as 1605 lemon juice was successfully used to keep scurvy at bay.

Bizarrely, it took the best part of two centuries for British sailors to develop the habit that earned them the nickname Limey, and in the meantime other anti-scorbutics were discovered, tested and haphazardly employed.

Writing in the early 17th century, Francis Bacon advised that travellers coming ashore after a long sea voyage be greeted with cider and oranges, 'an assured remedy for sicknesse taken at sea', and cider experts like John Worlidge referred to the drink's effectiveness against scurvy. One of the reasons for the success enjoyed by the cidermakers of South Hams in Devon was the proximity of Plymouth, first port of call for generations of scorbutic transatlantic voyagers. Cider's effectiveness against scurvy at sea was limited as an open barrel quickly spoiled, but some ships carried it to mix with water.

Then, in 1747, ship's surgeon James Lind conducted an experiment aboard his vessel, the Salisbury. Taking twelve of his scurvy cases, he gave fresh oranges and lemons to two, a daily quart of cider to a further two and, to the rest, various other popular remedies of the day. A month later, when the Salisbury sailed into Plymouth, the last eight were as sick as ever, while the tars fortunate enough to be given fruit were cured. The pair who had been given cider, meanwhile, showed a marked improvement.

It wasn't until the 20th century that scientists figured out the link between vitamin C and scurvy, by which time citrus fruit were the established treatment. Experiments conducted in the 1970s found only traces of the vitamin in cider, suggesting that Lind was mistaken. But in the early 1980s RK French set the record straight in '*The History and Virtues of Cyder*' (a must-read, incidentally);

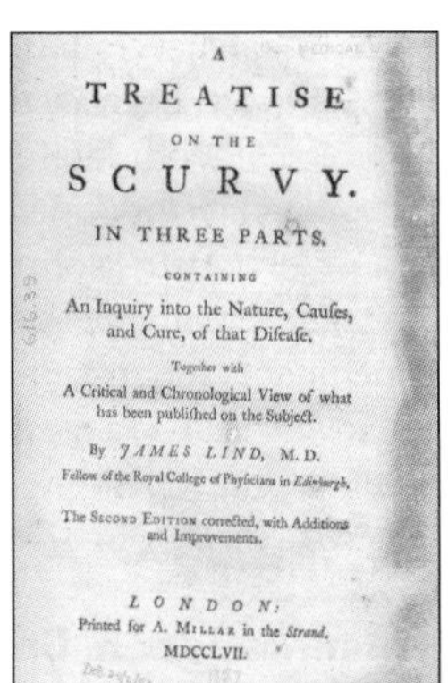

A
TREATISE
ON THE
SCURVY.
IN THREE PARTS.
CONTAINING
An Inquiry into the Nature, Caufes, and Cure, of that Difeafe.
Together with
A Critical and Chronological View of what has been publifhed on the Subject.
By JAMES LIND, M.D.
Fellow of the Royal College of Physicians in Edinburgh.
The Second Edition corrected, with Additions and Improvements.
LONDON:
Printed for A. Millar in the Strand.
MDCCLVII.

James Lind pioneered the use of citrus fruit to combat scurvy. He found that cider worked well too.

those researchers found only 3.3mg of vitamin C per litre, he wrote, because they were testing the wrong kind of cider – modern, filtered, watered-down, pasteurised, carbonated factory cider. By contrast a batch of single variety Strawberry Norman cider made in 1978/9 contained 33.8mg per litre. If, as Medical Research Council experiments suggest, 5mg of vitamin C per day is enough to prevent scurvy, a glass or two of strong cider a day would do the job nicely.

Five a day, anyone?

For years, Aspall concentrated on making and selling cyder vinegar, building on the health food craze of the 1970s.

Cider Vinegar Is Good For You – Isn't It?

When we visited Ye Olde Cider Bar in Newton Abbot recently, we came across a market stall selling vinegar. Surrounding the stall were laminated copies of an article from The Daily Mail:

> *Vinegar and honey cured my crippling arthritis, says delighted organist. When Sarah Gall was crippled by arthritis, the powerful painkilling drugs prescribed by her doctor brought no relief.*
>
> *Yet the 55-year-old church organist now claims to be completely pain-free thanks to a simple but startlingly effective cure she found in her kitchen cupboard – vinegar.*

In true Mail style the article trumpeted the unfortunate organist's claims that vinegar had done what the medical profession, with its dreadful waiting lists and evil painkillers, had failed to do, rounding off the article with a comment from a killjoy medic, "If it works for you that's great. It won't work for most people."

Yet many people do believe in the curative power of vinegar in general, and cider vinegar in particular. As well as arthritis people claim to have been cured of allergies, sinus infections, acne, high cholesterol, flu, chronic fatigue, candida, acid reflux, sore throats, contact dermatitis and gout. A daily dose of cider vinegar in water is said to control high blood pressure, and has been touted as a cure for diabetes, osteoporosis and obesity. Cider vinegar allegedly has anti-carcinogenic properties and will mitigate the ill effects of ageing – those antioxidants at it again.

Some of these health claims come straight out of apple mythology, but could any of them actually be true? What

The Virtues of 'Sider'

"This parish, wherein sider is plentiful, hath many people that do enjoy this blessing of long life; neither are the aged bedridden or decrepit as elsewhere; next to God, wee ascribe it to our flourishing orchards, first that the bloomed trees in spring do not only sweeten but purify the ambient air; next, that they yield us plenty of rich and winy liquors, which do conduce very much to the constant health of our inhabitants. Their ordinary course is to breakfast and sup with toast and sider through the whole Lent; which heightens their appetites and creates in them durable strength to labour."

Rev. Martin Johnson of Dilwyn, Herefordshire (1651-1698)

does cider vinegar have in it which is so powerful that one spoonful a day can prevent so many ailments? Is it stuffed full of vitamins? No. According to the United States Department of Agriculture, apple cider vinegar contains no vitamin A, vitamin B6, vitamin C, vitamin E, vitamin K, thiamin, riboflavin, niacin, pantothenic acid, or folate.

Is it full of calcium, potassium and other minerals? No more than you'd find in an apple. It doesn't contain much in the way of amino acids either. Nor ethyl alcohol, theobromine, beta-carotene, alpha-carotene, beta-cryptoxanthin, lycopene, lutein, or zeaxanthin.

What cider vinegar does have in it is acetic acid, and acetic acid really is good for you, in a modest sort of way. It can help your digestive system absorb calcium from greens, for instance, and it has also been shown to slow the breakdown of carbohydrates into sugars – which may prove to be good news for diabetics. But the best thing about cider vinegar – and no killjoy medic is going to dispute this one – is that it can make boring food taste good. So instead of slathering your chips or lettuce in fatty tartare sauce or mayonnaise you can sprinkle vinegar on them.

People attribute miraculous health-giving properties to cider vinegar.

How To Make Cider Vinegar

This might make seasoned cidermakers chuckle, because if there's one thing cider wants to do more than anything else, it's turn into vinegar. Fruit juice is full of acetobacteria, tiny beasties that turn fermented juice into acetic acid. They survive fermentation to live happily in the strongest cider, scorn sulphites, and get to work as soon as they come into contact with air. One of the main tasks of the cidermaker is to prevent this happening, by excluding air from the fermenting or maturing vessel. To make cider vinegar you just need to let nature take its course:

1. Get hold of some good quality farmhouse cider.
2. Take the lid off. Cover opening with muslin or similar to deter vinegar flies (fruit flies to the non-cidermaker).
3. Leave for a couple of months somewhere warm.
4. Test. When the cider has turned into vinegar, filter through a cloth to remove the sludge – 'the mother of vinegar' as it is known.
5. Use to dress greens or salad, or sprinkle on chips.
6. Live to be a hundred.

Traditional Devon Song

I were brought up on cider
And I be a hundred and two
But still that be nothing when you come to think
Me father and mother be still in the pink

And they be brought up on cider
Of the rare old Tavistock brew
And me granfer drinks quarts
For he's one of the sports
That were brought up on cider too.

SCARIEST CIDER COCKTAILS

PEOPLE HAVE BEEN DOCTORING THEIR CIDER FOREVER, BUT YOU HAVE TO WONDER WHY...

Cider and Black: Not really scary, except that adding blackcurrant turns your drink purple, not to mention your tongue and anything else that happens to get immersed in the stuff. Old boys have been doing this for years. Now cider companies are vying with each other to make the sickliest fruity hooch.

Snakebite: Presumably people used to mix a half of lager with a half of cider because the lager tasted better and the cider was cheap, but nowadays there's no excuse. Some youngsters seem to think it's illegal because landlords won't serve it to them. It isn't illegal, but it does taste horrible and it will make you puke.

Diesel, aka Snakebite and Black, Nasty, Purple Nasty: Yes, it's nasty and purple and it probably has a similar effect on your insides as drinking tractor fuel. Mix lager and cider together, add a drop of blackcurrant. Very popular in the North East, apparently.

Scri and Vi: A strange one from the streets of Street, where cider is known as screech. You take your screech and add to it a good glug of Vimto, the purple fizzy drink which was advertised by Purple Ronnie back in the day. And there you have it. Why? You'll have to ask someone from Street. Incidentally there's a cocktail that has nothing to do with cider, or Vimto for that matter, which is called a Cheeky Vimto. It's a mixture of port and blue WKD, which sounds challenging. A great name though.

Black Satin, aka Poor Man's Black Velvet: Half of Guinness mixed with a half of cider. Somehow doesn't sound quite as bad as Snakebite.

Tractor: This is a real peach. Pour a shot of Tia Maria into a pint glass. Add a half of Guinness then – get this – pour a half of cider from a great height into the glass. The result should be a massive foaming head which you're supposed to eat with a spoon. Yikes.

Black Silk Knickers: The name is quite intriguing but the drink is vile. Mix cider and Guinness, then add a shot of Jack Daniels and stir. Try pouring into a potted plant and see what happens.

Red Witch: A Goth favourite. Pour a shot each of vodka, Pernod and blackcurrant into a pint glass. Top up with cider. Enjoy. Or not.

Sheep Dip: Please don't try this at home... Mix 1 part gin, 2 parts vodka, 1 part white rum, 1 part Malibu and 1 part peach schnapps in a jug, with ice. Add a half pint of cider and fill with Seven-Up. Then add a few drops Blue Curacao until – wait for it – the contents turns green. Stir. Pour into cocktail glasses. Add fruit and umbrella. Ask yourself – what is sheep dip for? Drinking, or killing things?

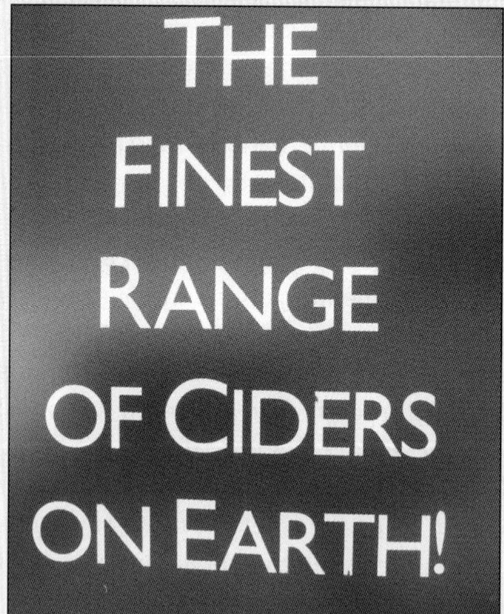
THE
FINEST
RANGE
OF CIDERS
ON EARTH!

That's quite a claim at The Apple, Bristol. But you won't find any of these concoctions on the cider boat...

TOP CIDER DRINKERS

It's all very well banging on about cider producers but we'd be nowhere without a faithful congregation of ciderheads. Most of us go about our business of keeping the cider industry going without recognition, forcing down cold pints on hot summer days and hot cups on cold winter nights, but let's at least acknowledge the efforts of our better-known comrades – the actors, musicians and others who are the stars in the cider-sozzled firmament.

Lily Allen has done her bit for home-grown cider. Good on you, Lily!

Lily Allen

The cider-sipping siren once had a can of Strongbow and a fag stuck permanently in her fingers. Motherhood may dull her thirst for a bit, but she'll be back.

Adge Cutler and The Wurzels

His thirty-fifth year behind him, AJ 'Adge' Cutler was unemployed and skint. But Cutler, who had worked on the cider press at Coates in Nailsea before becoming Acker Bilk's road manager for a spell, had three valuable talents: he could sing, he could make people laugh, and he knew Somerset.

Back in 1958 he had written *Drink up Thy Zider,* and as the Sixties started swinging he became a well-known face around the West Country's pubs and clubs. When his chance came he grabbed it, and on 2 November 1966 the Wurzels' first album was recorded live at the Royal Oak, just a short stumble from the Coates cider works in Nailsea.

Featuring Cutler-penned songs like *The Chew Magna Cha-Cha* and *When the Common Market Comes to Stanton Drew,* the album was released on Columbia Records – Bob Dylan's label. In December, *Drink up Thy Zider* became the group's first single, peaking at number 45 in the Hit Parade.

The album's sleeve notes describe an evening of merriment, with an audience of cider-quaffing Wurzel-lovers from every corner of Somerset; from Weston Zoyland to Monkton Combe. Nailsea's oldest inhabitant, wearing a top-hat for such a special occasion, was flanked by long-haired youths and mini-skirted girls. They were a bit restrained at first in front of them thar record men from Lunnon in town but soon livened up and drank the place dry.

It is impossible to define Wurzel-music, Bob Barratt's notes continue. It's not really pop – it's not really comedy. It has been disowned by the West of England Folk-Song Society and Adge was blackballed from the Long Ashton Jazz Appreciation Group on account of it. So lend an ear to this album and decide for yourself!

Scrumpy and Western caught on, and Adge was honoured by having a huge, 6000 gallon, cider vat named after him by his former employers, Coates. The BBC were there to film the unveiling, and capture staff and management singing along to Adge's signature tune.

Tales about Adge abound. Former Wurzel Melt Kingston tells how the frontman took him down to Dunne's Menswear in Bristol to get properly togged out in checked shirt, neckerchief and countryman's hat. When Melt emerged from the changing room in his new duds, Adge looked quizzical, took the brand new hat from Melt's head, threw it on the floor, jumped on it a couple of times and replaced it. 'That's better!' he said.

Although chart success eluded the band, the Wurzels kept playing sold-out shows around the West. Then, on the night of 5 May 1974, Adge was driving home from

The last resting place of Adge Cutler, only a few hundred yards from the Royal Oak.

Ten of the Best from Cutler of the West

- When the Common Market Comes to Stanton Drew
- The Champion Dung Spreader
- Drink Up Thy Zider
- Pill, Pill
- The Chew Magna Cha-Cha
- The Charlton Mackrell Jug Band
- Moonlight on the Malago
- The Somerset Space Race
- Sniff Up Thy Snuff
- The Shepton Mallet Matador

a gig when he flipped his sports car at the roundabout approaching the Severn Bridge at Chepstow and was killed. Somerset had lost its bard.

For the remaining Wurzels, Adge's death was the start of a new chapter in which songs like *Combine Harvester, Blackbird* and *I am a Cider Drinker* made them household names, but never again did their lyrics reach the heights of AJ Cutler at his best:

> *"Some say they seen a tank*
> *Of Portuguese vin blanc*
> *Jammed Pensford High Street t'other night"*

Wurzels Tommy Banner (left) and Pete Budd are still singing about cider. Picture Ivy Goatcher.

Traces of Adge survive around the place. You can hire his 1937 Bedford bus from John Woodham's Vintage Tours in Ryde, Isle of Wight, or visit his grave at All Saints Church, Nailsea. While his famous vat continues to perform its essential role, at Rich's Cider in Mark, there have been calls to give the bard of Somerset a more public memorial. If Liverpool has John Lennon Airport and Belfast has George Best, why shouldn't we have Adge Cutler International?

Prince Charles

Cider has a long association with royalty. Lord Scudamore and the cider-loving aristocracy of the Three Counties were avid supporters of the Cavalier cause during the English Civil War, and it was on the Restoration of Charles II in 1660 that the Golden Age of Cyder really got started. He wasn't called the Merry Monarch for nothing. Even Queen Victoria had a regular supply of Somerset's finest shipped in from Taunton, while George V was credited with inventing a new cider-based cocktail that had the gentry hooked. What about today? After years of drought you can now buy various bottled ciders at the House of Commons bars, while the future Charles III has often been snapped with his nose in a glass of posh bubbly cider. His Duchy Originals cider is not at all bad, if a bit pricey. And he's the biggest landowner in Herefordshire these days, just as Scudamore was in his.

Prince Charles likes a drop of apple juice. His Duchy Originals cider is not at all bad.

Prince William

Known as 'Steve' by fellow students during his time at St Andrews – a ruse designed to put tabloid newshounds off the scent – our future monarch has long preferred cider to beer. One right-leaning broadsheet that takes a particular interest in his drinking habits has reported him drinking a bottle of Scrumpy Jack with RAF chums at Scampton and an impressive three bottles of Strongbow at a London curry house. To honour his services to the cider industry the Prince had a new cider apple named after him in 2008, and you can now buy Prince William single variety cider from Thatchers; they grow the apple in their orchards around Sandford, Somerset.

Joe Strummer. Two legends met over a glass of cider when he visited Rog Wilkins at Land's End Farm. (Pic Frank Drake)

Joe Strummer

The Clash lead man spent the last part of his life in Broomfield, Somerset, within shouting distance of the old Taunton Cider factory at Norton Fitzwarren. A regular at Land's End Farm he is remembered in an interview torn from Q magazine, in which he describes a flagon of Wilkins as his idea of heaven. 'In Somerset,' Strummer said once, while sipping a hot spiced cider at the Cambridge Folk Festival, 'We take our cider seriously.'

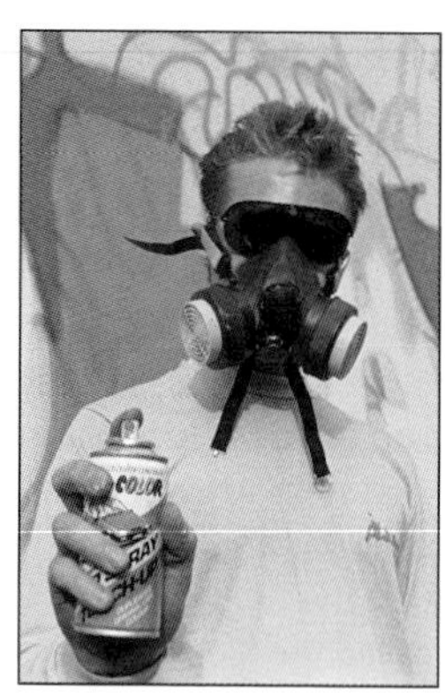

3D from Massive Attack used to enjoy a drop of cider before painting the streets of Bristol. (Pic Beezer)

The All-Party Parliamentary Cider Group

Next time someone's having a moan about our elected representatives, spare a thought for the poor souls who strive on our behalf at Westminster. Sandwiched between groups dealing with Chronic Pain and Citizen's Advice, the Parliamentary Cider Group was set up to 'promote the cause of cider as a drink; to raise its profile; and to inform and educate people about its role and importance, especially in rural areas.' Tory MP Bill Wiggin (Herefordshire North) is chair, and the NACM provides 'administrative support'. Wiggin got into a bit of a pickle during the 2009 Expenses witchhunt, but no mention was made of cider. But then he isn't drinking it for fun, is he?

On the subject of politics, the 2010 election has left Ciderland split along the lines of historic rivalries. Herefordshire is a sea of blue, while most of Somerset belongs to the Lib Dems.

Massive Attack

Former cider punk Robert '3D' Del Naja describes the halcyon Saturday afternoons of his youth:

"We used to go to Bixies cider mill on Hopewell Road,

which was like a proper old barn that would sell this stuff called Old Cripple Crock Cider which was like scrumpy and we would buy it in big plastic gallons and take that back to Castle Green and plough into all afternoon. I was done in by eight or nine after that stuff and would have to go to bed."

"Two large gins, two pints of cider... Ice in the cider."

Samuel Pepys

The man who described the Great Fire of London enjoyed a glass of the nation's favourite. Take this diary entry, from New Year's Eve 1662: 'Then to eat a dish of anchovies, and drink wine and syder, and very merry'. So that's why he managed to keep up his diary for all those years.

Withnail and I

Could this be where Magners got the idea from? The dishevelled thespians roll into a pub in Penrith armed with a pair of blues but with only minutes of drinking time. "Two large gins, two pints of cider," calls out the imperious Withnail. "Ice in the cider." Pub landlords up and down the country have since had to endure endless very pissed imitators. Ditto Lake District teashop owners, women called 'Mabs' and Paul McGann, who played 'I' and has the (mis)fortune to live in cider's capital city. If you see him, please refrain from bellowing 'We're not from London!' or 'Scrubbers!'

The Dymock Poets

For a couple of years before World War I, the Gloucestershire countryside east of Dymock played host to a group of poets, among them Robert Frost and Edward Thomas.

The poets were as poor as… poets and, like everyone else in the vicinity, they drank a lot of cider. Frost even wrote a rather odd poem in which he likens himself to a bubble in a glass of cider, and another about spending too long picking apples. A famously drunken cider supper enjoyed by the poets was re-enacted by the modern Friends of the Dymock Poets (www.dymockpoets.co.uk). Who knows? They may do it again.

Another of the poets was Lascelles Abercrombie, who later wrote: "I have lived in a cottage in the daffodil country, and I have, for a time, done what I wanted to do . . . I make no cider now, and I have no garden. But once I lived in Gloucestershire."

Robert Frost: The Cow in Apple Time

Something inspires the only cow of late
To make no more of a wall than an open gate,
And think no more of wall-builders than fools.
Her face is flecked with pomace and she drools
A cider syrup. Having tasted fruit,
She scorns a pasture withering to the root.
She runs from tree to tree where lie and sweeten
The windfalls spiked with stubble and worm-eaten.
She leaves them bitten when she has to fly.
She bellows on a knoll against the sky.
Her udder shrivels and the milk goes dry.

The apple character produced at Aardman Animations to promote Aardcore cider.

Aardman Animations

Back in 2009, some employees from Aardman Animations released their own cider, suitably titled 'Aardcore', on a regional level in Bristol to raise a bit of money for the company's charity The Wallace & Gromit Foundation. You could buy Aardcore for a while at The Orchard pub, it happens to be across the road from the animation company's new offices. It was made, so we are told, by Ben Crossman of Hewish.

Crossman's produced Aardcore to raise money for the Wallace & Gromit Foundation. It was on sale at The Orchard near Aardman's Bristol HQ.

John Lydon:

Not to be outdone by his old punk rival Joe Strummer, Johnnie Rotten showed up in Mudgeley with a Dutch TV crew and left us with a strangely compelling picture of Wilkins. "We've come 'ere for the cidah," announces the former Sex Pistol as he lurches towards Rog's barn. Lydon doesn't seem to have changed much since the days when ace producer John Waters described him as 'the boy you wouldn't ask to hand out the scissors'. But at one point Rog suggests he have a drop of gin in his cider – it'll go down well – and Rotten declines. Perhaps he is different, after all.

Blur

According to a report in the NME when the band were at the height of their fame, Blur's favourite bev was a half of cider and pernod. They do things differently in Essex.

Windy Miller (Camberwick Green)

This is a transcript of an episode of the odd British kids' show: "While Windy is watching the sails turn, Jonathan Bell arrives with some corn to grind. Windy offers him some cider but farmer Bell is driving so declines and Windy drinks the cider alone... Meanwhile, in Camberwick Green Mickey Murphy receives two large orders for cakes but finds he has run out of flour, so drives off to Colley's Mill with his children who find Windy asleep (having drunk too much cider)." And what, one might ask, is wrong with that?

John Irving's novel was made into a film and won two Oscars in 2000.

Annie Proulx

Best-selling author of *'The Shipping News'* and *'Brokeback Mountain'*, Proulx is not just a cider fan but an authority on the subject. Her book *'Cider: Making, Using and Enjoying Sweet and Hard Cider'* may not have the snappy title of her fiction but it's a thorough and deftly written guide to home cidermaking. Aimed at an American readership it's useful for cidermakers who don't have access to cider apples.

Acker Bilk

Adge Cutler was once his roadie and the Pensford-born jazz cat shared the Nailsea crooner's love of apple juice:

"Cider really is my favourite drink," wrote Acker in his foreword to the excellent book *'Cider's Story – Rough and Smooth'* by Nailsea resident Mark Foot. "I tasted it for the first time when I was seven," says Acker, "the farm workers kept the cider in a big jar in the shade… a few of my school mates and I couldn't resist it… I've loved it ever since… I'm talking about true scrumpy, of course."

Acker Bilk was introduced to scrumpy aged 7 and still found time to practise the clarinet.

The Cider House Rules

Almost as famous as Laurie Lee's classic, but for no good reason. The Guardian had this to say about the film version: 'A good two hours consisting, almost literally, of nonsense – gurning, emoting, self-regarding gibberish. evasive, unwholesome and deeply creepy.' Yes, but is Michael Caine a cider man? Anyone want to ask him?

Laurel and Hardy

Well, Oliver Hardy at least. In 1914, an unknown actor on the way up, he starred in silent comedy short *Good Cider*, playing a tramp who adds whisky to an undrinkable barrel of cider, making it the toast of the country fair. Who said cidermaking was difficult?

Thanks to this man no journalist can mention cider without making a pun on 'Rosie'.

Laurie Lee

Beautiful, wicked, earthy, poetic, nostalgic, tough… *Cider with Rosie* is justifiably a classic. Don't expect too much cider, but passages like this should keep you going:

"Never to be forgotten, that first long secret drink of golden fire, juice of those valleys and of that time, wine of wild orchards, of russet summer, of plump red apples, and Rosie's burning cheeks. Never to be forgotten, or ever tasted again..."

Meanwhile, Lee's autobiographical masterpiece has generated more than its fair share of puns with headline writers struggling to say anything about cider without alluding to the book. If in Dorset, look behind the bar for Cider by Rosie produced by the award-winning cidermaker and blogger, Rose Grant.

James Crowden

Having worked the press at Burrow Hill for years, the poet, former shepherd and countryside writer penned '*Cider – The Forgotten Miracle*' in 1999, then followed it up almost a decade later with '*Ciderland*', an award-winning survey of the West's cidermakers. He may be unique in his output of Cider Haiku:

Hard pressed, the stream of juice
Runs madly from the cheese –
Autumn careering out of control

Chris Martin

Coldplay front man's first child is called Apple. Gwyneth says the name is sweet and wholesome, but since Chris was outed as a cider-supping celeb you have to wonder.

Walter Raymond

A fine writer and minor literary legend, Raymond left a vivid portrait of village life on the edge of Exmoor, around 1905. His pen portraits of local characters like the mole catcher and the wheelwright are a bit sentimental in places but he had a meticulous eye for the detail of country trades and customs. In *The Book of Crafts and Character* he included a chapter on Cidermaking, which was then going through the revolution inspired by research conducted at Long Ashton.

Reef

Somerset's favourite indie stars penned the line 'Off to Mudgeley about the year's end' in their song '*Summer's in Bloom*'. At their April 2010 gig at the Academy in Bristol they apparently dedicated the song to Roger Wilkins and the village he put on the map.

From Temperley Kingsbury Episcopi to Temperley London, in one generation.

Alice Temperley

Julian's daughter is more famous than he is these days, but she hasn't forgotten her roots in the cider orchards of Somerset, where she was chased on occasion by an angry orchard pig. We had a similar experience with a Burrow Hill llama not long ago. The swallows are quite aggressive too. Can't think why...

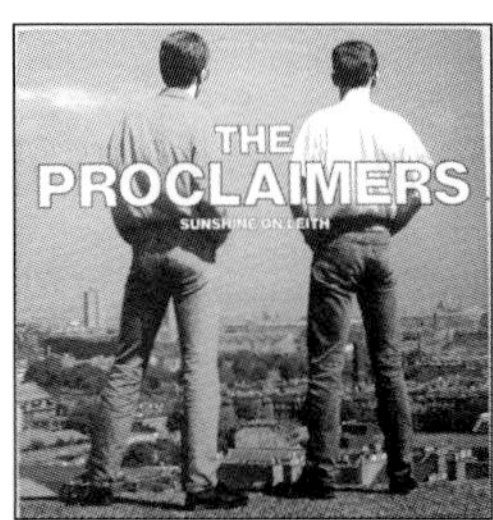

You'd walk 500 miles if a cold bottle of Oliver's perry was waiting at the other end.

Charlie Reid

The Proclaimer remembers drinking a great cider in a Basque restaurant in Madrid many years ago, but the crucial moment for him came when his tour manager started producing his own cider and perry. Can you guess who it was? You'll find out in the Three Counties section of the Areas chapter. Incidentally, Charlie has a simple solution to the vexed question of cider duty. Cut it! Good man.

Daniel Defoe

The author of *Robinson Crusoe* rode with the Duke of Monmouth at the Battle of Sedgemoor but escaped punishment. In his Tour Through England and Wales of 1724 he paused to enjoy a drop of Somerset cider: "So very good, so fine, so cheap..."

Linda Brava

The Swedish violinist, actress, model and rally driver dabbled in the cider business in the late 1990s. Her Linda Cider sold over 12 million bottles in two years, helped by a marketing campaign that included a 1998 calendar and personal appearances at supermarkets around the country, to which she travelled by helicopter.

Kate Moss

According to Aussie website Girl.com, it wasn't Magners that got everyone drinking cider... "Just like high waisted jeans and denim vests, trend-setter Kate Moss has started yet another craze, cider-on-ice. Along with other UK celebs, Kate Moss has turned cider-on-ice into the coolest drink over the UK summer."

Is Kate Moss really responsible for the cider revival? Well, it's said to keep you trim...

Matthew Fort

The Guardian food critic has described his enjoyment of Olivers perry: "And, sure enough, my head isn't blown off by a glass of his Three Counties medium-dry perry, but I am blown away by it, by its quiet, off-dry elegance, the suavity of its fruit, as debonair as a Savile Row suit, with a long, long finish."

Hugh Fearnley-Whittingstall

Hugh gave a crash course in how not to harvest perry pears when River Cottage visited Days Cottage in the autumn of 2009. Normally the pear collectors stay well clear while the tree is being shaken with the panking pole, but Hugh's producer apparently enjoyed watching him being bombarded by falling fruit. Winnie the Pooh gave us Poohsticks. Hugh F-W gave us Gloucestershire roulette. He made this, slightly dangerous remark while sipping a glass of perry with Dave Kaspar: "If I could only ever drink one alcoholic drink again for the rest of my life, and it was this, I would be quite happy."

Hugh puts his tastebuds to good use, judging at the Bath & West.

Stanley Donwood

The brilliant and enigmatic Radiohead cover artists is a well-known devotee of Real Cider and is said to have made his own in his West Country hideaway. Donwood is also thought to be working on an illustrated Lexicon of Cider terminology. But maybe that's the Hecks talking.

FESTIVALS AND COMPETITIONS

These days you could probably spend every weekend at some kind of cider event, which is good news in terms of choice, if slightly dangerous for the true fanatic. For cidermakers the various international, national and regional competitions offer an opportunity to meet other makers and make new contacts. And winning prizes gets you noticed. For those who are more interested in the consumption end of things there are numerous festivals, from the Real Ale and Cider festivals held by pubs to the annual competitions. Wassail around January 17 is one of the most important dates in the cider diary, but we haven't listed the Wassail events because there are so many of them. Many of the dates of the events in this section vary from year to year, so check websites for up-to-date information.

May
Sat 23rd, Sun 24th & Mon 25th
Starts 6pm Fri 22nd
THE
WELSH
PERRY
&
CIDER
FESTIVAL
2009
FREE ENTRY
Mid-day - 11pm
The Clytha Arms
Nr Abergavenny
Monmouthshire
South Wales, UK
LIVE Music, Hog Roast - Sunday
Food 9am - 9pm all weekend

Cider festivals are increasing in scale, quality and regularity. Good news all round.

Try your hand at cidermaking the old-fashioned way at a festival near you.

Powerstock Festival

Dorset, April

It sounds like a 100 megaton rock extravaganza but in reality the cult ciderfest is a village hall fundraiser that got a bit out of control. Back in 2001 Nick Poole was chairman of the village hall committee (an important job if you live in the country) and needed to make some money. So he thought, why not have a cider tasting? Strange as it may seem now, he struggled to find enough local cidermakers that first year – these days more than 30 turn up, and several of the local producers have gone commercial. Meanwhile, the number of ciderheads turning up to test the nectar has accelerated. When 1,000 showed up in 2009 the Old Bill had a quiet word, pointing out that the tiny village was unable to accommodate such numbers, even for one evening. In 2010 it was a ticket-only affair, as it will be from now on. Get yours early!

2010 also saw the first Powerstock cider competition, which had 36 entries, with contestants judging their own class. Nick is unsure what the future holds for the festival that was never supposed to be, but we suspect it will keep growing. See Listings for info.

Possibly the most beautiful phrase in the English language....

Camra National Cider And Perry Competition

Reading, May

Held during the Reading Beer and Cider Festival, this contest celebrates the CAMRA vision of Real Cider, generating plenty of publicity in the process. We're not sure that the ale campaigners' definition of Real Cider is particularly useful – their list of ciders 'not recognised as being real' is pointless and potentially damaging to companies that make full juice cider but choose to carbonate – but they have spent decades winning the respect of publicans, drinkers and the media.

Producers compete for Gold, Silver or Bronze in two classes: Cider and Perry. The judges are a bit more articulate than most. In 2010, the winner of the Cider Gold medal was Sandford Orchards Cider, which the judges described as 'having a fruity aroma with wonderful honeysuckle and banana notes, and a long, sweet aftertaste'. Not Wilkins, then.

The Big Apple Cider And Perry Trials

Herefordshire, May

Although the number of entries is approaching 200, the Big Apple competition is still very much a village do, with the local WI providing no-nonsense lunches and the best cup of tea you'll have all year.

The village of Putley lies just a few miles north of Much Marcle, with May Hill dominating the horizon like a friendly version of Mount Etna, and orchards cover the landscape in every direction. Even if the blossom is only just appearing the solitary perry pears and neat rows of orchard trees are a wonderful sight and a network of footpaths allows you to wander more or less at will around fields and orchards.

In 1989 a group of local cider and perry makers got together to launch the Big Apple Association, which aims to celebrate and promote all things apple- and pear-related in the parishes of the Marcle Ridge. Festivals in early May and October celebrate Blossomtime and Harvestime, with the former focused on Putley. The autumn festival is more of a cidermakers' open house, where you can visit local producers and even lend a hand with an antique stone mill at Hellens in Much Marcle. If you're entering the May competition be prepared: contestants are expected to judge each class they enter, which might mean tasting fifty-plus ciders or perries. Not that you have to drink much, but with extreme variations in quality (some of the Novice Perries can be challenging) it can be a shock to the system.

This takes place on the Saturday afternoon, after a frantic morning in which competitors from all over the UK try to get their precious demijohns to Putley in time for the 11.30am deadline. That's a lot of speeding cidermakers.

So Saturday the hall is packed with anxious or expectant producers, while Sunday and Monday belong to the fans. In 2010 £1.80 bought you a little plastic glass and six tiny homemade taster tickets – then came the tricky task of choosing half a dozen ciders and perries from the 180 on offer. You could always buy 30 sets of tickets and try the lot. We reckon that would be about 20 pints. 10 a day over 2 days? You might want a nap afterwards.

In 2012 James McCrindle's bottled perry stole the show, which featured 191 different entries. Definitely recommended. Visit www.bigapple.org.uk for this year's dates.

Cider festivals are a good place to observe old-fashioned cidermaking in action.

The Royal Bath And West Show

Somerset, Early June

The granddaddy of cider competitions, the Royal Bath and West Show has been handing out the silverware for as long as anyone can remember, but over the past decade the B&W's workaday cider section has blossomed

Local Festivals And How To Find Them

They're not always easy to track down, but on summer weekends there are cider festivals all over the place. We can't give details of events in a book like this, but we can give you some tips on how to find them:

CAMRA festivals: Local branches often include cider and perry in Real Ale festivals, and also run specialist cider festivals. Contact your local CAMRA to see what's going on.

Cider Sundays and other pub events: Check local media. They even have pub festivals in London. Some country pubs have camping.

Ciderfarm festivals, official and otherwise: Producers hold mini-festivals, with camping in some cases. The only way to find out about these events is to ask the makers, who may invite you along. Or not.

Sports club or village hall fundraisers, etc: Well, that's how Powerstock started… beer and cider festivals are fundraiser favourites. Keep an eye on the local media.

into an Orchards and Cider pavilion, with the number of people entering the competition topping 350 in 2009. Retired naval commander and fruit grower Rupert Best is the man behind this transformation, and his work was acknowledged with a special award in 2008. City folk may feel ever so slightly out of place at the show, which is a proper old-fashioned country fair, but the Orchards and Cider tent attracts the brightest and the best from across Ciderland. John Thatcher is usually on hand for the award ceremony, and you can expect to see Julian Temperley and other luminaries. Vigo and other orchard and cider-related businesses have stands and there's a book stall with an author or two invited along by the charming Mr Best.

Oh, and there's a bar. With cider. Get someone else to drive.

The competition itself has the usual range of classes but often produces some surprising results. If Somerset favourites tend to dominate – Perrys, Sheppys and Burrow Hill are frequent winners – there have been plenty of champions from elsewhere, while numerous unknowns have also taken the honours.

Check the website for dates and, if you're planning to enter, note that forms have to be in during April. www.bathandwest.com

Entries at the Bath & West await the judges' verdict.

The travelling press of Cider with Roadies appears regularly on the festival circuit.

Hereford International Cider Competition

Hereford, May

Based at the Cider Museum, this highly respected competition regularly attracts entries from Canada and the USA. Of the major competitions it is unusual in having a class devoted to in-bottle fermented cider or perry.

Perhaps this is unfair, but these days it doesn't seem to have quite the buzz of the Big Apple or the Bath and West. Maybe they need to borrow Rupert Best for a year or two…

The Welsh Cider And Perry Festival

Check website for venue

Celebrate the renaissance in Welsh cidermaking at a CAMRA award-winning pub. Bring the kids (or not). Eat. Drink. Camp. Look at the view. Sounds pretty good, doesn't it? www.welshcider.co.uk

Bath Cider Festival
Bristol Cider Festival

July/August and Jan/Feb

If you fancy an evening of roast hog and Scrumpy and Western, washed down with fine farmhouse cider, then look no further. The brainchild of Bath caterer and Mangledwurzel Chris Lilley, these events are organised by CiderFestivals.co.uk; Chris's people take care of the catering and, yes, the Mangledwurzels provide the Wurzels-tribute-style musical entertainment.

It sounds like a fantastic business plan, and the fans love it. With tickets less than a tenner, the festivals seem to sell out before the doors open, and there's plenty of good cider on offer from Thatchers, Hecks, Rich's, Mr Whitehead, Westons and other reputable cider providers.

Even better, Chris and team can help you organise your own cider festival, complete with Scrumpy and Western, in the comfort of your own venue. www.somersetmade.co.uk/ciderfestivals

The Big Apple hosts festivals in spring and in the autumn.

Three Counties Show

Malvern Showground, Worcester, summer

Top get-together for cider and perry producers in the region, with a bar run by the Three Counties Cider and Perry Association. Check out the trees in the National Collection of Perry Pears. Expect to stay the night.

Ross On Wye Cider Festival

Broome Farm, Ross, Late Aug/Early Sept

Mike Johnson's annual ho-down is legendary, but it's only one of many events held at Broome Farm during the season. Look out for opera, ceilidhs and music weekenders. And cider. And camping.

In 20 years Apple Day has become our unofficial autumn holiday.

Big Apple Autumn Festival

Much Marcle/Putley, October

Like the Spring Blossomtime festival, only in the autumn. And this time, instead of being squeezed into Putley Village Hall, you can get out and meet the makers on their own turf. Visit orchards, help with apple pressing and sample the wares of some top producers.

Apple Day

Everywhere, around 21 Oct

Where to start? Since its foundation in 1990 by Common Ground Apple Day has become the nation's favourite unofficial annual holiday. Apple and cider-related events go on all over the country, particularly at National Trust properties, Wildlife Trust sites and similar venues. Ask around for local events.

Autumn Cidermaking Festivals/ demonstrations

Everywhere, mid to late Oct

Again, there are too many of these to list. If there's a cidermaker nearby, the chances are they'll have some kind of autumn event. A few highlights include:

- Barrington Court, Somerset: help the National Trust collect and press apples using a Victorian press.
- Ralph's Cider Farm, Powys: the pioneering Welsh cidermaker hosts a working weekend, where you can have a go with Victorian scratters and presses of different kinds.
- Mill House Cider Museum, Dorset: two days of traditional cidermaking demonstrations with home-made equipment and some old-fashioned gear.
- Cider Museum, Hereford: hosts an annual festival with traditional cidermaking and other crafts. Look out for the apple varieties displayed on the old Bulmers boardroom table.

Mill House Cider Museum in Dorset hosts cidermaking demonstrations in October.

Q&A MARK SHIRLEY

CIDERMAKER AT ROCKINGHAM FOREST CIDER, MIDDLETON IN NORTHAMPTONSHIRE

What got you interested in cider and perry?
I started making cider in the late 80s, largely because where I live in the East Midlands, good cider was almost impossible to come by. The situation has improved a little over the last few years, but even so, outside of the traditional cidermaking areas, if you want to drink good cider, make your own!

Do you have a treasured memory of a particularly good cider or perry?
I have a particularly fond memory of drinking cider and perry at Jaspar Ely's smallholding at Framilode in Gloucs. I was cycling through the area and had heard about Jaspar through the grapevine. A real Gloucs character and proper cider man. He gave me a tour of the smallholding and we sat drinking his excellent cider and perry on the high wall which protected the cider house from the River Severn when in flood. Jaspar refused to take any money from a 'fellow cidermaker', even though I'd only made a few gallons at this point, and I was saddened to hear of his death a few years later before I had the opportunity to repay the kindness.

Do you have a favourite apple variety?
I like the rounded fruitiness, gentle tannins, and deep golden colour that Yarlington Mill brings to a blend. The best perry I've had was a crystal clear, pale as water, naturally sweet Malvern Hills from Days Cottage.

If you could drink cider in any time or place, where would it be?
In the 80s I recall holidays to the West Country where we would occasionally come upon a small farm gate sign advertising a very local cider for sale. Even then it was possible to find very small-scale farm cidermakers which were virtually unknown outside the local area. To have been able to journey the quiet backwaters of the West Country in the days when almost all farms made cider for farm workers and visitors would have been a treat.

How do you account for the recent surge of interest in cider and cidermaking?
I think the greater interest in cider and cidermaking is associated with the general rise in interest in the provenance of food and drink. More people are growing their own, keeping livestock, and seeking out quality, and/or locally produced food and drink, and cider naturally fits in to this pattern.

Any advice for the novice cidermaker?
Visit a cidermaker, buy some of their ciders and perrys, and ask as many questions as you can. You will rarely be disappointed.

Can you tell us about your best and/or worst moment as a cidermaker?
The most pleasurable moments of our cidermaking year are those spent harvesting fruit in beautiful old orchards. Most aspects of cidermaking are pretty hard work, the harvest included, but time spent in an old orchard, with nothing but woodpeckers, buzzards, and the occasional rambler for company, is a genuine privilege for us. Worst moments? Tennis Elbow, aching back, wasp stings…

What's your most precious bit of cider-related gear?
A small watercolour of an apple, painted for us by our friend Diana Fegredo, which we use in our logo. That's nice.

What can we do to ensure that orchards are still flourishing in 50 years' time?
Create a market for home grown fruit, whether for cidermaking or fresh fruit. Orchard produce is undervalued in the UK, and until this changes orcharding is always likely to be the realm of enthusiasts and hobbyists rather than a mainstream part of agriculture.

Places to Visit/Ciders to Try: Cidermakers, Cider Houses, Pubs & Museums

These listings are not intended to be comprehensive, but to offer a broad selection of cider-related places to visit, useful websites and further reading from the growing collection of excellent cider books. Choosing which pubs to include has been difficult because so many places are now adding a decent selection of ciders and perries, but may well have replaced them by the time you read this. So to qualify for inclusion, the pubs have to be well-established cider houses. If you would like to add a listing for consideration or update information, you can email us via the contact form at www.tangentbooks.co.uk or drop us a line at Tangent Books, Unit 5.16, Paintworks, Arnos Vale, Bristol BS4 3EH. Some of the cidermakers listed encourage visitors, while others have nowhere to put them. To avoid disappointment (or bothering a busy farmer) please check websites or phone before you travel.

DEVON

ASHRIDGE CIDER

Barkingdon Farm, Staverton TQ9 6AN
01803 840483
www.ashridgecider.com
This maker of gorgeous Champagne-style sparkling cider – Raymond Blanc's favourite apple-based tipple – has recently crossed over into the less pricey bottled cider market. One of the best around.

BRIMBLECOMBE

Farrants Farm, Dunsford EX6 7BA
01647 352783
Cider pressed through straw in a medieval cob barn. Call for information on pressing days in the autumn.

GRAY'S FARM CIDER

Halstow, Tedburn St. Mary EX6 6AN
01647 61236
Fifteen generations of experience go into this traditional Devon cider, which is dispensed from oak barrels in the barn behind the farmhouse. The lanes are narrow around there, so mind out when you're driving.

GREEN VALLEY CYDER

Darts Farm, Clyst St George EX3 0QH
01392 876658
The Darts Farm shop outside Exeter is one of the foodie success stories of the Southwest, and tucked in the back is a small but perfectly formed cider factory – a scion of the great Devon company Whiteways. Green Valley also runs an off licence with a fantastic range of

bottled ciders, from top-of-the-range bottle-fermented fizz to its own naturally sweet scrumpy.

HERON VALLEY

Crannacombe Farm, Hazelwood, Loddiswell, Kingsbridge TQ7 4DX
01548 550256
www.heronvalley.co.uk
Producer of organic juices and other drinks, plus good old-fashioned Devon cider. No additives of any kind, not even sulphites – this cider is Live! Visit the shop or order online.

HUNT'S CIDER

Higher Yalberton Farm, Paignton TQ4 7PE
01803 782309
www.huntscider.co.uk
The Hunt family has been making cider in Paignton for two hundred years or more, although there was a period in the mid-20th century when their apples went off to Whiteways instead. Today cider production is in full swing once again – you can go along and buy a flagon at the farm gate.

KILLERTON ESTATE CIDER

Killerton House, Broadclyst EX5 3LE
01392 881418
www.nationaltrust.org.uk
National Trust cidermaking at its best, with fine ciders made from apples grown on the estate – many of them rare local varieties. Look out for seasonal events and opportunities to get involved.

LUSCOMBE CIDER

Luscombe Farm, Colston Road, Buckfastleigh TQ11 0LP
01364 643036
luscombe.co.uk
Traditional award-winning and lightly sparkling Devon cider made only from weird and wonderful Devon apple varieties such as Sops in Wine, Tale Sweet, Pig's Snout, Quench, Slack ma Girdle, and Tom Putt.

LYME BAY CIDER

The Lyme Bay Winery, Shute, Axminster EX13 7PW
01297 551355
www.lymebaywinery.co.uk
Makers of cider, country wines and fruit liqueurs. Their enduringly popular Jack Ratt range is named after the notorious Lyme Bay smuggler Jack Rattenbury (1778-1844), whose hideaways and safe houses dotted the coastline from Weymouth to Topsham. Jack Ratt Vintage Dry won the 2012 Great Taste Award.

THE OLD FIRE HOUSE

50 New North Road, Exeter EX4 4EP
01392 277279
Lively Exeter pub, music venue and popular student haunt – you can always go in the holidays if you want to avoid the students. Wide range of ciders including local treats from Sandford Orchards and Winkleigh.

REDDAWAY'S FARM CIDER

Lower Rixdale Farm, Luton, Chudleigh, Newton Abbot TQ13 0BN
01626 775218
Devon farmhouse cider made in the traditional way from apples grown on the farm, and stored in oak barrels in the cellar under the farmhouse. Top prize-winner at the Devon County Show in 2010.

SANDFORD ORCHARDS

Lower Park Farm, Fordton, Crediton, Devon EX17 3PR
01363 777822
www.sandfordorchards.co.uk
Founded in 2003 by Barny and Marie Butterfield, Sandford Orchards is wowing the critics these days, with two gold medals at the 2012 Great Taste Awards – and deservedly so. They've also won the John Neason Award for Progressive Farming, which rewards Devon farmers who have found innovative ways of improving their businesses. Pop along to the farm shop or look out for bottled Devon Red and Shaky Bridge.

WINKLEIGH CIDER

Western Barn, Hatherleigh Road, Winkleigh, Devon EX19 8AP
01837 83560
www.winkleighcider.com
A scion of famous Devon cidermakers, Inch's Cider, which was taken over by Bulmers in the 1990s. When production moved away from Winkleigh, chief cidermaker David Bridgman decided to stay put and carry on, and since then the family-run business has gone from strength to strength.

YE OLDE CIDER BAR

99 East Street, Newton Abbot TQ12 2LD
01626 354221

Through the ups and downs of the cider industry, Ye Olde Cider Bar has been serving its clientele of regulars and tourists. As you'd expect, there's a great range of ciders and also fruit wines. The place is first stop for the town's youth on Saturday night, but midweek the old boys hold court. One not to be missed.

DORSET

CASTLE INN

The Castle Inn, West Lulworth BH20 5RN
01929 400311
www.thecastleinn-lulworthcove.co.uk

Dorset seems to have more than its fair share of good cider pubs and this thatched inn is no exception. You can even check out the available ciders online before you go…

CIDER BY ROSIE

Winterbourne Houghton
01258 880543
www.ciderbyrosie.co.uk

Rose Grant doesn't have a shop on site but you can find her fabulous cider in numerous local pubs – her website has a handy map showing where they all are. Anyone starting out in small-scale commercial cidermaking should have a read of her blog, which covers just about every aspect of the business in a chatty, informative style.

MILL HOUSE CIDER MUSEUM

Owermoigne, Nr. Dorchester DT2 8HZ
01305 852220
www.millhousecider.com

Open all year round (closed Mondays), the Mill House Cider Museum aims to show visitors just how cider is made the traditional way. Look out for seasonal demonstrations, particularly the autumn cidermaking days.

RED LION, SWANAGE

63 High Street, Swanage BH19 2LY
01929 423533

Lots of cider on offer at this family-run pub, mostly from Westons. B&B available if you're enjoying yourself too much to leave.

ROYAL PORTLAND ARMS

40 Fortuneswell, Portland DT5 1LZ
0871 951 1000

Quirky local with plenty of good cider, including Cider by Rosie when available.

THE SQUARE AND COMPASS

Worth Matravers, Swanage BH19 3LF
01929 439229
www.squareandcompasspub.co.uk

A pub you have to visit at least once in your life. Not only does it possess glorious views over the coast and its own Fossil Museum, it also has an excellent range of ciders, including those made on site by owner Charlie Newman. Plenty of live music, and you can camp within easy walking distance. Probably better to do the cliff walk before the cider, rather than the other way round.

THE STABLE

The Bull Hotel, East St, Bridport DT6 3LF
01308 422878
www.thestabledorset.co.uk

If you needed evidence of the great Dorset cider revival, here it is – a brand new ciderhouse with an ever-increasing range of products from top national makers (not so many locals, though). They sell pizzas too. With plenty of places to stay nearby, this could be an ideal destination for the cider connoisseur.

CORNWALL

CORNISH ORCHARDS

Westnorth Manor Farm, Duloe, Liskeard PL14 4PW
01503 269007
www.cornishorchards.co.uk

Andy spent his formative years at the Cider Bar in Newton Abbot. The National Trust tenant farmer put his training to good use and makes excellent, beautifully packaged ciders from rare Cornish varieties. These include Ellison's Orange, Beauty of Bath, Cornish Longstem, Tommy Knight and Colloggett Pippin.

THE GURNARD'S HEAD HOTEL

Nr Zennor, St. Ives TR26 3DE
www.gurnardshead.co.uk

Fabulous location and they sell Skreach dry cider, which is produced on a deliberately small scale by Hugh Chapman in nearby St. Buryan. Skreach in Zennor? It's a must.

HEALEY'S CORNISH CYDER FARM

Callestick, Penhallow, near Truro TR4 9LW
01872 573356
www.thecornishcyderfarm.co.uk

The Cornish Cyder Farm – formerly known as Cornish Scrumpy – is the largest cidermaker in Cornwall, best known outside the county as the producer of Cornish Rattler. If you're in the area, why not go along for a tractor ride around the orchards or a tour of the production facilities, including the press house, bottlery, jam kitchen, cyder museum, brandy distillery and cellars.

HELFORD CREEK CIDER

Mudgeon Vean Farm, St. Martin, Helston TR17 6DB
01326 231341
www.helfordcreek.co.uk

Cider made from local apple varieties such as Manaccan Primrose, Pigs Snout, John Broad and Tommy Knight, which are grown in the producer's own orchard and at several others nearby.

THE LIZARD CIDER BARN

Predannack, The Lizard TR12 7AU
01326 241481

Produces cider as well as Cornish Cream Liqueur, mead and elderberry wine. Shop sells excellent local ciders, such as Helford Creek and Roskillys, which may otherwise be hard to find, plus there's a vintage cider press outside.

SOMERSET

ASHILL CIDER

Ashtons Farm, Ashill, Illminster TA19 9NE
01823 480513

Just off the A358 between Ilminster and Taunton, Ashill Cider sells good Somerset farmhouse cider. Enjoy a break from the road and a few minutes of peace and quiet.

BARRINGTON COURT

Barrington, near Ilminster TA19 0NQ
01460 242614
www.nationaltrust.org.uk

Since they revived cidermaking here the cider has gained quite a reputation. Harvest and pressing is done by volunteers, so get in touch if you want to help out. You can buy cider from the shop but expect it to be gone by summer.

BRIDGE FARM CIDER

East Chinnock, Nr Yeovil BA22 9EA
01935 862387
www.bridgefarmcider.co.uk

After twenty years the Bridge Farm travelling cider tent is now a welcome sight at festivals and fairs around the country; you can visit the farm shop too and buy a bottle similar to the one presented recently to the Queen (and no doubt snaffled by Prince Charles). Makers of proper Somerset cider and now also a Somerset Cider Brandy distilled at... well, you can guess where.

BRISTOL AND EXETER INN

135 St John Street, Bridgwater TA6 5JA
0871 951 1000

A tiny, rundown local pub that has made it into the online cider guides somehow. Not a place you can pop into surreptitiously.

BURROW HILL CIDER & SOMERSET CIDER BRANDY

Pass Vale Farm, Kingsbury Episcopi TA12 6BU
01460 240782
www.ciderbrandy.co.uk

If you can visit one cider farm in Somerset it has to be Burrow Hill. Walk up the hill and around the orchards. Admire Josephine and Fifi, the alembic stills that turn farmhouse cider into fine cider brandy. And when you visit the shop, note the huge antique press that serves as a kind of impromptu shelving system.

PAUL CHANT CIDER

Midsomer Norton, Somerset
07940 853099
www.paulchant.com

The other half of the Frank Naish cidermaking operation, Paul also makes his own authentic Somerset ciders, which are not for the faint-hearted. His Badger's Spit will make your eyes water, then have you crying for more...

CROSSMANS CIDER

Mayfield Farm, Hewish, Weston-Super-Mare BS24 6RQ
01934 833174

Ben Crossman is the 4th generation of cidermakers at Mayfield Farm and his cider is a firm favourite in the Bristol region. Hewish is just off the M5 near Weston, so why not drop by? They have a nice new sign, so you can't miss 'em.

ELI'S AKA THE ROSE & CROWN

Huish Episcopi, Langport TA10 9QT
01458 250494

Characterful local pub explored in detail by Ian Marchant in his book *The Longest Crawl*. Though the days of self-service from the barrel are gone, the pub with its warren of stone-flagged rooms is well worth a visit.

HALFWAY HOUSE

Pitney Hill, Langport TA10 9AB
01458 252513
www.thehalfwayhouse.co.uk

The recipient of numerous awards, this quiet, characterful country pub has ciders from Hecks and, when available, Wilkins.

HECKS

9-11 Middle Leigh, Street BA16 0LB
01458 442367
www.hecksfarmhousecider.co.uk

Hecks is unrivalled in its range of single variety ciders and remains a firm favourite of many dedicated cider drinkers. A visit to the shop is the perfect antidote to an afternoon buying shoes at Clarks down the road.

LAMB AND FOUNTAIN

57 Castle Street, Frome BA11 3BW
01373 463414

Another local pub lost in time. Farmhouse cider on tap, to accompany the 70s décor.

NAISH'S CIDER

Piltown Farm,West Pennard, Glastonbury BA6 8NQ
07940 853099 (Paul Chant)

Frank Naish is a legend, a cidermaker who was pressing apples before World War II. He keeps things simple so expect a properly challenging, dry Somerset farmhouse cider. Take your own container and call before you set off.

ORCHARD PIG

West Bradley Orchard, West Bradley, Nr Glastonbury BA6 8LT
01458 851222
www.orchardpig.co.uk

Not really a place to visit, but they do have regular events and festivals, and the location is stunning. Check the website for information and to find out the best places to find Orchard Pig cider.

PARSON'S CHOICE

Parsonage Farm, West Lyng TA3 5AP
01823 490978

Proper farmhouse cider with no frills and no fuss, made with vintage cider apples in the place they grow best. What more could you ask for? You'll find Parsonage Farm between Taunton and Glastonbury, a couple of miles from King Alfred's old haunt at Athelney.

PENNARD CIDER

Avalon Vineyard, The Drove, East Pennard, Shepton Mallet BA4 6UA
01749 860393
www.pennardorganicwines.co.uk

Organic juice pressed through straw is the basis for this old-fashioned Somerset cider.

PERRY'S CIDER MILLS

Dowlish Wake, Ilminster TA19 0NY
01460 55195
www.perryscider.co.uk

A venerable Somerset cider company that regularly wins prizes, not surprising as their Vintage Cider and single varieties like Dabinett are top-notch. The museum is well worth a look, and there's a good shop and cafe. Dowlish Wake was the home of Speke, intrepid explorer of the Nile.

PILTON CIDER

Pilton, Somerset
01749 830 205
www.piltoncider.com

Makers of an excellent keeved sparkling cider which you can buy in up-market shops. Close to a hundred different apples find their way into the mix, gathered in four Somerset orchards. That's dedication for you.

PLOUGH INN

75 Station Road, Taunton TA1 1PB
01823 324404
www.theploughtaunton.co.uk

Handy for the station and the cricket ground, the Plough does its bit for local cidermakers by selling Tricky Cider and other brands you won't find in too many pubs around the country.

RICH'S

Mill Farm, Watchfield TA9 4RD
01278 783651
www.richscider.co.uk

Another entertaining little museum, and you can wander through to admire the giant vats that were rescued from Coates in Nailsea. The shop caters to holidaymakers and even sells cider in miniature glass kegs – possibly the world's smallest cider containers. They sell by the gallon too, of course. Popular restaurant and regular events, including a major wassail.

SHEPPY'S FARM & CIDER CENTRE

Three Bridges Farm, Bradford-on-Tone TA4 1ER
01823 461233
www.sheppyscider.com
One of the oldest Somerset cider companies (they've been at it more than 200 years) and producer of some wonderful bottled ciders, both single varieties and blends. Their (bottled) Somerset Draught Cider is among the best in its class. Pull off the M5 at Junction 26 to visit the farm shop, take a stroll around the farm and orchards or nose round the museum, which is jam-packed with old farming gear and cidermaking equipment. If you see Sheppy's on draught anywhere, grab some quick.

SOMERSET RURAL LIFE MUSEUM

Abbey Farm, Chilkwell Street, Glastonbury BA6 8DB
01458 831197
If you're interested in Somerset history then this is a must, with plenty of exhibits and books relating to cidermaking. Look out for exhibitions such as Bill Bradshaw's travelling photography show, IAMCIDER, and special events such as apple pressing and wassail. The Rifleman is just round the corner if you fancy a glass of Wilkins after your exertions.

THATCHERS CIDER COMPANY

Myrtle Farm, Sandford BS25 5RA
01934 822862
www.thatcherscider.co.uk
It's changed a bit since the days when you got your cider from a barrel in the shed, except that you still get your cider from a barrel. Here you will find all your favourites on draught and a great selection of bottled blends and single varieties. If you want to see more, take a walk up the lane next door and cast your eye over several generations of orchards. The Railway down the road has a lovely garden and lots of Thatchers – not surprising as it's owned by the company.

TORRE CIDER FARM

Washford, Watchet TA23 0LA
01984 640004
www.torrecider.com
Farmer-cidermakers who produce the alarming-sounding Sheepstagger and Tornado ciders. Have a taste while the family admire pygmy goats at the farm or drink tea in the café…

TRICKY CIDER

The Old Bakery, Honiton Road, Churchinford TA3 7RF
01823 602782
www.trickycider.com
Originally made at Tricky Warren Farm, in the wilds of the Blackdown Hills, Tricky is a proper Somerset cider with one of the more imaginative labels around… Look out for the mobile bar at a festival near you.

WEST CROFT CIDER

West Croft Farm, Brent Knoll TA9 4BE
01278 760762
Maker of Janet's Jungle Juice, West Croft offers visitors draught cider from the barrel and a fine example of ciderhouse décor. For anyone wanting to leave Magners behind and explore Somerset cider, a quick detour off the M5 to Brent Knoll is highly recommended.

WILKINS

Land's End Farm, Mudgley BS28 4TU
01934 712358
www.wilkinscider.com
The most famous farmer-cidermaker of them all, Roger Wilkins still divides his time between cider barn and cattle. Land's End Farm is practically a holy site to thousands of fans, so expect a crowd if you visit in summer. Excellent, no frills Somerset cider, the closest thing you'll get to an old-fashioned village ciderhouse, and some very good cheddar from Westcombe.

WOOKEY HOLE INN

High Street, Wookey Hole, Wells BA5 1BP
01749 676677
www.wookeyholeinn.com
The antique exterior belies the renovations within, in a bright modern style one reviewer described as 'Austin Powers'. Not the cheapest eating in town but they do sell the good stuff from Mudgley (see above).

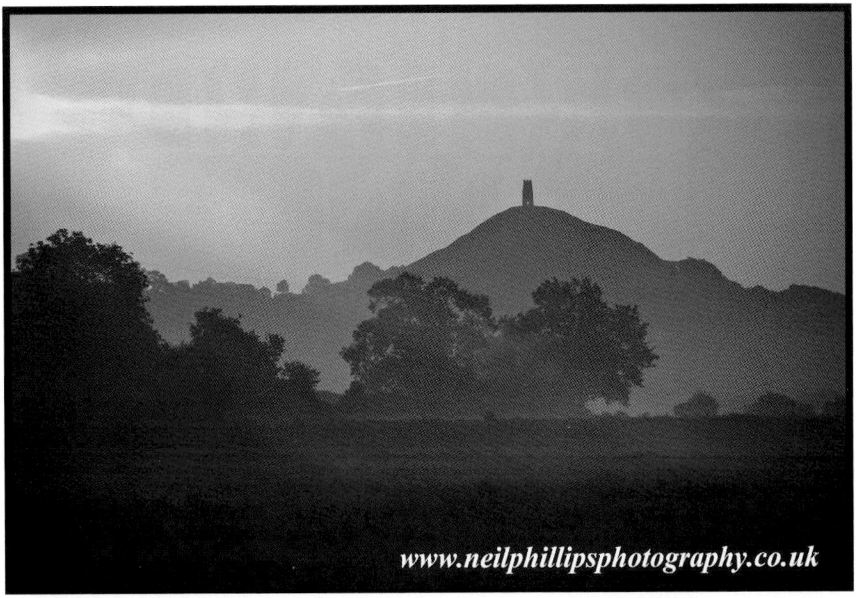

www.neilphillipsphotography.co.uk

WORLEY'S CIDER

No 55, Dean, Shepton Mallet BA4 4SA
07855 951718
www.worleyscider.co.uk

Neil Worley's cidermaking career took off when he won First Prize at the Bath & West at the first time of asking. Life in the tiny hamlet of Dean has never been the same since…

THREE COUNTIES

BARBOURNE CIDER

www.barbournecider.co.uk

Small-scale Worcestershire cider and perry maker selling online and via Worcester pubs like The Plough. Look out for their Blakeney Red Worcestershire Perry.

BARNFIELD WINERY & CIDER MILL

Broadway Road, Broadway, Worcestershire WR12 7HB
01386 853145
www.barnfieldcidermill.co.uk

Visit the shop and try a range of fruit wines, cider and perry as you admire the antique stone mill and presses.

CAFÉ RENE

31 Southgate Street, Gloucester GL1 1TP
01452 309340
www.caferene.co.uk

Unobtrusive French-themed bar/restaurant hidden away behind an arch. Good range of ciders and food if you fancy it.

CIDER MUSEUM & KING OFFA DISTILLERY

21 Ryelands Street, Hereford HR4 0LW
01432 354 207
www.cidermuseum.co.uk

A museum established in the old Bulmers factory after the company expanded in the 1960s, this is a fascinating day out for cider enthusiasts. The shop sells a range of top local ciders, as well as cider brandy. Check the website for details of regular events through the year, including the International Cider Competition.

THE CROWN INN

Woolhope, Herefordshire HR1 4QP
www.crowninnwoolhope.co.uk

Classy local, whose owners used to run the Scrumpy House restaurant at Westons. With contacts like these, you can expect some decent cider. Look out for Oliver's…

DUNKERTONS CIDER MILL

Pembridge, Leominster HR6 9ED
01544 388653
www.dunkertons.co.uk

Anyone who claims that you can't make a commercial success out of a fully organic cider operation should visit Dunkertons, the first cidermaker to gain Soil Association accreditation. Black Fox is an outstanding cider, widely available in upmarket stores such as Waitrose.

THE FLEECE INN

The Cross, Bretforton, Nr Evesham, Worcester WR11 7JE
01386 831173
www.thefleeceinn.co.uk

Gorgeous old Vale of Evesham pub now owned by the National Trust after being in the same family for centuries. Home of the British Asparagus Festival Day in May and the Apples and Ale Festival in October. The landlord sells his own Ark Cider, which is made at the pub.

GREGG'S PIT CIDER AND PERRY

Much Marcle, Herefordshire HR8 2NL
01531 660687
www.greggs-pit.co.uk

Living proof of what you can achieve making cider on a small scale, Gregg's Pit is a frequent award-winner and a favourite among people who know a good perry when they see one. Visit during the Big Apple autumn festival, or look at the website for information on what's available – you have to be on the ball to get your hands on that fine perry.

GWATKIN CIDER

Moorhampton Park Farm, Abbey Dore, Herfordshire HR2 0AL
01981 550258
www.gwatkincider.co.uk

An extremely popular and highly respected cidermaker, Gwatkin has a habit of wowing CAMRA judges. A fine range of ciders and perries, and well worth visiting.

HARTLAND CIDER

Tirley Villa, Tirley, Gloucester, Gloucestershire GL19 4HA
01452 780480

Long-standing family cider business formerly run by legendary countryman Ray Hartland. They make a decent farmhouse perry.

HELLENS

Much Marcle, Herefordshire HR8 2LY
01531 660504
www.hellensmanor.com

Just down the road from Westons, Hellens is a fine old mansion with an avenue of perry pears. It's open to the public part of the time and in the autumn you can go along to press perry pears. Check website before you travel.

HENNEY'S CIDER

Bishops Frome, Herefordshire WR6 5AP
www.henneys.co.uk

Included here because Henney's Dry is one of the best ciders available in supermarkets - a reasonably priced, consistently delicious cider. Novice cidermakers beware: Mike Henney started out fermenting 5 gallons in the airing cupboard for fun… Now produces 200,000 gallons plus per year.

HEREFORDSHIRE CIDER ROUTE

www.ciderroute.co.uk

Very useful website promoting the county's cider and perry attractions, with cycle routes to download and lots of information about the county's top producers. The route from Ledbury around the Marcle Ridge is particularly recommended.

THE HOP POCKET

Hop Pocket Craft Centre, New House Farm, Bishops Frome, Herefordshire WR6 5BT
01531 640592
www.hoppocketwine.co.uk

Shop selling cider and perry among a vast range of drinks. Regular tastings, or you can order by phone.

LIVE AND LET LIVE

Bringsty Common, Bringsty, Worcester WR6 5UW
01886 821462
www.liveandletlive-bringsty.co.uk

Lovely thatched pub serving Oliver's cider and perry, among others.

LYNE DOWN CIDER AND PERRY

The Cider Barn, Lyne Down, Much Marcle, Herefordshire HR8 2NT
07756 108501
www.lynedowncider.co.uk

Long-established company that was run for many years by the brilliant Jean Nowell. Look out for their prize-winning Roaring Meg cider.

MCCRINDLE'S CIDER

Little Loiterpin, Blakeney Hill, Blakeney, Gloucestershire GL15 4AH
01594 517 387

James McCrindle makes cider and perry in small batches; his new champagne-method perry is a winner.

MILLETS FARM SHOP, EVESHAM

Evesham Country Park, Evesham, Worcestershire WR11 4TP
01386 423970

A range of unusual draught ciders and perries available in their Cider Corner.

MINERS ARMS

New Rd, Lydney, Gloucestershire GL15 4PE
01594 562483
www.minersarmswhitecroft.com

Excellent Free House with a good range of regional ciders.

THE MONKEY HOUSE, DEFFORD

Woodmancote (A4104), Defford, Worcs WR8 9BW
01386 750234

Much-loved old cider house. Phone before you go to make sure it's open, as the hours are mildly irregular.

NORBURY'S NORREST FARM & CIDER CO

Holywell Farm Buildings, Storridge, Nr Malvern, Worcestershire WR13 5HD
01886 83 22 06

Fruit farm offering seasonal PYO and maker of the fierce-sounding Norbury's Black Bull cider.

OLIVER'S CIDER AND PERRY

Moor House Farm, Ocle Pychard, Herefordshire HR13QZ
01432 820569
www.theolivers.org.uk

One of the finest craft producers around, Oliver's is the kind of outfit the government should cherish and protect. But there's not much chance of that, so it's up to us to go along (Saturdays only) or visit the website and buy lots of cider and perry. Highly recommended, particularly the Normandy-style perry. American readers should look out for Gold Rush Cider – an epoch-making transatlantic collaboration between Tom Oliver and Greg Hall of Virtue Cider, Chicago IL.

ONCE UPON A TREE & DRAGON ORCHARD

Dragon Orchard, Putley, Ledbury HR8 2RG (note for Sat Nav users - the postcode will take you next door - look for sign)
01531 670263
www.onceuponatree.co.uk
Weds-Sun

A marvellous example of creative thinking in agriculture, Dragon Orchard is partly sustained by a cropshare system. Its owners also work closely with neighbour Simon Day, expert winemaker and founder of Once Upon a Tree. Not surprisingly his ciders and perries are excellent, and you have to try the ice cider. Visit Weds-Sun, or check the website.

THE ORCHARD CENTRE

Blackwells End, Hartpury GL19 3DB
www.tasteandexplore.com/cider-perry-centre.shtml

Visitor centre at the heart of the National Collection of Perry Pears, and the venue for many of the events run by Peter Mitchell through his Cider and Perry Academy. Hindlip Ciders and Hartpury Perries are produced at the Centre. A must-visit for perry fans.

THE PLOUGH, WORCESTER

23 Fish Street, Worcester WR1 2HN
0871 951 1000

Eccentric, old-fashioned city centre pub noted for its friendly atmosphere. Cider from Barbourne, Hogans and other small-scale producers.

THE RAILWAY INN

Station Road, Newnham-On-Severn GL14 1DA
01594 516 317
www.newnhamonsevern.co.uk

Unpretentious local pub with a staggering selection of ciders, many of them from regional producers and otherwise hard to find. You could conceivably go there by train, if you don't mind a lengthy walk from Lydney.

ROSS-ON-WYE & BROOME FARM CIDER AND PERRY

Broome Farm, Peterstow HR9 6QG
01989 769556
www.rosscider.com

Mike Johnson is one of those people whose influence is acknowledged by many other cidermakers. A frequent award-winner, his ciders and perries are of course top notch. Try them at the shop on-site and check for details of seasonal events – the autumn cider festival is highly recommended. If Ross is too far to travel, you can buy Mike's ciders and perries online at www.cideronline.net.

SEVERN CIDER

The Old Vicarage, Awre GL14 1EL
01594 510282
www.severncider.com

Severn Cider has revived production in one of the legendary parishes of Ciderland using timeless local varieties like Hagloe Crab to produce a range of delicious, characterful ciders and perries. Visit the Cellar at the Old Vicarage to sample and buy.

STROUD FARMERS' MARKET

Cornhill Market Place, Stroud
fresh-n-local.co.uk/markets/stroud.php
Saturdays

This great farmers' market features cider and perry from Lyne Down Farm, Days Cottage and other notable local producers. Check the website for other market's in the area.

THREE COUNTIES CIDER SHOP

5a The Homend, Ledbury, Hereford HR8 1BN
01531 670263
www.threecountiescider.co.uk

New venture from Once Upon a Tree offering up to a dozen ciders and perries on draught and many more in bottles. Also sell hampers of local treats.

WESTONS

The Bounds, Much Marcle HR8 2NQ
01531 660233
www.westons-cider.co.uk

Every cider lover should visit Much Marcle, ideally during the Big Apple autumn festival. Westons is always worth a look, not just for the shop, where you can buy cider by the pallet-load, and the restaurant. The Bounds is a very cool place, with its 18th century farmhouse and 21st century storage tanks.

SOUTHERN ENGLAND

CIDERNIKS

7 High Street, Kintbury, Hungerford, Berkshire RG17 9TJ
07885 296789
www.ciderniks.com

Tasty dry ciders include Combe Raider and Dab Hand.

COTSWOLD CIDER COMPANY

54 Coleshill, Oxfordshire SN6 7PT
www.cotswoldciderco.com

Exciting, stylish cider company that supports Common Ground – good for them! Their Coleshill House bottle-fermented cider won its class at the Bath & West in 2012, mostly for its full, dry flavour but also for its wonderful packaging.

GODSHILL CIDER

High Street, Godshill, Isle of Wight PO38 3HZ
01983 840680
godshillisleofwight.co.uk

Local orchards supply Porter's Perfection, Somerset Redstreak, Sweet Cleave, Tan Harvey, Taunton Fair Maid and a host of other apples, which are pressed in the traditional manner. Look out for the posh hand-crafted cider jars. Who knew the Isle of Wight had such treasures?

HANDMADE CIDER

Slaughterford Mill, Chippenham SN14 8RJ
07590 264 804
www.handmadecider.co.uk

Engineer and cidermaker Denis France sources his fruit from two old Somerset orchards, and makes a range of bottled and draught ciders. He somehow found time to build his own bar, which you can hire for weddings and other events…

MILLWHITES CIDER

The Cider Mill, Bourne End Farm, London Road, Hemel Hempstead HP1 2RH
07904 525865/07710 525220
www.millwhites.co.uk

Don't be fooled by the address: Millwhites is made from cider apples grown on the company's own Somerset orchards. It's available all over the country these days - powerful stuff, too.

THE NATIONAL COLLECTION OF CIDER AND PERRY

Middle Farm, Firle, Lewes, East Sussex, BN8 6LJ
01323 811324
www.middlefarm.com

Cider? Perry? Sussex? Well it all makes sense because the National Collection occupies middle ground between the Eastern Counties and the West. Within easy distance of London you'll find a massive range of ciders and perries and plenty of help choosing.

NEW FOREST CIDER

Pound Land, Burley BH24 4ED
01425 403598
www.newforestcider.co.uk

For many years Barry Topp has been Ciderland's unofficial ambassador to London, selling his and other people's cider at Borough Market. You can also visit him in the New Forest, where there's a shop and a handy B&B.

SEDLESCOMBE VINEYARD

Cripp's Corner, Sedlescombe, nr Robertsbridge, East Sussex, TN32 5SA
01580 830715

An organic vineyard also specialising in organic cider. You can visit most days through the summer and autumn, with guided tours available if you book in advance.

UPTON CIDER

Upton Fruit Farm, Upton, Didcot, Oxfordshire OX11 9JE
www.uptoncider.co.uk

Stan Lynch planted a 10-acre orchard in the early 1970s to provide fruit (including Michelin, Dabinett, Yarlington Mill) for Taunton Cider. A decade later he started making cider himself, and the tradition continues today. Good strong farmhouse cider.

VIRTUAL ORCHARD

Nr Milton Keynes, Buckinghamshire
www.virtualorchard.co.uk

Laurence Conisbee is a brave soul. Not only is he an example of that rare creature, the Buckinghamshire cidermaker, he also sources his fruit from a bewildering number of small, privately owned orchards. AND he recently gave up his day job to make cider full time. It does help that his Hard Core cider has won CAMRA's top prize… Website links to a Google map of his Virtual Orchard. Love it!

EASTERN COUNTIES

BADGERS HILL CIDERY

Chilham, nr Canterbury, CT4 8BW
01227 730573

A pioneer of Kentish cider during the slow years before Magners, Badgers Hill started up when the supermarkets' stranglehold on the fruit market made fruit growing economically unviable. Today you can visit the farm shop between March and December, buy their Pippin Cider and see what's on offer entertainment-wise for the kids.

BIDDENDEN

Biddenden Vineyards, Gribble Bridge Lane, Biddenden, Kent TN27 8DF
01580 291726
www.biddendenvineyards.com

The most established cidermaker in Kent, Biddendens makes some of the strongest cider we've come across. You can find it at Chimes in Pimlico and at other London pubs, or visit the shop, taste wine and cider, and take a stroll round the vineyards.

BROGDALE HORTICULTURAL TRUST

Brogdale Farm, Faversham, Kent ME13 8XZ
01795 535286
www.brogdale.org

Home of the National Fruit Collection, Brogdale Farm offers visitors an opportunity to see and taste all manner of fruit, from apples to hazelnuts. A must for orchard fans, and there are cider-related events and festivals too – check website for details.

CASTLINGS HEATH COTTAGE ORGANIC CIDER

Castlings Heath Cottage, Castlings Heath, Groton, Sudbury, Suffolk CO10 5ES
01787 210899

Made by Tom Norton, landlord of The White Horse pub in nearby Edwardstone. Good, strong, dry cider made the East Anglian way.

THE CIDER SHED

98-100 Lawson Road, Norwich NR3 4LF
01603 413153
www.theshednorwich.co.uk

Norfolk's new ciderhouse has its roots in Gaymer country. Ciders from Burnard's include Montys Dog Dry, and Gilberts Growler Perry is sometimes available. Check website for music events and up-to-date cider listings.

ESSEX CIDER SHOP

166 Moulsham Street, Chelmsford, Essex CM2 0LD
01245 264177
www.theessexcidershop.co.uk

Crikey. This new shop stocks over a hundred ciders and perries, not only from Thatchers and Westons, but also from a diverse range of smaller producers. Rather like the Bristol Cider Shop, in fact…

NORFOLK CIDER COMPANY

Wroxham Barns, Tunstead Road, Hoveton, Norfolk NR12 8QU
01603 784876 (day); 01953 860533 (eve)
www.norfolkcider.com

Traditional East Anglian cider made since the mid-1980s and continuing a centuries-old Norfolk tradition. Look out for the yellow Kingfisher Farm label in pubs around Norwich and the Broads.

PAWLEY FARM CIDER

Kimberlea, Pawley Farm, Painters Forstal, Faversham, Kent ME13 0EN
01795 532043

Kentish cider made to a 200-year old family recipe. Phone for info on orchard tours, etc.

PICKLED PIG

Stretham, nr Ely, Cambs
www.pickledpig.co.uk

Porker's Snout? Sweet Little Pig? Next time you're in the Ely area, see if you can get your hands on one of Pickled Pig's all-natural ciders. Check website for availability and outlets.

ROUGH OLD WIFE

Cork Farm, Hawkins Rough Orchard, Long Hill, Old Wives Lees, Canterbury CT4 8BN
01227 732414
www.rougholdwife.com

Up-and-coming Kent producer that sells to local pubs and farm shops, and also welcomes visitors. In the past they've offered a Juice Your Own service and enjoyed having people help out with harvest and pressing, so contact them if you'd like to get involved.

WHIN HILL CIDER
Stearman's Yard, Wells-next-the-Sea NR23 1BT
01328 711033
www.whinhillcider.co.uk
Unusually for an Eastern Counties producer, Whin Hill Cider uses vintage cider apples grown in a North Norfolk orchard. Visit the shop in downtown Wells-next-the-Sea, buy some cider and drink it on the beach – perfect!

LONDON

THE BREE LOUISE
69 Cobourg Street, NW1 2HH
0207 681 4930
www.thebreelouise.com
Down-to-earth backstreet pub round the corner from Euston Station. Don't expect glamorous surroundings or fine dining. Do expect a stimulating range of draught ciders, from Westons to small producers like Ciderniks, and a choice of pies. Friendly discounts for CAMRA, students, NHS & armed forces.

CHIMES RESTAURANT
26 Churton St, SW1V 2LP
0207 821 7456
www.chimes-of-pimlico.co.uk
A restaurant specialising in English food, with a longstanding reputation as a place to drink cider and perry. As well as some well-known national favourites, look out for Biddendens and Merrydown, which has a staunch local following.

THE CIDER TAP
190 Euston Road, London, NW1 2EF
www.eustontap.com
Claims to be London's only dedicated cider bar, and they certainly have plenty to choose from. What is it about Euston that attracts so many ciderheads? Look out for Wilkins, Oliver's Perry, Sandford Orchards and more.

THE DUCHESS OF CAMBRIDGE
320 Goldhawk Road, Stamford Brook London W6 0XF
0208 834 7336
www.theduchessofcambridgepub.com
Sister pub of the Bree Louise, with a similar range of ciders available.

THE GREEN MAN
36 Riding House St, London W1W 7EP
0207 580 9087
www.thegreenmanw1.co.uk
A Cider House and Kitchen in the heart of Fitzrovia? An early champion of the London cider revival, the Green Man offers quirkily stylish surroundings, good pub grub and a youthful crowd. Has its own Green Man Special Cider alongside an eclectic mix of real and, er, less real ciders.

THE HARP TAVERN
47 Chandos Place, London WC2N 4HS
0207 836 0291
www.harpcoventgarden.com
Crowded little pub full of character and probably the best selection of craft cider and perry in the capital. Don't be put off by the impressive display of real ales – the cider's in the fridge and you order from a menu…

HERMIT'S CAVE
28 Camberwell Church Street, SE5 8QU
0207 703 3188
Friendly haunt of Camberwell art students and proper old-fashioned regulars.

JOLLY BUTCHERS
204 Stoke Newington High St, N16 7HU
0207 249 9471
jollybutchers.co.uk
Solid real ale pub with a decent selection of ciders.

NEW FOREST CIDER
Borough Market, Southwark St, London SE1 1TL (London Bridge tube)
Thurs-Sat
www.newforestcider.co.uk
Barry Topp was one of the first stallholders when Borough Market started up again a few years back, and now his boldness is paying dividends. Think of a food and you can probably buy it in this bustling market, then wash it down with a jar of New Forest. Burrow Hill and other ciders also available.

ORCHARD PRESS CIDER
Greenwich Market, Greenwich, SE10 9HY
www.orchardpresscider.com
Purveyor of upmarket sparkling ciders, with a stylish vintage website. Great excuse to visit Greenwich Market.

PEMBURY TAVERN
90 Amhurst Road, Hackney, E8 1JH
0208 986 8597.
www.individualpubs.co.uk/pembury
Vast old corner pub that was resurrected a few years ago by the Individual Pubs group. They've had some good ciders since, and you should find at least one on draught.

SOUTHAMPTON ARMS
139 Highgate Rd, NW5 1LE
www.thesouthamptonarms.co.uk
A pub of genuine independence and character, which only sells ale and cider from equally characterful and independent brewers and cidermakers. Cash only. No bookings. Unsurprisingly, others have tried to emulate the Southampton's charms (see website for details)…

BRISTOL & BATH

THE APPLE
Welsh Back BS1 4SB
0117 925 3500
www.applecider.co.uk
All aboard! Yes, The Apple is a boat packed with cider drinkers, and a fine vessel she is too. Half a dozen draught ciders, usually including Hecks and Thatchers, plus numerous bottles. The DIY Ploughman's makes a great Saturday lunch.

THE APPLE TREE
27 Philip Street, Bedminster
0117 966 7097
Legendary Bedminster cider house. The Barley Mow, which has a similar ambience, is a short stumble back towards Asda.

ARNOLFINI CAFÉ BAR
16 Narrow Quay BS1 4QA
0117 917 2300
Cider from Bristol Cider Works. Have a couple, then go and look at the art. It's more fun that way.

BRISTOL CIDER HOUSE
8-9 Surrey Street BS2 8PS
0117 942 8196
www.bristolciderhouse.co.uk
If you're not that fond of shopping, escape Cabot's Circus for this characterful old drinking den. Open Monday to Saturday for a pint of decent cider, or you can book for a group tasting session in the upstairs bar.

BRISTOL CIDER SHOP
7 Christmas Steps BS1 5BS
0117 3821679
www.bristolcidershop.co.uk
The first and best cider shop in the land, selling bottled and draught cider and perry from producers located within a fifty-mile radius of Bristol (a bit of choice, then). Peter and Nick try every cider and perry they sell, and know most of the producers personally, and they'll do their utmost to find a drink for every taste (except bad taste). Also run cider- and perry-making days, and other events throughout the year.

THE CAT & WHEEL
207 Cheltenham Road, BS6 5QX
0117 942 7862
A Moles pub – that's the brewery, not the burrowing mammal, so expect their various ciders and more.

THE CORONATION TAP
8 Sion Place Clifton BS8 4AX
0117 9739617
www.thecoronationtap.com
What can we say? This famous old ciderhouse has been a second home to generations of Bristol University students, and recently it has gained quite a reputation as an intimate music venue. If you've never been Corried, it's probably about time you were.

COTHAM PORTER STORES
15 Cotham Road South BS6 5TZ
0117 903 0689
Once upon a time pub toilets were usually outdoors and at Cotham Porter Stores they still are! A pub of character, or should that be 'characters', and one that must rank as one of the nation's narrowest.

DAYS COTTAGE
Bristol Farmers' Market, Corn Street, Wednesdays
www.dayscottage.co.uk
Days Cottage perry was good enough for Hugh Fearnley-Whittingstall, and we have to admit that their draught cider fuelled much of the writing of this book. You won't find Days Cottage in any pubs, but you can buy cider

and perry – as well as apple juice and apples in season – from the stall.

THE DUKE OF YORK

2 Jubilee Road, Baptist Mills BS2 9RS
0117 941 3677
Splendidly eccentric pub, outside and in, and well worth a visit. Perries are quite lethal.

THE GREEN MAN

21 Alfred Place, BS2 8HD 0117 930 4824
Organic pub that has had Sheppys on draught in the past, along with bottled ciders like Luscombe.

THE NOVA SCOTIA

Nova Scotia Place, Hotwells BS1 6XJ
0117 929 7994
www.novascotiahotel.co.uk
Can you beat sitting outside the Nova on a sunny afternoon with a pint of cider, watching the old boys potter about with their boats? No, didn't think so…

THE OLD DUKE

45 King Street, BS1 4ER
0117 927 7137
www.theoldduke.co.uk
Jazz meets cider at an old Bristol favourite. Can get very busy, and hot, which is a good excuse to drink more cider.

THE ORCHARD INN

12 Hanover Place BS1 6XT
0117 9262678
www.orchardinn.com
Just round the back of the ss Great Britain, the Orchard is unique in the range and quality of its farmhouse ciders and perries. We don't know of any other pub with a dozen, constantly changing brands on offer, including such obscure favourites as Brimblecombe and Ashill. Expect a varied crowd, from Aardman whizkids to old boys who remember when this was the heart of the working docks.

THE STABLE

Canon's Road, Harbourside BS1 5UH
0117 927 9999
www.stablepizza.com
The first Stable cider and pizza bar was opened by Richard and Nikki Cooper in Bridport in 2009 and by the time Fullers bought a large chunk of the company in 2014, there were six Stable bars across the West Country. This is the modern face of the cider house. Loads of craft ciders served in stylish, family-friendly bars along with pizza and pies.

THE SUGAR LOAF

51 St Marks Road, Easton BS5 6HX
0117 939 4498
www.sugarloafpub.co.uk
Lively Easton local which is only a minute's stumble from Stapleton Road station. Pick up a curry from Bristol Sweet Mart on the way home.

TUCKER'S GRAVE

Faulkland, Radstock, Bath, Somerset BA3 5XF
0871 951 1000
Tiny pub with a cult following, and Cheddar Valley on tap. Having been a pub for over 200 years – it was named after the burial place of Edwin Tucker, who committed suicide in 1747 – the place closed in 2011, only to return from the dead a couple of months later. Hooray! According to CAMRA, this is one of only 11 British pubs that doesn't have a bar. So now you know.

WALES

BLAENGAWNEY CIDER

Blaengawney Farm, Mynydd Maen, Hafodyrynys, Caerphilly NP11 5AY
01495 246629
Prize-winning maker of traditional ciders, including Hallets Real Cider. Swept the board at the 2011 Welsh Perry and Cider Championships, then hosted the 2012 event, winning Champion Perry. Just wait till their new orchards reach maturity…

BILL BLEASDALE'S WELSH MOUNTAIN ORCHARDS

Prospect Orchard, Prospect, Newchapel, Llanidloes, Powys, SY1 6JY
01686 411277 / 0779 0071729
A cidermaker himself, Bill sells a wide range of eating, cooking and cider apple trees, both vintage and new, and does all sorts of grafting and orchard renovation-type stuff. He's also the author of the hilarious, informative 'How to Grow Apples and Make Cider', which is hand-written and hand-drawn. Do you know how to create a Vole Zone of Doom around an apple sapling? Read Bill's book and find out.

BLUEBELL INN

Rhosesmor Road, Halkyn, Flintshire CH8 8DL
01352 780309
www.BlueBell.uk.eu.org

Family-run, award-winning Free House that lists its ales and ciders online and adds descriptions of the drinks and pen portraits of their producers. Lots of music and fun events like murder mystery nights. Oh to be in Halkyn!

GWYNT Y DDRAIG

Llest Farm, Llantwit Fardre, Pontypridd, Rhondda Cynon Taff CF38 2PW
01443 209 852
www.gwyntcider.com

The tearaway success of the Welsh cider renaissance, Gwynt y Ddraig is now competing with the big boys in Bristol and beyond. Visit during the annual Open Day and for other events, or check the website to find out where you can buy Fiery Fox and other ciders.

THE PENRHYN ARMS

Pendre Rd, Penrhynside, Llandudno, Conwy LL30 3BY.
07780 678927
www.penrhynarms.com

A splendid selection of ciders and perries makes this one of the best cider pubs in Wales. Look out for the Penrhyn Arms House Ciders, Old Digger and Red Ruby; groups of up to eight can stay at Ruby's Apartment next door.

RALPHS CIDER & CIDER HOUSE

Old Badland, New Radnor, Presteigne, Powys LD8 2TG
01544 350304
www.ralphsciderfestival.co.uk

One of few proper ciderhouses left, Ralphs is well worth visiting. Look out for their amazing collection of old cidermaking gear, much of it still in use today. You can also see Ralphs out and about on the festival circuit.

ROSIE'S TRIPLE-D CIDER

Dafarn Dywyrch Farm, Llandegla, Wrexham, Denbighshire LL11 3BA
01978 790222

Cidermaker Steve Hughes has an excellent relationship with the Bluebell Inn (above); once a year he takes his vintage scratter and press to the pub, to make Rosie's Blue Bell Cider.

TOLOJA ORCHARDS

01570 471295
tolojaorchards196.vpweb.co.uk

Cidermaker based on a smallholding overlooking Cardigan Bay. Look out for bottled ciders in shops in and around Lampeter: Lancelot, Guinevere, Merlin's Potion and other products with an Arthurian flavour.

TROGGI SEIDR

Lower House Cottage, Earlswood, Monmouthshire
01291 650653

Founded in 1984, Troggi specialises in whole juice cider and perry.

TY BRYN CIDER

Upper House Farm, Grosmont, Abergavenny, Monmouthshire NP7 8LA
01873 821237

Lovely traditional ciders from producer Tony Watkins. Apples grown on the farm. Also offer a pressing service.

TY GWYN CIDER

Whitehouse Farm, Crossways, Newcastle, Monmouthshire NP25 5NR
01600 750287
www.tygwyncider.co.uk

Oz Clarke and Kate Humble are fans of this award-winning company, which is run by the brothers Ben and Alex Culpin.

THE MIDLANDS

HOGAN'S CIDER

Lower Barn Buildings, Haselor, Alcester, Warwickshire B49 6LX
01789 488 433
www.hoganscider.co.uk

Apples and perry pears from the Three Counties blended to create draught and bottled ciders and perries; double winner at Bath and West 2012. Visit the shop, buy online or use the search tool on their website to find the nearest pint…

THE OFFIE, LEICESTER

142 Clarendon Park Rd, Leicester LE2 3AE.
01509 413970 (day) 0116 2701553 (eve)
www.offie.hostei.com

Good selection of ciders and perries, including Thatchers, Westons, Dunkertons.

ROCKINGHAM FOREST CIDER
54 Main Street, Middleton, Market Harborough, Leicestershire LE16 8YU
01536 772001
rockinghamforestcider.moonfruit.com
A blend of Worcestershire cider apples and local sharps, pressed, fermented and matured in the heart of the Welland valley. They make perry too, using pears from an unsprayed orchard in the Three Counties.

SIGNAL BOX INN
Lakeside Station, Kings Road, Cleethorpes DN35 0AG
01472 604657
www.cleethorpescoastlightrailway.co.uk
Couldn't resist putting this in, as it claims to be – and probably is – the world's smallest pub. Stocks most of Westons range. Closed Mondays.

SKIDBROOKE CYDER
The Grange, Skidbrooke, Louth, Lincolnshire LN11 7DH
www.skidbrookecyder.com
If you thought wassail was strictly a West Country thing, come along in January and see the Grimsby Morris in action. Lots of other events and tours and, of course, cider.

TORKARD CIDER
Hucknall, Nottinghamshire
0115 968 0709
www.torkardcider.moonfruit.com
Nottinghamshire's finest, if not only, producer of real cider. Their Cross Border Conflict sounds like a proper 'fighting cider', but the name in fact refers to the unusual mix of local fruit with imports from Herefordshire.

UP NORTH

AMPLEFORTH ABBEY CIDER
Ampleforth Abbey, York YO62 4EN
01439 766778
www.abbey.ampleforth.org.uk
Centuries after the Dissolution of the Monasteries, cider is being made and sold at Ampleforth, using apples from the abbey's own orchards. Cider brandy is available too, distilled from Ampleforth cider by the Somerset Cider Brandy Company.

THE ARKWRIGHT ARMS
Chesterfield Road, Sutton-cum-Duckmanton, Chesterfield S44 5JG
www.arkwrightarms.co.uk
Old-fashioned pub with a healthy – and permanent – range of ciders.

CHESHIRE CIDER
Eddisbury Fruit Farm, Yeld Lane, Kelsall CW6 OTE
0845 0941023
www.cheshirecider.co.uk
An award-winning Eastern Counties-style cider (ie with cookers and eaters, rather than vintage cider varieties) available at the farm shop.

THE CROWN AT WORTHINGTON
Platt Lane, Worthington, Standish, Wigan, Lancashire WN1 2XF
08000 686678
www.thecrownatworthington.co.uk
Look out for real ciders from West Croft Farm, Oliver's and other top producers.

CUMBERLAND ARMS
Ouseburn, Byker, Newcastle upon Tyne, NE6 1LD
0191 265 6151
www.thecumberlandarms.co.uk
Lively, friendly pub with B&B, a venue that hosts music and comedy nights, and some top ciders, including Ross-on-Wye and Gwynt Y Ddraig, which are sourced by local producer Solway Cider. Regional CAMRA winner.

DOVE SYKE CIDER
Dove Syke Nursery, Eaves Hall Lane, West Bradford, Clitheroe Lancashire BB7 3JG
01200 428417
www.dovesykecider.co.uk
There can't be too many cidermakers in Lancashire but here's one, producer of Ribble Valley Gold. A new orchard of cider apple varieties suggests good things for the future.

THE HARLEQUIN
108 Nursery Street, Sheffield S3 8GG
0114 275 8195
www.theharlequinpub.co.uk
Friendly traditional pub where you'll find a range of ciders from the familiar to the uniquely local. Udders Orchard anyone?

HOP AND VINE

24 Albion Street, Hull, HU1 3TH
07787 564 264
www.hopandvinehull.co.uk
Do the good people of Hull know how lucky they are? Bustling CAMRA award-winning pub with a fascinating online log of ciders. While you're at it, why not have a go at the Hull Cider Crawl, as described here: www.ukcider.co.uk/wiki/index.php/Hull_Cider_Crawl

THE MALTINGS

Tanner's Moat, York YO1 1HU
01904 655387
www.maltings.co.uk
Real ciders on tap, plus an array of fruit wines. Originally known as the Railway Tavern, the pub is three minutes from York station (on the way there, at least).

MOORLANDS FARM CYDER AND APPLE JUICE

Moorland Farm, Cliffe Road, North Newbald, York YO43 4SR
01430 827 359 / 07970 252 119
www.moorlandsfarmcyder.co.uk
When Rob and Caroline Gibbon were forced to diversify from the rearing of cattle they went to visit the cidermaking monks of Ampleforth and caught the cider bug. Several years on they've won awards from CAMRA and are growing fast. Check the website for outlets.

NOOKS YARD CIDER

Little Leigh, Cheshire
01606 891 541/07976 746 339
www.nooksyard.com
Makers of Cheshire Perry and a range of strong, dry ciders that combine cooking apples with vintage cider varieties. Have a look at their lively blog.

OLD POET'S CORNER

Ashover, Derbyshire
01246 590888
www.oldpoets.co.uk
Former CAMRA Cider Pub winner and stockist of multiple real ciders, as well as the odd perry.

THE PRINCE OF WALES

Foxfield, Broughton-in-Furness LA20 6BX
01229 716238
www.princeofwalesfoxfield.co.uk
Former CAMRA Cider Pub winner, which caused the landlord some astonishment. They should have at least one scrumpy on the go, so if you're stuck in the Lake District with no cider, hop on the train to Foxfield for a pint.

THE STUBBING WHARF

King St Hebden Bridge, West Yorkshire HX7 6NW
01422 844107
www.stubbingwharf.com
Celebrate Apple Day, take the stage on open mic night and enjoy some proper cider. Mind out for the canal though, eh.

THISTLY CROSS CIDER

South Belton, Dunbar EH42 1RG
07956 655123
www.thistlycrosscider.co.uk
Cider in Scotland? Yes indeed. As far as we know this is the most northerly cider you can buy commercially – see the website for details.

UNICORN GROCERY

89 Albany Rd, Chorlton, Manchester M21 0BN
www.unicorn-grocery.co.uk
Co-operative grocery with a decent range of bottled ciders, including Dunkerton's Black Fox, Heron Valley and Crones.

THE VALLEY BAR

51 Valley Road, Scarborough, North Yorkshire YO11 2LX
07866 582818/01723 372593
www.valleybar.co.uk
Scarborough's finest! Half a dozen real ciders to choose from. Sandwiches for a pound and only a short walk to the beach…

USEFUL ORGANISATIONS & RESOURCES

THE BIG APPLE

www.bigapple.org.uk

Since the 1980s The Big Apple has run twice-yearly festivals to celebrate all things apple- and cider-related along the Marcle Ridge. The Blossomtime cider and perry trials are excellent experience for novice makers, with an opportunity, in 2010, to test more than 150 ciders and perries.

THE CIDER AND PERRY ACADEMY

www.cider-academy.co.uk

Training courses run by award-winning cidermaker Peter Mitchell, mostly in Hartpury, Glos. He's also lecturing in the USA these days. How the times are a-changing!

THE CIDER BLOG

theciderblog.wordpress.com

Entertaining, informative blog run by Bristolian Nick Morris. Has reviewed many a pub, cider and perry.

CIDER PUNK

http://ciderpunk.com

Buy farmhouse/artisan cider online - featuring Wilkins, West Croft, Olivers, Ross on Wye, Severn Cider and more.

THE CIDER WORKSHOP

www.ciderworkshop.com

Fabulous online group devoted to craft cidermaking. Advice and info from Dr Andrew Lea and other luminaries. Ask a sensible question and be amazed at the response. Also has a valuable archive of discussions and articles.

FRUIT SHARK UK

www.fruitshark.co.uk

Importers of the Czech Fruit Shark range of electric scratters. A good investment for anyone making more than a few gallons of cider a year.

GLOUCESTERSHIRE ORCHARD GROUP

www.gloucestershireorchardgroup.org.uk

Established to preserve and promote Gloucestershire orchards, GOG offers all kinds of information for orchard owners. There's an orchard skills centre at Days Cottage where you can learn about grafting and pruning, and lots of annual courses and events.

IAMCIDER

iamcider.blogspot.co.uk

Bill Bradshaw's lively cider-related blog, illustrated with his own pictures.

MARCHER APPLE NETWORK

www.marcherapple.net

A group set up to research and preserve apple varieties in the Marches. Recently produced a beautifully illustrated Pomona.

NATIONAL ASSOCIATION OF CIDER MAKERS

www.cideruk.com

The main industry body works with government and is generally a bit high-powered for the small producer. But the website has all sorts of important and useful information, from legal stuff to news about trends in the industry.

NATIONAL ORCHARD FORUM

www.nat-orchard-forum.org.uk

A good starting point for anyone thinking about planting an orchard – or looking for a source of fruit. Has links to numerous regional organisations and groups.

OLD TIME CIDER

www.oldtimecider.com

THE place to find out what's going in the burgeoning North American cider community; their North American Cider Map shows just how much is happening these days. NB If you're in the USA, don't forget to ask for 'hard cider', otherwise you'll get your apple juice unfermented…

ORCHARD HIVE AND VINE

www.orchard-hive-and-vine.co.uk
Online cider and perry outlet, based in Leominster. Sells products from some of the region's best makers.

SOUTH WEST OF ENGLAND CIDER MAKERS ASSOCIATION.

Contact: Bob Chaplin, Kilver Street, Shepton Mallet BA4 5ND
01749 334000
A subsidiary to the NACM, the SWECMA is much more helpful for small-scale craft producers, especially those thinking about going commercial.

THREE COUNTIES CIDER AND PERRY ASSOCIATION

www.thethreecountiesciderandperryassociation.co.uk

THREE COUNTIES PERRY

www.threecountiesperry.co.uk
Two useful websites for people who want to find out more about cider and perry in the Three Counties.

VIGO LTD

www.vigoltd.com
The Number One supplier of cidermaking equipment in the UK, from mills and pumps to pasteurizers and bottle fillers. Set up in 1984 by Alex Hill, Vigo also sells books, packaging equipment, chemical additives and just about anything else you can think of. Visit their website or go along to their annual Open Day.

WELSH PERRY AND CIDER SOCIETY

www.welshcider.co.uk
An important force in the ongoing Welsh cider revival, the society hosts an annual competition and serves as a forum for producers in Wales. An essential resource for the novice.

Further Reading

Calvados: The Spirit of Normandy, Charles Neal (Wine Appreciation Guild, 2012)

Cider: Making, Using and Enjoying Sweet and Hard Cider, Annie Proulx and Lew Nichols (Storey, 2003)

Cider, The Forgotten Miracle, James Crowden (Cyder Press 2, 1999)

Ciderland, James Crowden (Birlinn, 2008)

The Common Ground Book of Orchards (Common Ground, 2000)

Craft Cider Making, Andrew Lea (The Good Life Press, 2008)

How to Grow Apples and Make Cider, Bill Bleasdale (Welsh Mountain Books, 2010)

In Search of Cider, Alan Stone (Somerset History, 2010)

Manmade Eden, James Russell (Redcliffe Press, 2007)

The New Book of Apples, Joan Morgan & Alison Richards (Ebury, 2002)

Somerset Cider Handbook, Alan Stone (somersethistory.co.uk, 2009)

A Somerset Pomona, Liz Copas (Dovecote Press, 2001)